Capital Markets Trading and Investment Strategies in China

Xiaojiang Zhang

Capital Markets Trading and Investment Strategies in China

A Practitioner's Guide

 Springer

Xiaojiang Zhang
Beijing
China

ISBN 978-981-10-8496-6   ISBN 978-981-10-8497-3   (eBook)
https://doi.org/10.1007/978-981-10-8497-3

Library of Congress Control Number: 2018934864

Printed on acid-free paper

This Springer imprint is published by the registered company Springer Nature Singapore Pte Ltd.
part of Springer Nature
The registered company address is: 152 Beach Road, #21-01/04 Gateway East, Singapore 189721,
Singapore

Contents

Introduction

As each large, modern trade nation evolves over different developmental stages, its capital markets inevitably embrace various market liberalizations to cater for the need from domestic and international investors. Amid those significant changes, the Chinese capital market has experienced substantial growth in size, breadth of instruments, and diversity of participants over the recent years, with its fixed income market well over 5 trillion USD, and onshore FX market daily trading volume on a typical day around 30 billion USD. In addition to huge complexity presented by all large capital markets, where trade, business, monetary condition, policies all change and interact instantly with huge momentum, this market presents a unique challenge to financial professionals worldwide, especially those with vested business interest in China, who are desiring a structural analytical approach that can help them to conform domestic solution with their global trading and investment standard.

The content of this book is aimed at financial practitioners who have already possessed in-depth knowledge in their perspective capital markets area regarding foreign exchange, money market, fixed income, and related derivative products, and have keen interest in gaining a deep insight into the Chinese market to develop or strengthen their strategy application and risk management practice related to China and global markets.

This book covers in details the building blocks of Chinese capital markets at the financial instrument level, the basic analytical pricing term structure of those instruments, the macro and industry economic framework and progress of market liberalization process at work that these capital markets instruments reside in, the interaction of various participants in the market, their trading and investment objectives and rationales, some of the most applied trading and investment strategies, and frequently used risk management techniques.

All data series were collected from domestic and international public sources to reduce possible ambiguity or conflict. I am grateful for their presence, upon which we can build common understanding with objectivity and facilitate the growth and collaboration of international investment community.

Chapter 1
Building Blocks of an Investment Portfolio

1.1 Foreign Exchange Instruments

1.1.1 Onshore CNY FX Instruments

1.1.1.1 Global Context

A quick summary of the current state of global foreign exchange market is necessary to provide a context within which detailed discussion on China foreign exchange market can be correctly presented. Since the beginning of this century, the global FX market rose significantly amid the rapid expansion of international trade, which was supported by the newly inclusion of many emerging economies into the global trade system, the falling cost of transportation and rise of the internet that facilitated the information sharing across the globe. More recently, the FX market encountered headwind, especially in the area of spot trade, coinciding with the general decline of international trade. The lack of growth in the FX trading will continue as long as global economy and international trade growth do not pick up speed.

© Springer Nature Singapore Pte Ltd. 2018
X. Zhang, *Capital Markets Trading and Investment Strategies in China*,
https://doi.org/10.1007/978-981-10-8497-3_1

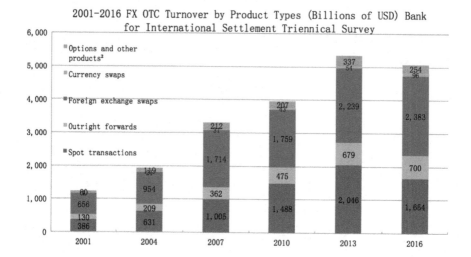

From the perspective of each traded individual currency, USdollar has remained the most important currency in the global FX market since 2001, based upon triennial survey of central banks by Bank of International Settlement. The market share of the second most important currency, the Euro, headed lower, with some of its share replaced by the increased presence of other currencies including AUD, MXN, CNY. From 2001 to 2016, CNY as a traded currency made some market progress, capturing about 2% of the FX OTC turnover out of 100% in 2016.

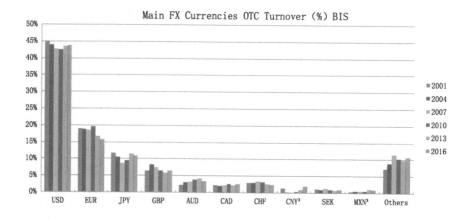

From the perspective of traded currency pair, the most important pair is EUR/USD, followed by USD/JPY, USD/GBP and USD/AUD. EUR/USD had lost some market share over the recent years, with that space being filled by currency pairs formed by USD coupling with some emerging market currencies, including USD/CNY, which had 3.8% share of the market in the 2016 BIS survey.

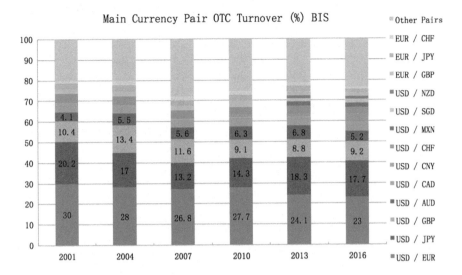

From the perspective of traded products, FX swap provides better FX interest rate exposure management than FX forward for its lack of spot risk, but its execution needs a functional money market of each underlying currency. For the main currency markets, the mixture of product types showed slightly lower percentage of FX Swap regarding CNY and JPY, relatively to EUR and USD, illustrates the room for further possible market development in the underlying CNY and JPY money markets.

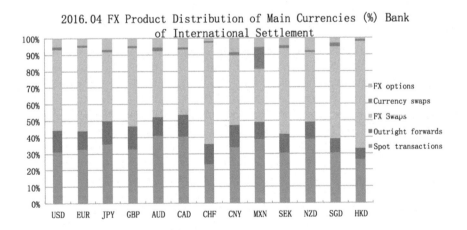

From the perspective of geographical trading activity congregation, partly due to the expansion of electronic trading and trading firms looking for physical proximity during price finding and execution, UK and US have consolidated their leads in FX trading and these countries advantage have increased over the recent years.

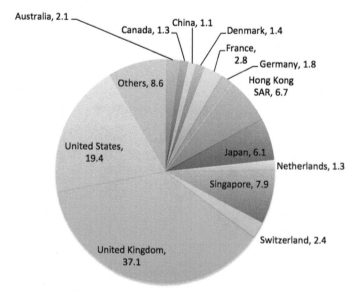

2016 FX OTC Turnover by Region (%) BIS

1.1.1.2   The Market Place

The development of onshore China FX market in the last of decades has experienced the following periods:

1980–1985 Prior this time, excess foreign exchange funds were returned to the government, then redistributed to those with various need. In the end of 1978, China started profound market reform. Rapid economic growth and international trade growth soon followed. To better serve the market reform and economic need, Foreign Exchange Redistribution Market was created between 1980 and 1985, where mostly state-owned entities possessing foreign exchange were allowed to sell excess funds to other state-owned entities with currency need. The price of transactions was limited to within 10% of published spot rate. During this period, CNY price was lowered specifically for the goods sector versus service sector, aimed to support the export industry that generally lacked competitiveness. This policy has created two sets of official FX prices that led to international criticism.

1985–1993 As market reformed progressed and inflation started to pick up, the limitation of relatively rigid trading price became evident. After series of reforms were put into place, the FX market enjoyed substantial growth. The most significant reform policy was the creation of FX Redistribution Market, where the trading counterparties were allowed to set their own price and permitting more entities to participate in the FX trading. In 1987, the total amount of foreign exchange flows in and out of China was 70 billion USD and the trading volume in the FX

Redistribution Market was 4.2 billion USD. With the reform taking hold, the trading volume in the Redistribution Market grew to 62.6 billion USD in 1988, and 251.05 billion USD in 1992. During this period, the policy to lower the FX price specifically for the goods exporting sector was eliminated. But as the FX Redistribution Market price was different from the official published price, and different dealing centers within the country were not electronically connected to each other, price divergence still existed.

1994–2005 In 1993, the Foreign Exchange Redistribution Market's market share was 80% of the total Chinese foreign exchange market, while the other 20% of the FX transactions were still conducted in the older official FX rate. The pricing divergence was finally solved by one-time devaluation of the official FX rate and merging various regional markets into a single FX market in Shanghai in 1993. The merger of the different markets had the following impact:

1. Created a single computerized market with increased trading liquidity and pricing transparency;
2. Set up a two-tier market structure. One tier was designed for banks to deal with their various clients, and the interbank market as the other tier, where banks trade with each other and the central bank. This stricture is consistent with the international norm, and within this framework, central bank can manage price fluctuation and regulate FX flows.
3. Trading can be conducted, with dealer quotes, or market order matching. Market orders were ordered based upon prices to match buy and sell side;
4. The interbank market members can be classified into proprietary trading type or broker type. Proprietary trading members can handle both broker business and proprietary trading business, while the broker members are not permitted to conduct a prop trading business;
5. Centralized the settlement process. CNY is settled via a two-tier settlement process. The local tier counterparties settle against each other, while in the central tier different local centers settle the net amount between each other. On the other hand, FX is settled with one tier mechanism;
6. Central bank intervention in the foreign exchange market could be conducted with increased efficiency.
7. Eliminated the regulatory FX reservation requirement.

As the result, the current Chinese FX market started to form in 1994. A single FX rate based upon market condition at 8.7 was set. Everyday PBOC would published USD CNY exchange rate based upon yesterday's market condition, and exchange rate of CNY against other currencies based upon USD CNY rate and other currencies' market conditions from yesterday. Banks would trade within a range of those published rate based upon current market conditions. In 1996 the business activity category realm within which related FX exchange could be conducted was expanded to allow for all trade-related activities. During Asia financial crisis between 1997 and 1998, the USD/CNY rate stayed stable and actually rose to 8.28.

After China entered WTO, between 2001 and 2005, capital account was gradually opened, a natural progressive stage after the partial opening of current account.

2005–Present On July 21st, 2005, more ambitious FX market liberalization was started. As the first step, PBOC, the central bank, published new regulation, defining daily closing CNY's trading price to be given by PBOC. This daily closing price was changed from referencing against USD to a basket of currencies, and would be used as the mid price for next day's trading. USD-CNY pair will be traded with plus or minus 0.3% of this published mid price. PBOC may adjust this price based upon changing macro and market condition. CNY rose to 8.11.

In 2006 Market dealer system was introduced. In 2007, the trading band was widened from 0.3 to 0.5%.

CNY FX rate gradually rose over time. Under the extraordinary circumstance of global finance crisis, between July 2008 and June 2010, FX market liberalization was suspended. CNY was made to center around 6.83, as a measure to maintain market stability during the 1st Quantitative Easing program that lasted between Nov 2008 and Apr 2010.

On June 19th, 2010, FX reform was resumed with CNY rate again referenced against a basket of currencies. CNY market started to form in Hong Kong (China). A year after this, on June 17th 2011, CNY was at 6.47. 21.8% above 8.11 when FX reform was started in 2005.

On April 16th 2012, USD-CNY daily trading band was widened from 0.5 to 1%. On March 17th 2014, USD-CNY daily trading band was widened from 1 to 2%. EUR, JPY, GBP and HKD versus CNY trading bands were set at 3%. Russian Ruble was at 5%. South Africa's ZAR was at 10%.

In August of 2015, new reform was introduced for mid price regulation. Mid price will be mainly decided by the market closing of the previous day, plus any market and demand change expected by the market makers up to the next opening. There is no restriction regarding day-to-day mid price change. This was designed to introduce a pricing mechanism that is more market-oriented.

Over the last several decades, we have witnessed significant changes occurring in the CNY market and Chinese economic landscape. A spot rate time series for the past 10 years has reflected the change of economic condition from a competitive export industry with a continuously strengthening currency in a managed floating exchange rate regime, to a more balanced trade industry with a relatively neutral currency rate and more flexible exchange rate management system.

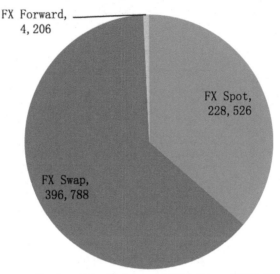

FX Trading Volumes 2014.04 – 2017.03
($100M) China Money 外汇交易中心

As the economic development entered a more maturing stage during the last decade, the onshore foreign exchange market also progressed to reach certain level of more sophistication, with FX Swap/Forward trading volume dominating the simpler Spot product in the interbank dealer market.

When compared against more sophisticated global FX trading centers, two key differences could still be observed. First, the FX trading is still mostly driven by the need of Chinese international trade, for there is a concentration of FX transaction centered on CNY-related currency pairs. Second, there is a lack of deep FX option market, which could be attributed to a variety of reasons.

Regarding trading practice convention the onshore FX market mostly observes international norm. For example, a forward transaction is often split into a Spot plus Swap trade package, a typical practice for forward traders to lock in the interest rate parity, while let a spot trader to deal with spot risk. The pricing mechanism has defined the market as a two-tier structure. The interbank CFETS, which is a dealer market reserved for banks, adding spread based upon international market price. Additional spread is added to CFETS price to create the retail market price.

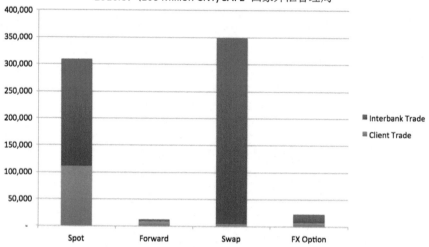

Foreign Exchange Client Trade and Interbank Trade Comparison 2016.01 - 2016.07 (100 Million CNY) SAFE 国家外汇管理局

During the first half of 2016, FX Spot and FX Swap constitute the majority of the trading activities. Most of the non-spot transactions are conducted on the interbank market, China Foreign Exchange Trade System CFETS. On CFETS, given bid and ask quotes are matched based upon best price and time, and spot clearing is done on T + 1 basis.

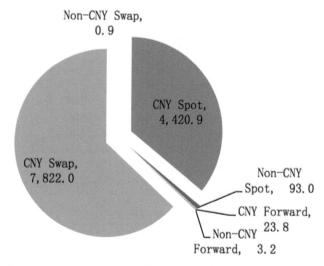

Trading Values 2016.04 ($100M) CFETS 外汇交易中心

As mentioned earlier, most of transactions in Chinese FX market centered on CNY, for spot, forward and swap transactions, an indication of the market focus on CNY market, and deep liquidity offered by USD in China's international trade. In addition, it is the prevalent practice among large trading houses to use USD in their desk's P&L procedure and that also contributes to trader's reluctance in taking non-USD position.

1.1.1.3 FX Spot

While pricing quoting in the interbank market mostly follows the international convention, when dealers and brokers refer to a currency being bought or sold, since most of the transactions centered on CNY, the convention is to quote on the non-CNY currency, not the contract counter convention as defined in international trading convention. Also specific to domestic FX market is the spot delivery date includes today and O/N to facilitate daily mid price trading band regulatory requirement enforcement.

In the interbank market, USD CNY was the dominating currency pair being traded. The USD CNY's prevalence was not expected to change soon, for the interbank FX market was still driven largely by international trade originated within China, hence the presence of CNY. At the same time, US Dollar is still the preferred settlement currency in international trade originated from China; and the common practice of splitting of non-USD trade currency pair using USD as the split currency also contributes the to dominance of USD. Even though the size of the US market as China export destination is comparable to that of Euro Zone, EUR CNY transaction volume is only slightly more than 1% of USD CNY volume.

After excluding USD, trading volume distribution pattern by currency becomes a better reflection of their respective export market share, with EUR, JPY, HKD and SGD being the most frequently traded currencies. Next to the important European and Japanese markets, Hong Kong (China) and Singapore also play significant role in China's international trade. While rapidly improving ports and other international trade services have become more competitive from some Chinese cities, especially in Shenzhen Shanghai and Tianjin, large amount of international trade of China still flows through more established international trading outpost Singapore and Hong Kong (China).

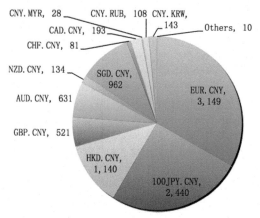

CFETS FX Spot Trading Volumes Excluding
USD–CNY Pair 2014.04 – 2017.03 (100 Million
CNY) China Money 中国货币网

Monthly FX spot trading volume can be the combined effect of both commercial trade-related activities and capital markets volatility. Between June and July of 2015, there was a large equity market crash that took the Shanghai equity index value from above 5,100 to between 3,000. Flight to safety after the index dive led to large purchased of US dollars. In the end of 2015 and 2016, in both cases, Federal Reserve was expected to raise fed fund rate in their December meetings, and that caused strong buying sentiment for USD. There was a noticeable decrease of USD buying from January to February in 2016. While USD was still preferred due to the solid US recovery, some of the published data suggested that the US growth was less strong than expected, therefore probability for Fed future rate increase was lowered temporarily, the USD buying sentiment was weaker in February than January.

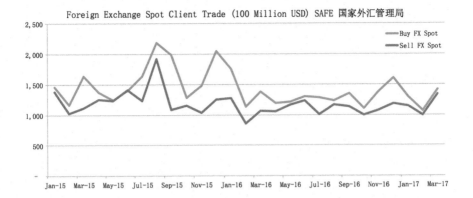

Foreign Exchange Spot Client Trade (100 Million USD) SAFE 国家外汇管理局

In the last couple of years, simultaneous US economic recovery and China growth slowdown caused international capital flow to overshadow the more typical commerce-related currency flow. Prior this more recent development, FX trading volume often spiked up before the yearend due to holiday season shipmen originated from China. February was traditional a low month for currency trading due to long holiday week for the Chinese Spring Festival.

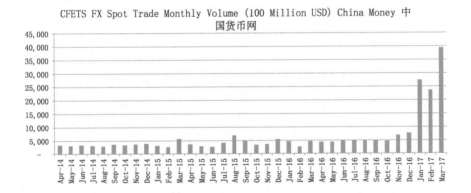

CFETS FX Spot Trade Monthly Volume (100 Million USD) China Money 中国货币网

Some of the conventions related to FX trading in the interbank market:

(a) Definition: members exchange RMB and FX at contracted currencies, amount and exchange rate, and settle or deliver within two business days;
(b) Trading Mechanisms: anonymous trading and bilateral trading;
(c) Instruments: USD/CNY, EUR/CNY, JPY/CNY, HKD/CNY, GBP/CNY, AUD/CNY, NZD/CNY, SGD/CNY, CHF/CNY, CAD/CNY, CNY/MYR, CNY/RUB, CNY/THB (Regional Trading), CNY/KZT (Regional Trading);
(d) Trading Hours: Beijing time: 9:30 a.m. to 11:30 p.m., trading hours for CNY/KZT and CNY/THB are 10:30 a.m. to 4:30 p.m. and 9:30 a.m. to 4:30 p.m. respectively, excluding Chinese statutory holidays;

(e) Method of Clearing and Settlement: for anonymous trading, the CFETS provides the centralized clearing service as the central counterparty; for bilateral trading, the trading parties clear and settle with each other according to the agreement;

(f) Trading Eligibility: eligible banks, other non-banking financial institutions, and non-financial corporations, can apply to CFETS (Chinese Foreign Exchange Trade System) for RMB spot trade eligibility. Non-financial corporations need additional filing with SAFE (State Foreign Exchange Administration of the People's Republic of China/State Administration of Foreign Exchange) for record-keepings after the initial approval of CFCS.

1.1.1.4 FX Forward

Solid business demand and good market making effort exist across major FX Forward standard tenors in USD CNY pair trading. This resulted in good liquidity for 1M, 3M and 1Y forward tenors.

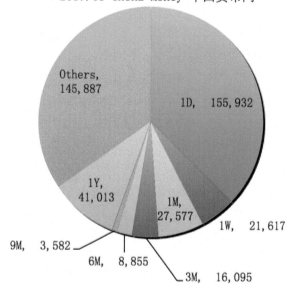

CFETS FX Forward Trade Tenor Distribution (USD Millions) 2014. 04 – 2017. 03 China Money 中国货币网

On the FX trading maturity ladders, short maturity 1D and 1W tenors are often used for international trade-related settlement activities and treasury position management. Currency movement expectations were often expressed on the longer maturity tenors including 1 month or more. There was a clear differentiation in terms of tenor application when dealing with temporary events or fundamental economic shift. 2015.08 buying of USD forward was the result of domestic equity market crash. 2016.06 buying was the result of BREXIT. These two buying spike were caused by liquidity or political events hence less substantial versus the economic fundamentals underlying the USD appreciation expectation around 2016.01 and 2017.01. The FX tenors in 2016.01 and 2017.01 were 3M and 1Y, longer than the 1M tenor applied for 2015.08 and 2016.06 USD purchasing. As the picture of US economic growth became clearer in the beginning of 2017 versus 2016, the FX forward tenor traded was also extended from 3M to the longer 1Y tenor.

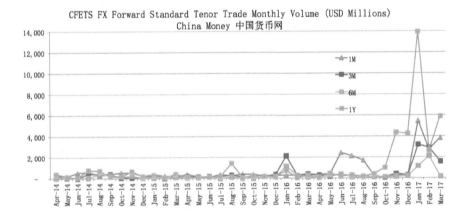

US dollar's safe heaven status in the FX forward trading can be inferred from both the tenor and the amount traded. FX forward buy sell amount has been a clear indicator for market participant sentiment regarding the future direction of expected currency movement. During the beginning of 2016, US economy was very strong, so was the expectation for Fed's action on raising interest rate and the rise of US dollar and this was substantiated with strong purchase of USD. In February of 2016, a flurry of news came out regarding retail sales, manufacturing index, all suggesting a solid but more moderate US economy. The buying of USD versus selling became muted, until July when the strength of US economic growth became more established.

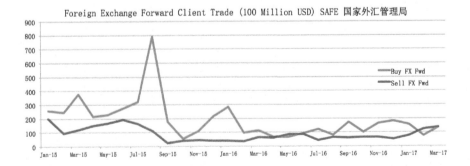

In addition to the direction of buying and the tenor traded, FX forward trading volume is also important for measuring market sentiment in China regarding the relative direction of USD and CNY. Throughout the large events of 2015.08 and 2016.06, and during the strengthening of US economy at the end of 2015 and 2016, the FX forward volume increased substantially suggesting the relative strengthening of USD versus CNY.

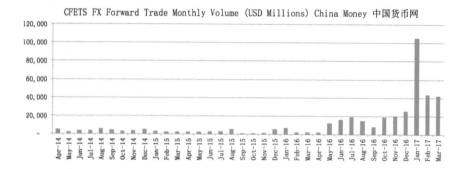

Some of the FX forward trading convention in China's interbank market:

(a) Definition: RMB/FX forward trading is a binding obligation between the trading parties in the national interbank FX market to buy or sell a certain amount of foreign currency at a contracted rate of exchange on a certain date in the future (at least two business days from the trading date;

(b) Specification: items, such as currencies, amount, maturity, exchange rate, margin and settlement arrangement etc., are to be negotiated by the two parties;

(c) Trading Mechanism: bilateral trading;

(d) Instrument: USD/CNY, EUR/CNY, JPY/CNY, HKD/CNY, GBP/CNY, AUD/CNY, NZD/CNY, SGD/CNY, CHF/CNY, CAD/CNY, CNY/MYR, CNY/RUB;

(e) Trading Hours: Beijing time: 9:30 a.m. to 11:30 p.m., excluding Chinese statutory holidays.

(f) Method of Clearing and Settlement: the clearing is done according to the agreement by the two parties, mainly bilateral clearing at present;

(g) Trading Eligibility: Inter-bank Spot-trade Eligible financial institutions, with the relevant approval from regulatory agencies for derivatives business, can apply for one or all inter-bank RMB derivatives products trading eligibility approval based upon business need.

1.1.1.5 FX Swap

An FX product designed to capture interest rate parity without spot risk, FX swap has gained its acceptance in the interbank market, evidenced by its larger than FX forward trading volume in the dealer market. Many of the forward positions were traded back-to-back to offload position risk, and it is more efficient to offload forward positions in FX swap versus uncovered FX forward.

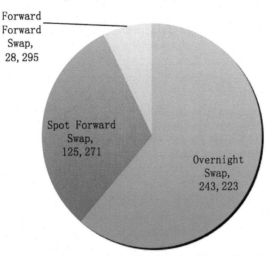

CFETS FX Swap Trade Tenor Distribution
(100 Million USD) 2014.04 – 2017.03
China Money 中国货币网

Swap monthly trading volume change closely followed FX forward volume change, with large increases that could be observed in the second half of 2015, the beginning of 2016 and the beginning of 2017.

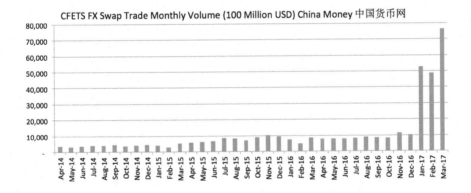

Compared with liquid application of FX swap that was intended for currency risk management, short-dated currency position management was still the most important function of FX swap trading in the dealer market, illustrated by the large volume of overnight index swap.

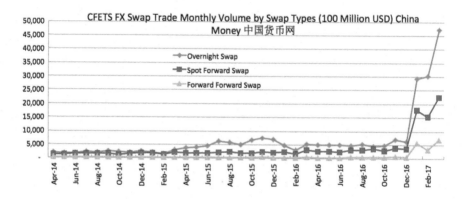

Similar to FX forward, FX Swap is also an instrument where the market expectation of currency relative strength can be inferred via the buy and sell amount of underlying currency, specifically on the forward leg of the swap. In 2015, forward leg sell of USD suggested that some market participants were still less clear about the direction of USD CNY exchange rate movement. Strong buying of USD in 2016 indicated the firmed up consensus that US economic growth and China structural reform would form the fundamentals underlying USD CNY for some time to come.

Some of the FX swap trading convention in China's interbank market:

(a) Definition: RMB/FX swap involves the actual exchange of two currencies (RMB against FX) on a specific date at a rate agreed in the contract (the short leg), and a reverse exchange of the same two currencies at a date further in the future at another rate (generally different from the rate applied to the short leg) agreed in the contract (the long leg);

(b) Specification: The object currency of the swap is the foreign currency, and the currency, amount, tenor, exchange rate, price (swap point) and settlement arrangement are to be negotiated by the two parties;

(c) Trading Mechanism: bilateral trading;

(d) Instruments: USD/CNY, EUR/CNY, JPY/CNY, HKD/CNY, GBP/CNY, AUD/ CNY, NZD/CNY, SGD/CNY, CHF/CNY, CAD/CNY, CNY/MYR, CNY/RUB;

(e) Trading Hours: Beijing time: 9:30 a.m. to 11:30 p.m., excluding Chinese statutory holidays;

(f) Method of Clearing and Settlement: the clearing is done according to the agreements by the two parties. Bilateral clearing is the dominant clearing mode employed at present;

(g) Market Eligibility: inter-bank Spot-trade Eligible financial institutions, with the relevant approval from regulatory agencies for derivatives business, can apply for one or all inter-bank RMB derivatives products trading eligibility approval based upon business need.

1.1.1.6   FX Option

FX Option is a relative new product on China's interbank market. Due to the fact that CNY is still a managed float currency, effect of option usage is still limited. As the globalization of CNY progresses, wider usage of FX option is expected in the future.

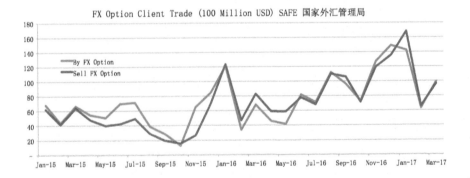

Some of the FX option trading convention in China's interbank market:

(a) Product definition: an RMB/FX options trading (hereinafter referred to as an "options trading") refers to any trading giving one party the right to trade a certain volume of FX assets at an agreed exchange rate on a given trading day. The option buyer acquires such a right by paying an option premium; the option seller collects the option premium and performs its obligation when the buyer chooses to exercise its right (vanilla European options);

(b) Product description: in an options trading, the subject matter is the foreign currencies bought and sold. The currencies, amount, period, pricing parameters (volatility rate, execution price, spot price/forward exchange rate, domestic and foreign currency interest rates), transaction price (option premium) and settlement arrangements, etc., are agreed upon through negotiations between the two parties to the transaction;

(c) Trading method: bilateral inquiry;

(d) Quotation targets: currency pairs such as USD/CNY, EUR/CNY, JPY/CNY, HKD/CNY and GBP/CNY, and implied volatility rates corresponding to 25 Delta Call, ATM and 25 Delta Put;

(e) Trading hours: Beijing time: 9:30 a.m. to 11:30 p.m. The market is closed during statutory holidays in China;

(f) Settlement method: the two parties to the transaction settle through the agreed method. Currently, most transactions are settled bilaterally;

(g) Market Eligibility: inter-bank Spot-trade Eligible financial institutions, with the relevant approval from regulatory agencies for derivatives business, can apply for one or all inter-bank RMB derivatives products trading eligibility approval based upon business need.

1.1.1.7   Cross Currency Pair Trades

This refers to Non-RMB FX Spot, Forward and Swap transactions conducted on CFETS. Their relatively low trading volumes indicated their minor roles in China's interbank FX market.

Some of the cross currency pair trades trading convention in China's interbank market:

(a) Trading Mechanisms: anonymous trading and bilateral trading;

(b) Instruments: EUR/USD, AUD/USD, GBP/USD, USD/CHF, USD/HKD, USD/CAD, USD/JPY, EUR/JPY, USD/SGD;

(c) Trading Hours: Beijing time: 7:00 a.m. to 11:30 p.m., excluding Chinese statutory holidays;

(d) Method of Clearing and Settlement: for anonymous trading, the CFETS provides the centralized clearing service as the central counterparty; for bilateral trading, the trading parties clear and settle with each other according to the agreement;

(e) Trading Eligibility: eligible banks, other non-banking financial institutions, and non-financial corporations, and their authorized branches, can apply to CFETS (Chinese Foreign Exchange Trade System) for cross currency pair trade eligibility.

1.1.2   Offshore CNY/CNH FX Instruments

1.1.2.1   The Market Place

Since the market liberalization process of CNY resumed in 2010, policy and regulatory changes were put into place to allow offshore trade-related CNY settlement and open currency flow between onshore and offshore CNY market.

Based upon PBOC 2015 report on CNY internationalization, in 2014, onshore CNY daily trading volume was 55 billion USD, while offshore CNH daily trading volume was at 230 billion USD. The offshore CNH market was composed of spot, forward, FX swap, FX option and NDF. There was also a small CNY NDF market.

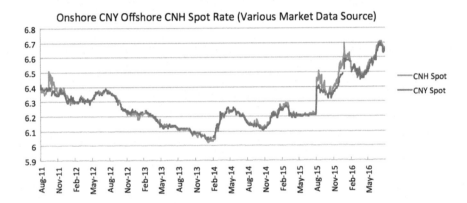

1.1.2.2   Deliverable Versus NDF

CNY NDF was an instrument developed in the 1990s when CNY trade account control was still in place. It gained its popularity especially during the 2008–2010 period, when expectation for CNY appreciation was strong and trade-related need for CNY was high, but there is no offshore deliverable CNY market for hedging and other risk management need.

As offshore CNY, dubbed CNH market came into force, CNH-denominated instrument as the deliverable alternative took over NDF. NDF trading volume, based upon various industry surveys, is much smaller than the deliverable CNH trading volume. Nevertheless, at times NDF still plays an important role as a leading price sentiment indicator.

1.1.2.3 FX Forward Trade

CNH forward trading practice follows the global currency trading norm. While CNH is already an important currency in global trading system in term of volume, due to the segregation of the CNY domestic market from international market, CNH pricing mechanism is subject to the change of the relatively small offshore liquidity pool that can make CNH price from time to time vary substantially from theoretical interest rate parity-derived price, in this case, the parity between offshore CNH and global USD interest rate. For market to express its view on the future CNY price without the liquidity interference, the NDF CNY still has an important role to play, hence the coexistence of both the deliverable CNH and non-deliverable CNY in the international FX market. The CNH forward trade can be set up back-to-back against CNH spot and CNH swap.

1.1.2.4 FX Option

There is a market for CNH option. Though CNH can float in any direction without trading limit band, but its ultimate value, the same as other international currency, is linked to CNY investment value when it is cycled back to the market back into China, therefore the nature of managed float of CNY exchange rate decides the offshore CNH rate is also managed float in nature. This to certain extend makes CNH option expensive, and that is expected to remain so until CNY globalization gains more maturity.

1.2 Traded Money Market Instruments

1.2.1 Onshore CNY Market

1.2.1.1 Diversified Participants

There are two main places where participants engage in onshore MM activities. The larger of the two markets is China Foreign Exchange Trade System, CFETS, which is managed by PBOC. Vast majority of traditional dealer money market activities, such as instrument issuance, market making, buying and selling, are conducted on CFETS. The other relatively smaller market refers to various exchanges, including Shanghai Stock Exchange and Shenzhen Stock Exchange. On those exchanges, both institutional dealers and retail customers except banks are present to conduct transactions. Corporate bond carry trade created a very large repo financing demand on exchanges. Due to the much larger influence of banks have in financial systems in China, CFETS money market volume and financing rate are watched closely by both regulators and market institutions.

1.2.1.2 Liquidity and Historical Development

From 1984 central planning gradually started to give away and PBOC assumed its central bank role. Still at the time economic policy was conducted mainly through lending management including both the types and the amount of loan activities. The objective of monetary policy was to support and supplement the implementation of various lending targets. Addressing economic concerns through lending management tools lacked precision and was partially responsible for the high inflation in the late 1980s. From 1993 to 1997, PBOC began turning to monetary tool to drive its economic policy agenda and started publishing monetary supply statistics, hoping to rein in the high inflation though achieving certain preset monetary targets. In 1998, lending control of the national commercial banks was eliminated and the landscape of the current money market began to take shape. As China entered WTO in 2001 the country embarked on interest rate liberalization. After a temporary halt caused by the 2008 financial crisis, interest rate liberalization resumed in 2010. With the more recent introduction of Short-term Liquidity Operations (SLO), Standing Lending Facility (SLF), MLF Mid-term Lending Facility (MLF) and Pledged Supplementary Lending (PSL), Interbank market has become a more mature and active capital market for participants to borrow when in shortage and lend in excess. Policy makers also use money market to (a) stabilize short end market liquidity volatility, (b) set short end interest rate target, and (c) transmit its policy signal through various market operations. The transmission mechanism has been fine-tuned and considered achieving its full effectiveness since 2015.

1.2.1.3 The Markets Maturity Distribution

Main types of traded instrument include Loan/Deposit, Outright Rep and Pledged Repo. Market liquidity is ample for 1 day, 1-week, 2-week instrument, up to 3M.

1.2.1.4 Pledged Repo and Reverse Repo

Among Repo/Reverse Repo, Outright Repo/Outright Reverse Repo and Loan Deposit, Repo, also referred to as Pledged Repo, is the most important money market financing instrument in the interbank market. Banks often use interest rate instrument, such as Treasury bonds and policy bank bonds as the underlying collateral in repo transaction, and by doing so, they have eliminated the need for both issuer and counterparty credit limit allocation. Credit risk elimination has led to deep liquidity of repo trades in interbank market.

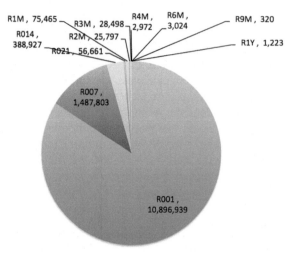

Interbank Repo Traded Amount by Maturity
2014.04-2017.03 (100 Million CNY) China
Money 中国货币网

In the above graph, R refers to Repo transactions, while D, M and Y refer to maturity units in days, months and year.

Trading on 1D and 7D is very liquid. 1D repo is used frequently to cover both short-term funding imbalance and provide funding on long-term leveraged positions.

While most of the Repo trades are conducted for overnight, the repo liquidity extends beyond 1-day maturity. An important observation to be made was, similar to LIBOR, SHIBOR as a pricing benchmark encountered the difficulty in lacking accurate pricing rationale. As a result, Repo rate has became indicative for SHIBOR loan/depo for standard maturities.

Monthly Interbank Longer Than 1D Repo Trading Volume by Maturity (100 Million CNY) China Money, 中国货币网

Some of the Repo trading convention in China's interbank market:

(a) Definition of Instrument: pledged repo is a type of short-term financing business where bonds are used by both trading parties as a pledge of rights. It refers to a financing act in which borrower (positive repo party), pledges bonds to lender (reverse repo party) for funds, and at the same time two parties agree upon that when at a future date positive repo party returns the amount of funds calculated at the specified repo rate to the reverse repo party, the reverse repo party shall lift the pledged rights on the pledged bonds;

(b) Trading Mechanism: Bilateral trading;

(c) Terms: the terms of pledged repo range from 1 day to 365 days. Through the trading system, the trading volume and price of pledged repo is publicly released as a total of 11 terms including 1-day, 7-day, 14-day, 21-day, 1-month, 2-month, 3-month, 4-month, 6-month, 9-month and 1-year;

(d) Trading Hours: Beijing time: 9:00–12:00 a.m., 1:30–4:30 p.m., excluding Chinese statutory holidays;

(e) Market Participants: commercial banks and its authorized branches, rural credit cooperatives, urban credit cooperatives and other deposit-taking financial institutions, insurance companies, securities companies, fund management companies and their managed funds, portfolios, insurance products, financial companies and other non-bank financial institutions which all have bond trading qualification, and foreign-funded financial; institutions which conduct RMB business, can all enter into the bond market for transaction.

(f) Method of Clearing and Settlement: the two trading parties, at the specified date, shall handle gross settlement of funds at their own risk in accordance with deal sheet. Depository bond settlement is carried out through the China Central Depository and Clearing Co., Ltd, while funds settlement is conducted through the China National Automatic Payment System of PBC. Three types of settlement, namely "payment after delivery", "delivery after payment" and "DVP", are available.

1.2.1.5 Outright Repo and Reverse Repo

Outright Repo and Reverse Repo, while not as liquid as Repo trades, still constitute an important segment in the interbank money market. Similar to Repo market in terms of maturity distribution, most of the transactions are conducted with 1D and 7D maturities.

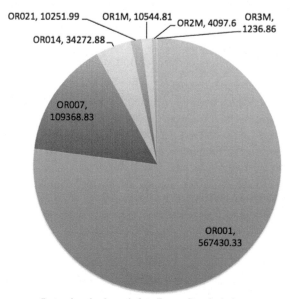

Interbank Outright Repo Traded Amount
2014. 04 – 2017. 03 (100 Million CNY) China
Money 中国货币网

OR in the graph refers to Outright Repo. D, M and Y refers to maturity units in days, months and year.

The monthly trading volume pattern resembles that to the pledged repo, with typical low point in the February for 2015, 2016 and 2017. The large volume in the first half of 2015 was corresponding to the large issuance of local government debt and a short equity boom and bust. The low in mid 2016 was partly corresponding to the BREXIT that slowed liquidity outflow due to US economic resurgence. Later low was partly due to US election and fed policy uncertainty.

Monthly Interbank Outright Repo Trading Volume by Maturity (100 Million CNY)
China Money, 中国货币网

Different from Pledged Repo that requires the placement of collateral into a custodial account, Outright Repo requires collateral to be transferred temporarily to the lender, until the trade matures, when the collateral is back into the hands of its original owner. Outright repo and reverse repo therefore contain less risks for the lender by imposing more stringent collateral requirement on the borrowers, who typically have less credit standing in a specific outright repo transaction. The poorer credit quality in these transactions determines there usually will be a relative compensating spread when compared with Repo.

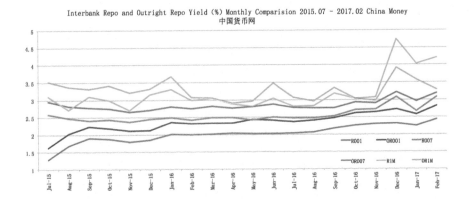

Interbank Repo and Outright Repo Yield (%) Monthly Comparision 2015.07 – 2017.02 China Money
中国货币网

Some of the Outright Repo trading convention in China's interbank market:

(a) Definition of Instrument: outright repo refers to a trading business where in time of a bondholder (positive repo party) selling bonds to a buyer (reverse repo party), the two parties at the same time agree upon that when at a future date such a positive repo party shall buy from the reverse repo party the equal number of the same-type bonds at a pre-defined price;

(b) Trading Mechanism: bilateral trading;

(c) Terms: the terms of outright repo range from 1 to 91 day. Through the trading system, the trading volume and price of outright repo is published as a total of 7 terms including 1-day, 7-day, 14-day, 21-day, 1-month, 2-month and 3-month;

(d) Trading Hours: Beijing time: 9:00–12:00 a.m., 1:30–4:30 p.m., excluding Chinese statutory holidays;

(e) Market Participants: commercial banks and its authorized branches, rural credit cooperatives, urban credit cooperatives and other deposit-taking financial institutions, insurance companies, securities companies, fund management companies and their managed funds, portfolios, insurance products, financial companies and other non-bank financial institutions which all have bond trading qualification, and foreign-funded financial institutions which conduct RMB business, can all enter into the market for transaction;

(f) Method of Clearing and Settlement: the two trading parties, at the specified date, shall handle gross settlement as per deal ticket. Depository bond settlement is carried out through China Central Depository and Clearing Co., Ltd., while funds settlement is conducted through the China National Automatic Payment System of PBC. Three types of settlement, namely "payment after bonds", "bonds after payment", and "DVP", are available.

1.2.1.6 Interbank Lending

Unlike Repo with interest rate collateral, loan/deposit requires credit limit allocation when money is lent out to a counterparty. Same as Repo and Outright Repo, most of the trading is executed for 1D and 7D maturity, while 14D, 1M and 3M still possess certain liquidity depth.

In practice, the lending activities are further categorized based upon maturities. Those with very short term, typically 1D, could also be referred to as interbank funding, with their principal purpose designed to cover short-term funding shortage. While those of longer term, may be referred to as interbank lending, with their principal purpose designed to provide lending on projects.

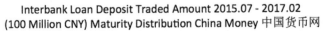

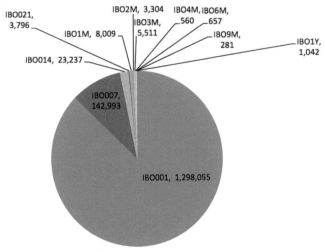

Because conditions underlying money market demand and supply for funds can change instantly, month-to-month loan deposit trading volume can also have large volatility. The factors driving condition changes include international macro economic factors, domestic macro economic factors, monetary policy factors, capital market events concerning bond issuance/maturity and large equity issuance, and many other factors.

Loan and deposit activity is not as liquid as repo trades, but its liquidity beyond 7D is consistent, hence a venue for participants in interbank market to gain access to funds when they need them.

Some of the Interbank Lending trading convention in China's interbank market:

(a) Definition: refers to no-guarantee financing business, which is dealt through the trading system of the CFETS by and among financial institutions, which link the CFETS via the network;

(b) Trading Mechanism: bilateral trading;

(c) Terms: for interbank lending, the shortest term is 1 day, and the longest term is 1 year. The CFETS is responsible for calculating and publishing the weighted average rates in accord with a total of 11 terms including 1-day, 7-day, 14-day, 21-day, 1-month, 2-month, 3-month, 4-month, 6-month, 9-month, and 1-year;

(d) Trading Hours: Beijing time: 9:00–12:00 a.m., 1:30–4:30 p.m., excluding Chinese statutory holidays.

(e) Market Participants: market participants include commercial banks and their authorized branches, rural credit cooperatives, urban credit co-operatives, financial companies and securities companies and other relevant financial institutions which are approved by PBC and have independent legal entity qualifications, and foreign-funded financial institutions which can conduct RMB business by the PBC approval.

(f) Method of Clearing and Settlement: both trading parties, at the specified date, shall handle gross settlement at their own risk in accordance with deal sheet. The speed of settlement is T + 0 or T + 1.

1.2.1.7 Interbank Deposit

Interbank deposit is referring to excess liquid assets deposited by financial institutions in banks. The interest earned on interbank deposit is less versus interbank lending (loan deposit), but the amount of deposit can be much larger than interbank loan deposit. The deposit tends to be cash and earns a floating rate return.

1.2.1.8 FX Deposits

Instruments: Lending transaction for USD, EUR, HKD with a term less than 1 year.
    Trading Hours: Beijing time: 7:00–23:30, excluding Chinese statutory holidays.
    Access Qualifications: banks, non-bank financial institutions, non-financial enterprises or their authorized branches having FX interbank lending business qualification, can all make application of being an FX deposits member.

1.2.1.9 Commercial Paper

Commercial paper is a short-term fixed income instrument, with maturity within a year. Regulations require the amount issued outstanding should not exceed 40% of the issuer's net asset value. Both issuer and the debt have to be rated. It takes about 2–3 months for issuance registration process to finish.

1.2.1.10 Short Commercial Paper

With maturity within 270 days, short commercial paper (SCP) is more comparable to US commercial paper than commercial paper in China. Since inception, it has quickly gained popularity over commercial paper. The main difference between commercial paper and short commercial paper, besides maturity, is that CP issuance approval requires the rating of both the to-be-issued CP and the issuer, while SCP does not require the rating of SCP, but only the rating of the issuer itself. It also takes less time to process an issuance registration for SCP. There is no significant difference between the two on issuing cost.

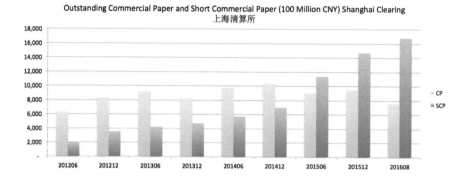

Outstanding Commercial Paper and Short Commercial Paper (100 Million CNY) Shanghai Clearing
上海清算所

1.2.1.11   Central Bank Bill

From 1990 up to 2008 financial crisis, years of large international trading surplus and investment capital inflow, created large quantities of foreign exchange in banks that had to be swapped into CNY for domestic application. Central bank PBOC bought FX from banks to create so called "funds outstanding for foreign exchange". In return banks have received large amount of CNY for various lending activity. To absorb this excess liquidity that could otherwise potentially have destabilizing inflationary consequence, one method was to increase banks' reserve requirement. Since the excess CNY liquidity was not evenly distributed among all financial institutions, an alternative method used by PBOC was to issue large quantity of central bank bill. Issuance of central bank bills could be either openly sold on market or specifically allocated to banks with large excess liquidity and very active lending activities. On this regard, central bank bill served its purpose very well.

The second intended objective of central bank bill was to create the short end benchmark interest rate, the same as the Treasury bill. One problem was that the central bank bill was not issued by the Treasury Department, but by the PBOC, therefore central bank bill does not obtain the same tax-exempt status as treasury-issued instruments. Hence the so-called dematerializing effect, referring to US Treasury bond pricing converges with US Treasury bill pricing when their remaining maturities overlap with each other, does not happen to China Treasury bond. Eventually the market chose Repo instrument yield using interest rate bond as the collateral becomes the benchmark rate for the short end of interest rate yield curve.

1.2.1.12   Sec Lending

Definition of Instrument: securities lending refers to a financing business where borrower borrows bonds from a lender by using a certain number of other bonds as a pledge, and at the same time they agree upon that at a future date the borrowed bonds shall be returned and the lender shall return corresponding pledged bonds. CFETS provides quotations, transaction, recording and information services for security lending transaction.

Monthly Bond Sec Lending (100 Million CNY) China Bond
中债登

Some of the Sec Lending trading convention in China's interbank market:

(a) Trading Mechanism: bilateral trading;
(b) Terms: the term of security lending is determined by both parties through consultation, but the term shall not exceed 365 days. CFETS classifies security lending instruments into a total of 11 terms of 1-day, 7-day, 14-day, 21-day, 1-month, 2-month, 3-month, 4-month, 6-month, 9-month and 1-year;
(c) Trading Hours: Beijing time: 9:00–12:00 a.m., 1:30–4:30 p.m., excluding Chinese statutory holidays.

1.2.1.13 Forward Rate Agreement

Definition of Instrument: forward rate agreement refers to a financial contract in which both trading parties agree to exchange the interests which are respectively calculated at a fixed rate and a reference rate for a certain amount of nominal principal on a agreed date. Between the two parties, in the forward rate agreement, the buyer pays the interest at a fixed rate while the seller pays the interest at a reference rate.

Some of the FRA trading convention in China's interbank market:

(a) Trading Mechanism: bilateral trading and one-click trading;
(b) Forward rate agreement transaction can be conducted through the trading system of CFETS, by telephone, by fax and in other manners. For the concluded transaction not going through the trading system of CFETS, relevant financial institutions should deliver transaction records of forward rate agreement to CFETS for recognition before 12:00 a.m. of the next business day after such a transaction was concluded;

(c) Reference Rate: reference rate for forward rate agreement should be a benchmark market rate for the national interbank bond market released by CFETS and other organizations under the authorization of the PBC, or a benchmark rate announced by the PBC. Specific rate is agreed upon by both trading parties;
(d) Market Participants: of the national interbank bond market participants (referred to as market participants), financial institutions having a market maker or clearing agency business qualification, can conduct forward rate agreement transaction with all other market participants, and other financial institutions can conduct forward rate agreement transaction with all financial institutions, but non-financial institutions can only carry out hedge-purposed forward rate agreement transaction with the financial institutions having a market maker or clearing agency business qualification;
(e) Trading Hours: Beijing time: 9:00–12:00 a.m., 1:30–4:30 p.m., excluding Chinese statutory holidays.

1.2.1.14 Cross-Border CNY Financing with Loan/Depo

Often offered as a product, this is a package of trades, aimed at providing low cost financing to international trade exporter, with deposit collateral as risk-mitigating tool, meanwhile sharing the interest rate differential profit between a bank and its client.

There are two main types of this product. The first is when a client starts with an existing interest-earning FX deposit. Based upon client's request, the bank will execute forward sell FX trade and obtain a CNY loan. Upon maturity, FX deposit will be cashed out to settle FX forward sell. The received CNY will be used to pay back CNY loan. The key of this successful product package is that since FX asset is acting as a collateral, there is no risk for banks, therefore an exporter can obtain low-cost financing in CNY.

The second is when client starts with an existing interest-earning CNY deposit. CNY deposit can be used as collateral to receive an FX loan. Upon maturity, CNY deposit will be cashed out and obtain FX, via either a prearranged FX forward or FX window trade. Obtained FX from this CNY sell will then be used to pay back FX loan. In this case, CNY deposit is acting as collateral for banks and an exporter can obtain low-cost financing in USD or other FX currencies.

1.2.1.15 CD

Large Negotiable Certificate of Deposit was introduced in the end of 2013 in China. The main difference between CD and commercial paper, is for the former, the fund used to purchase the instrument is classified as a deposit, for the later, it is classified as a debt investment. As a short maturity credit product, with an active secondary market, CD played an important role in the US interest rate liberalization process. Not only with return on the CD not subjected to Regulation Q's rate ceiling restriction, and also as a termed deposit the instrument provided more funding stability for the issuer, CD was popular to both investors and banks when it came to the market.

In China, CD is preceded by Interbank CD, which was aimed at only institutional investors, issued mainly by share-holding commercial banks and rural commercial banks. CD instrument, on the other hand, based upon guideline issued in the June of 2015 by PBOC, is issued by deposit-taking financial institutions including commercial banks, policy banks, rural coops and other financial institutions, aimed at a much broader investor base, including both institution and individual investors.

As a form of loan, when compared to interbank borrowing that is benchmarked against repo, CD investment is a form of deposit that will be covered by deposit insurance and is also subject to deposit-to-loan ratio, therefore it is a safer investment and slightly more expensive to issuer than interbank CD, hence in theory its yield is expected to be slightly lower than interbank CD with equivalent maturity.

To an investor, the main reason for CD's popularity is that it is a form of termed loan that has an active secondary market, therefore a more liquid investment instrument than term loan. Its advantage is proved by its huge growth since its 2013 inception, significantly surpassing short commercial paper and commercial paper in terms of amount outstanding. To a bank issuer, it optimizes the balance sheet by precisely matching the term of the funding requirement. To the market itself and regulators, with an active secondary market, CD also is better than SHIBOR deposit in signaling the market condition for the short end of the credit market.

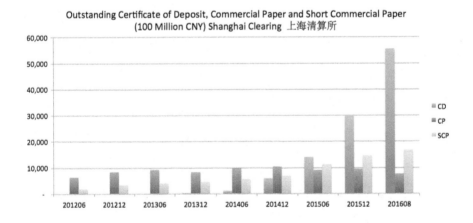

Outstanding Certificate of Deposit, Commercial Paper and Short Commercial Paper (100 Million CNY) Shanghai Clearing 上海清算所

1.2.1.16 MM Funds

Both fixed income and money market funds have grown in recent years. Each offered competitive advantage in their respective investment class. Bond fund is viewed as a safer alternative versus volatile equity fund, while money market fund is viewed as a preferred alternative versus cash account with higher return.

The strong driving force behind MM fund was the interest rate market liberal-ization. An analogy could be drawn between this relatively recent MM fund growth in China and the past experience of MM fund in the US in the late 1970s and early 1980s.

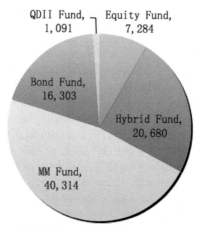

Mutual Fund Assets by Investment Asset Type 2017. 03 (100 Million CNY) AMAC 中国证券投资基金业协会

MM funds invest in instrument within one-year maturity. Most of their investment is interbank deposit. Different from retail cash or saving deposit that usually offer less than 1%, interbank deposit offers competitive market interest rate that can be reach 3–4%, and early redemption is possible for important buyers. In 2016 year-end filing of YueBao, the largest MM fund in China, the fund stated that 73% of the investment had maturity within a half year. About 70.27% of its investment was interbank deposit. Trading Financial Investment was mostly in short-term bonds.

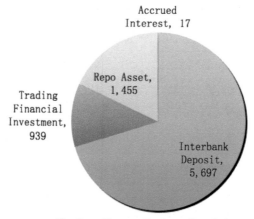

YueBao Money Market Fund Asset Allocation (100 Million CNY) 2016 Year End Fund Annual Filing

1.2.1.17 Different MM Indices

SHBOR (Shanghai Interbank Offered Rate) is calculated, announced and named on the technological platform of the National Interbank Funding Center in Shanghai. It is a simple, no-guarantee, wholesale interest rate calculated by arithmetically averaging all the interbank RMB lending rates offered by the price quotation group of banks with high credit rating. Currently, the Shibor consists of eight maturities: overnight, 1-week, 2-week, 1-month, 3-month, 6-month, 9-month and 1-year.

The price quotation group of Shibor consists of 18 commercial banks. These quoting banks are primary dealers of open market operation or market makers in the FX market, with sound information disclosure and active RMB transactions in China's money market. Shibor Working Group of PBC decides and adjusts the panel banks, supervises and administrates the Shibor operation, and regulates the behavior of the quoting banks and the specified publisher in accordance with the Implementation Rules of Shibor.

National Interbank Funding Center is authorized to calculate and publish Shibor. At 9:30 a.m. (Beijing Time) each business day, Shibor of the eight maturities will be published at www.shibor.org after arithmetically averaging all the quotations of the 18 banks, with the four highest and four lowest quotations excluded.

Interbank Fixing Repo Rate/7 Day Weighted Moving Average Fixing Repo Rate is a benchmark rate based on repo trading rate for interbank market between 9:00 and 11:30 a.m. every trading day, and the calculation method is compiled with international experience. Fixing Repo Rate is released to the public at 11:30 a.m. on each trading day. The calculation method of fixing repo rate is as followed:

(a) It is calculated based on all trading rates of overnight repo (R001), 7-day repo (R007), and 14-day repo (R014) between 9:00 and 11:30 a.m. (including 9:00 and 11:30 a.m.) on each trading day. In particular, if some transactions have the same counterparty and trading rate (same or opposite transaction direction), only one transaction will be selected in the samples;

(b) Sort overnight repo rate, 7-day repo rate, and 14-day repo rate respectively in ascending order. The maximum sequence number of sorting order is N, and the interest rate at the [N/2] (integer value is assumed) + 1 location shall be the fixing rate of that day;

(c) Overnight fixing repo rate, 7-day fixing repo rate, and 14-day fixing repo rate are respectively flagged as FR001, FR007, and FR014. Fixing repo rate is released to the public at 11:30 a.m. on each trading day.

(d) Treatments of Abnormal Cases. If there are no transaction data between 9:00 and 11:30 a.m., the corresponding period Shibor*365/360 will be taken as fixing rate of that day.

The main difference between fixing repo rate and 7-day repo weighted moving average rate for interbank market (the original benchmark for interest rate, released on October, 2004) is that fixing repo rate is an intraday rate, and average 7-day repo rates is a closing rate. In addition, the difference in calculation methods is that the median algorithm is adopted for fixing repo rate, and the weighted average algorithm is adopted for 7-day repo weighted moving average rate.

For 7-day repo weighted moving average rate in interbank market (i.e. the original "benchmark of interest rate," hereinafter referred to as weighted moving average rate), its data are based on 7-day repo rate (R007) in interbank market. As a statistically integrated instrument, R007 actually covers pledged repo transactions with terms of 2-day, 3-day, 4-day, 5-day, 6-day, and 7-day, and is a conventional definition in line with market practice. The calculation process involves three stages of abnormal data treatment, intraday weighted data generation and moving average rate calculation.

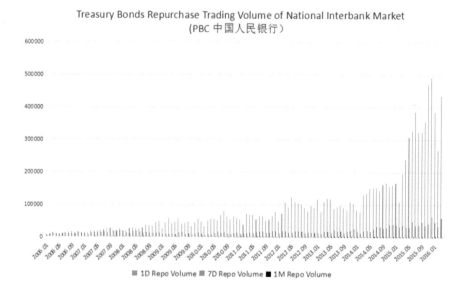

The volume of repo trades has grown substantially over the years, and has became a significant source of short term financing in the interbank market, where the collateral is government bonds, hence credit risk is only limited to the counterparty but not instrument issuer. Its status as the short-term benchmark interest rate, makes it comparable to LIBOR in the Euro Dollar market or Fed Fund rate in the US interest rate market.

1.2.2 Offshore Money Market Management

To facilitate domestic clients conducting trade-related activities, many domestic institutions often set up offshore operations and offer international financial services. Offshore money market management is an important part of the asset liability management for these offshore operations. Frequently used offshore money market instruments include repo, loan deposit, commercial paper and FX swap.

1.2.2.1 Repo and Reverse Repo

A common financial instrument used in conducting short term financing, repo is structured as such that in the first exchange, collateral is given for cash received; in the second exchange, cash borrowed is returned to the lender with interest payment included and collateral is returned to the borrower. Repo is thus viewed as a type of borrowing activity. Reverse Repo is a Repo transaction viewed from the other side of the Repo trade, described as such that in the first exchange, collateral is received for cash lent out; in the second exchange, cash is received with interest payment included and collateral is returned to counterparty. Reverse Repo is thus viewed as a type of lending activity.

Outright Repo and Outright Reverse Repo are all repo transactions. The difference is that in a Repo transaction, asset used as collateral does not change its ownership unless repayment is in question, while under outright Repo the ownership of the collateral does change hand twice to mitigate credit risk in lending.

Repo and Reverse Repo are widely used in international markets. With collateral, the risk is assumed to be limited when compared against traditional loan deposit transaction. In international markets repo usage is popular among hedge fund.

1.2.2.2 Loan Deposit

Loan and deposit are traded following global market standard. Trades are often executed via Reuters and other terminals, with broker quotes and counterparty quotes. CNH loan deposit played a significant role for companies taking advantage of interest rate differential between the domestic and international market. CNH can only be recycled back into Chinese market via designated clearing banks, thus the trading volume and yield is subject to PBOC regulatory policies.

1.2.2.3 Commercial Paper

Commercial paper is an unsecured instrument with maximum maturity of 270 days. Issued by companies with good credit standing and each CP issuance itself rated by main rating agencies, they are considered as low risk instruments. The exception was asset-backed commercial paper based upon credit obligation that exited market after the credit crisis.

1.2.2.4   FX Swap

Offshore FX Swap follows global FX swap trading conventions. Trades are executed via Reuters and other terminals, with broker quotes and counterparty quotes.

Usually client will initiate a request for forward quote. Based upon interest rate parity, swap points are being giving by the forward traders. A market quote of spot at the time, plus swap points, will result a complete package of trades including a spot and a swap. With the external forward trade taking client request, and the spot and swap trade together provide the back-to-back hedge for a bank's forward position.

1.3   Fixed Income Instruments

The history of Chinese bond market went back to 1950, when the first public bond was issued with complete success. At that time, to increase the appeal of the issuance, the bond value was indexed against a basket of different products, including wheat, fabric and coal. Between 1954 and 1958, 4 more issuances were conducted. All were normal fixed rate bonds with coupon rate at 4%.

1981–1991 Without effective trading and distribution venues, the fixed income market was mainly retail OTC market, where bonds were allocated to and held by various institutions or individuals until maturity.

1988–1991 The main distribution and trading venues were set up using banks' retail offices in 1988, and 1991, Shanghai Stock Exchange was created to also handle physical bond custodial service and trade book-entry government bonds. At this time, the framework for fixed income trading was set up to mainly have distributed bond trading through the outlet network, supplemented with centralized bond trading at exchanges. Government sold bonds to cover budget deficit and fund development project. Macro economic management was not the main consideration for bond issuance.

1991–1997 Since the creation of the stock exchange, trading activities gradually moved towards exchanges. In the May of 1995, there was a large incident regarding bond future trading caused the bond future contract to be delisted from exchanges. In the same year, the thought was book-entry bond trading should only be conducted centralized trading places and bond trading in OTC market was stopped. In 1997, large amount of bank funds went into the equity market via repo transaction, causing an equity market speculative rise. Banks funds are pulled out of exchanges.

1997–2001 To address issues concerning fixed income trading encountered on the exchange, the interbank market was created in 1997 with 16 main banks as its members. In 1998, insurance companies were allowed to participating in the market. In 1999, hundreds of credit coops, some securities firms were added. In

2000, financial companies were permitted into the interbank market. By that time, it had over 690 institutions, covered the most of the financial universe in China. Between 1999 and 2000, the interbank market became the main fixed income market in China. Trading volume, including repo activities, took off. The coming of the interbank market, created a venue for PBOC to conduct its open market operation, implement monetary policy and push for interest rate market liberalization.

2002–Current More fixed income products came into the market place during this period, including central bank bill in 2002, bank subordinated deb in 2004 and asset-back securities in 2006. 2008 saw medium term notes, and 2009, local government bond and Small-and-Medium Enterprise Collective Notes (SMECN). MTN and SMECN were instruments aimed at meeting the financing need of private sector, and local government bond was aimed at meeting the need of local development.

At this time, the market place is composed of three segments: exchanges, interbank market, and retail market. (1) The exchange market has both institutional and individual participants, and thus a mixture of both retail and wholesale market characteristics. (2) The interbank has only institutional players, thus an OTC wholesale market. (3) Commercial bank's OTC retail market, which is an extension of OTC wholesale market to reach retail customers. Some bond types could be simultaneously listed on multiple markets, sold to retail, institutional customers.

The bond market itself has mostly accomplished centralized service for bond registration, custodial service, clearing and settlement. For those services to be provided, corresponding organizations have been set, the most important are China Money, China Bond and CSDC (China Clear).

1.3.1   Instruments Types

Based upon data published on China Bond, by the end of 2016, the total value of bonds outstanding was 37.78 trillion CNY. Out of those, the largest issuer was the Treasury department, followed by local government and China Development Bank. Together, National government, local government, and three major policy banks (CDB, Export-Import Bank of China, ADBC account for more than three quarters of bonds issued. This has contributed to the sufficient liquidity to the interest rate section of the bond market. The development of a liquid interest rate section forms the basis for the credit market, for a credit premium/spread computation drives credit market spread/risk trade-off assessment.

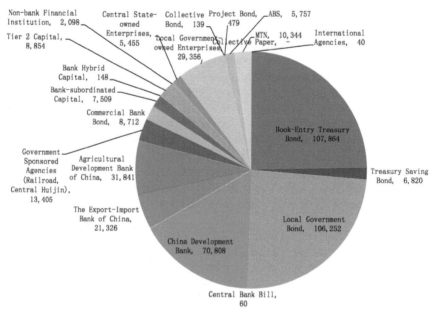

2016.12 Bond Outstanding Amount (100 Million CNY) China Bond 中债登

The most significant development from 2014 to 2016 was the introduction of local government bond. It was used to reduce the level of local government debt payment by swapping local government loan with local government bond, which had lower coupon rate. Treasury bond amount was increased to add fiscal stimulus to the economy, while ADBC bond amount increase was a more agriculturally targeted financial stimulus. MTN outstanding amount was reduced partly because of higher issuing cost as interest rate moved up in the last couple of years.

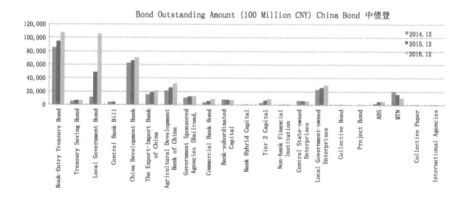

Majority of the bond investments were held by various banks, which include national commercial banks, urban commercial banks and rural commercial banks. Adding insurance companies, the buy-and-hold is still the behavioral norm for bond asset class.

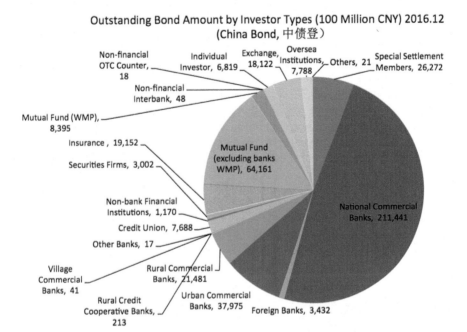

Outstanding Bond Amount by Investor Types (100 Million CNY) 2016.12 (China Bond, 中债登)

While large banks still retained their influence in the fixed income asset class partly due to their increased positions in illiquid local government bonds, mutual funds clearly expanded their presence in the more liquid space. This was also the case for urban and rural commercial banks. In general, market became more dynamic and different institutional increased their fixed income asset class participation to meet end investors' diversified needs.

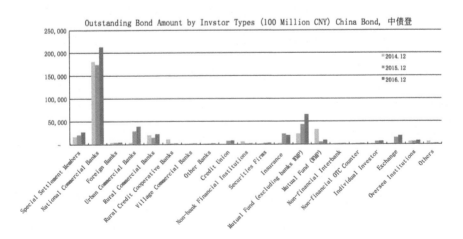

Outstanding Bond Amount by Invstor Types (100 Million CNY) China Bond, 中债登

1.3.1.1 Book-Entry Treasury Bond

China Department of Treasury issues book-entry bonds on exchanges and the interbank bond market. Book-entry bonds are different from individual Treasury saving bonds that people can by over the counter from designated commercial bank. Individual Treasury saving bonds can either deliver single final redemption payment with accumulated coupon and principal, or make separate coupon payments that earn saving deposit rate before withdrawal. Due to the liquidity associated with the amount being issued, book-entry Treasury bonds are often used as the benchmark for the debt market.

Treasury bond issuance is carefully managed to maintain an even distribution across the term structure so demand from various groups of investors can be met. 7 year has always been a problem for its lukewarm demand. Local government debt was aimed at swapping out local government loan so the average term is much shorter at between 3 and 5 year maturity.

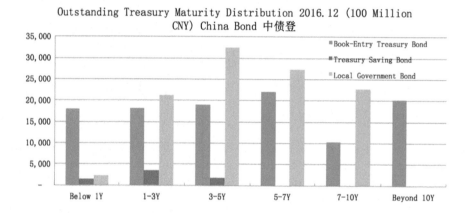

Outstanding Treasury Maturity Distribution 2016. 12 (100 Million CNY) China Bond 中债登

Under the current tax code, treasury bonds', as well as local government bonds' interest income is tax-free, and it does not require risk capital allocation during the investment holding period, thus no need for credit limit allocation. For these reasons, treasury bonds have been favored by both national commercial banks and urban commercial banks. As country's interest rate liberalization progresses, the cost of deposit for banks gradually rises, and banks are holding less Treasury bonds, while other institutions step into use Treasury bonds for liquidity management with better return.

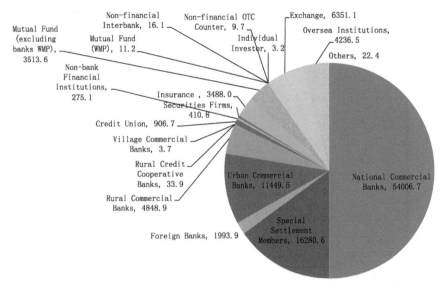

Treasury Bond Held by Investor Types 2016.12 (100 Million) China Bond, 中债登

The investment demand change causes fixed income yield level change that is often benchmarked by Treasury bond yield level. One important note is that banks are not allowed to deal with equities directly, so the attractiveness of the interbank bond assets versus other asset classes, including loans, is not necessarily linked to the liquidity condition in the equity market, which refers to stocks listed on Shanghai and Shenzhen stock exchanges.

The Investment demand change also causes the term structural level change. Unlike the dollar debt market, where the term spread of interest rate curve is measured by the 2Y–10Y spread, the term spread in Chinese treasury market is measured by the 1Y–10Y spread. One of the two large spikes occurred in the end of 2008, when government injected large liquidity into the market to stabilize the economy after US financial crisis and short end yield came down. The other large spike occurred in the middle of 2015. To deflate the equity speculation bubble, regulation was tightened and liquidity flew from equity market into the interbank bond market. The massive liquidity flow drove down the short-term treasury yield and created the large spike of term structure.

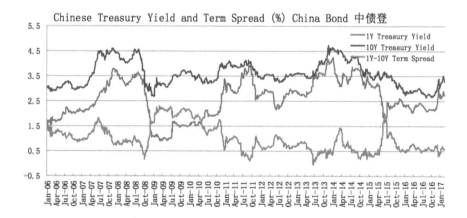

The investment demand change causes specific bond yield differences. Treasury bonds are more liquid for recent issuance, which is the case across the world. One distinction of the China bond market versus US bond market is the tax-exempt status of the treasury bonds, which renders its dematerialization less effective. Typically, when a bond is issued, its coupon rate is close to the current market yield. As market yield moves away from issuing market yield as a bond ages, since higher coupon with more tax-exempt effect can be more desirable for institutional investors compared to more recent issuance with lower coupon rate, even when two issuances have comparable remaining maturities, a 10-year maturity issuance that was issued 5 years ago may not be considered exchangeable with a newly issued 5-year bond. More recently issued bonds can therefore be more liquid as their coupons rates are closer to market condition and there is less tax idiosyncrasy concern.

1.3.1.2   Local Government Bond

There are two types of local government bonds. The first type refers to those issued by Treasury Department on behalf of local government, with Department of Treasury as its guarantor, hence requires no risk capital allocation. Vast majority of local government bonds are issued directly by local government requiring risk capital allocation at 20%. Historically, default by local government is very low, therefore the credit spread on these issuance is not high.

The history of local government bond could be dated back to early 1990s. The local government used to collect tax and spend collected tax on various public services, with local revenue surplus being turned over to central government. The consequence was certain coastal areas with large amount of tax income would try to report their surplus as small as possible. Central government lacked resource to help less developed areas or support national projects. This picture was changed once tax income began to be split between local and central government. While tax revenue to local government was decreased, majority of civil responsibilities still fell upon local government thus the substantial need for local financing was created.

There are three ways for local government to borrow. There was relatively small amount of bonds issued by Dept. of Treasury on behalf of local government. Local government could also issue bonds or borrow from banks via so-called platforms, conduits set up by local government to go around the regulation that prevented local government from directly borrowing from either bank or capital markets. In fact, a large amount of credit bonds traded are in essence local government liabilities issued by those platform conduits. These platform enterprises also borrowed loans on behalf of local government, with land or other income-generating assets used as collaterals, and their largest source of income was usually from land usage sales. This became a problem when property sales in 3rd tier and 4th tier cities stalled, and banks were facing huge loan default risk. To solve this problem, refinancing effort was orchestrated by central bank and other government agencies. Local government issued bonds at provincial level, which was considered less risky, therefore at much lower interest rate, between 3 and 4% compared with enterprise loan borrowed by local enterprises that sometimes reached 10%. Also maturity of the newly issued bonds can be much longer than the maturity of those replaced loans. The result was that local government reduced their interest liability in an economy with growth speed became moderate, and banks have reduced their loan principal risk exposure.

Local Govy Bond	By Treasury	General Obligation	Revenue Bond	Local Platform
VAT Tax Rate	0	0	0	25%
Risk Weight	0	20%	20%	100%
Redemption by	Treasury	Local Budget	Project Revenue	Implicit Guarantee

While a huge success in terms of risk reduction, the issuance of local government bond for loan swapping also had its own problems. The most prominent one being that the amount issued has been very large and the major banks are saddled with such a quantity it crowded out funds available for investment on other asset classes. Measures were taken, for example, to make the bond type eligible for PSL collateral aimed at mitigating the crowding effect. Sometimes analogies were made between the local government bonds as PSL collateral to US quantitative easing program. The second issue is that the risk spread is considered to be too low by many analysts, and this leads to a somewhat illiquid secondary market for local government bond.

1.3.1.3 Policy Bank Bond

There are three policy banks China Development Bank, The Export-Import Bank of China, and Agricultural Development Bank of China, each plays an important role in its perspective area.

Unlike commercial banks, policy banks do not have extensive retail branch to take personal deposit, hence most of their financing was achieved via the more expensive bond market, about 66–71%, based upon their recent annual filings. Those bond offerings, frequent and in large amount, have contributed to the general liquidity to the bond market. As investors have relative stable expectation for spreads among the three issuers, each new offering, regardless from which issuer, sets the mark-to-market process of the whole fixed income market in motion, thus brings transparency to the whole policy bank bond segment of the bond market.

All policy bank bond issuances, including those issued by China Development Bank, The Import Export Bank of China and Agricultural Development Bank of China, are under the supervision of PBOC.

1.3.1.4 China Development Bank (CDB)

Based upon information available on its portal, China Development Bank (CDB) was founded in 1994 as a policy financial institution. It was incorporated as China Development Bank Corporation in December 2008, and officially defined as a development finance institution in March 2015.

CDB has a registered capital of RMB 421.248 billion. Its shareholders include the Ministry of Finance of the People's Republic of China (36.54%), Central Huijin Investment Ltd. (34.68%), Buttonwood Investment Holding Co., Ltd. (27.19%) and the National Council for Social Security Fund (1.59%).

CDB provides medium to long-term financing facilities that serve China's major long-term economic and social development strategies. By the end of 2015, its assets grew to RMB 12.3 trillion, and non-performing loan (NPL) had been kept below 1% for 43 consecutive quarters, with consistently outstanding market performance. Professional credit rating agencies including Moody's and Standard & Poor's have rated CDB at the same level as China's sovereign rate.

CDB is the world's largest development finance institution, and the largest Chinese bank for foreign investment and financing cooperation, long-term lending and bond issuance. It ranked 87th on the Fortune Global 500 list in 2015.

The risk weighting of CDB financial bonds bought by commercial banks is 0%, which also serves as the basis for regulating CDB bond investments by securities and insurance institutions.

Maturities of CDB bonds vary from three months to 50 years, including fixed rate and floating rate bonds (pegged to 1-year time deposit or Shibor) and bonds with options, making CDB a leading innovator in China's bond market. Its bond issuance system incorporates blanket key term benchmark bonds, general financial bonds and targeted financial bonds. Specifically, blanket key term benchmark bonds are issued weekly through tender via the PBOC's bond issue system.

CDB financial bonds receive active subscriptions among various financial institutions, including commercial banks, credit cooperatives, insurance companies, funds, wealth management plans of commercial banks, securities companies and overseas organizations. In 2015, spot CDB financial bond and pledged repo transactions totaled RMB 25.1 trillion and RMB 115.8 trillion respectively, accounting for 29 and 25% of the total trading volume of spot bonds and pledged repos on the interbank market, making them the most actively traded bonds in China. China Central Depository & Clearing Co., Ltd. compiled a series of CDB bond indexes in 2004, including wealth indexes, full-price and net-price indexes, to objectively reflect the market trends for CDB bonds. Aside from government bonds, CDB bond indexes are the only indexes released for an individual bond issuer in China.

CDB bonds are favored by institutional investors in general, with the exception of the special settlement members that are not profit-driven and prefer treasury bonds for their tax-exempt status and liquidity comparable to CDB bonds.

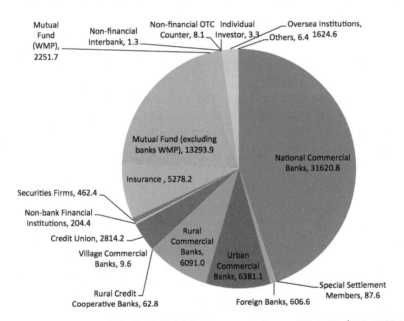

CDB Bond Held by Investor Types 2016.12 (100 Million CNY)
China Bond, 中债登

Starting from 2014 to 2016, the general monetary environment can be categorized as ample amount of liquidity. To pursue higher yield, urban commercial banks, rural commercial banks, credit union and bond funds had all increased their purchase of CDB bonds, while large commercial banks liquidity was focusing local government bonds.

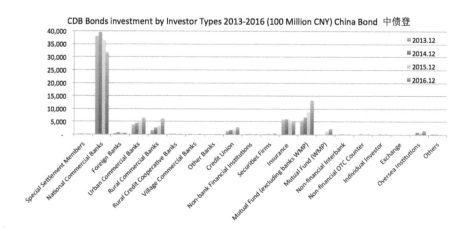

Besides their low risk while making relative higher interest payment than treasury, their availability in large quantities in long maturity between 7 and 10 years makes CDB bonds very attractive for insurance companies.

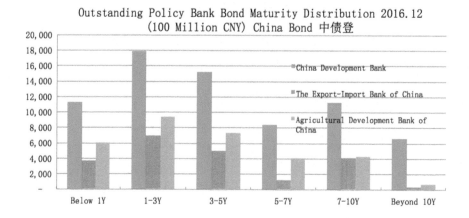

1.3.1.5 The Export-Import Bank of China (EIBC)

Founded in 1994, the Export-Import Bank of China is a state bank solely owned by the government. Its international credit ratings are the same as China's sovereign ratings. The Bank has established correspondent banking relationship with more than 1,000 banks. The Bank's main mandate is to facilitate the export and import of Chinese mechanical and electronic products, complete sets of equipment and new- and high-tech products, assist Chinese companies with comparative advantages in their offshore project contracting and outbound investment, and promote international economic cooperation and trade.

The Bank's approved on-balance-sheet loans totaled RMB1,101.6 billion, total contracted loans stood at RMB1,180.9 billion, and total loan disbursement reached RMB1,077.4 billion. As of the end of 2015, the Bank's outstanding on-balance sheet loans amounted to RMB2,148.2 billion, its off-balance-sheet on-lending stood at USD14.6 billion, and its on-balance-sheet and off-balance-sheet assets totaled RMB2,935.2 billion. The Bank's international credit ratings remained the same as China's sovereign ratings.

On its 2015 annual report, its stated mission objectives were: supporting the development of the real economy and facilitating economic structural adjustment, transformation and upgrading; promoting China's import and export optimization and increasing competitiveness of Chinese products and equipment in the international market; implementing China's overseas development strategy and promoting its economic cooperation with other countries.

Some of its capital markets routines include raising funds in domestic and international capital markets and money markets; international inter-bank loans, organizing or participating in international and domestic syndication loans; CNY inter-bank borrowing/lending and bond repurchases; Foreign exchange transaction.

In its 2015 filing, the bank's balance sheet size stood at 2.833 trillion CNY. More than 70% was outstanding loan. 76% of the financing was achieved via bond issuance. Among the loans being made in 2015 filing, 43% were foreign trade loans, and majority of foreign trade loan is for import of goods; 27% were international cooperation loans, most of which were loans for overseas contracting; 23% was loans for supporting greater openness, most of which was loans for transformation upgrading and loans for infrastructure.

Regarding bonds issued by EIBC, the investor base for EIBC bond is similar to CDB bond. EIBC bond offers slighter higher yield versus CDB bond to compensate its relatively lower liquidity.

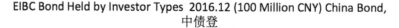

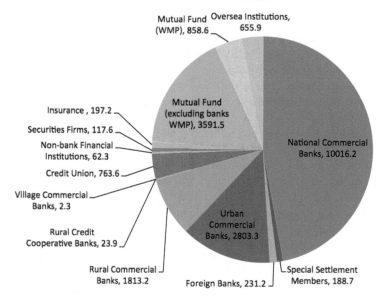

EIBC Bond Held by Investor Types 2016.12 (100 Million CNY) China Bond, 中债登

The investor base that prefers buying CDB bond rather than buying Treasury bond also prefers buying EIBC bond rather than buying CDB bond for the same reasons. For those institutions that prefer Treasury bond, such as special settlement members, EIBC bond slightly higher yield is not enough to compensate for treasury tax-exempt advantage.

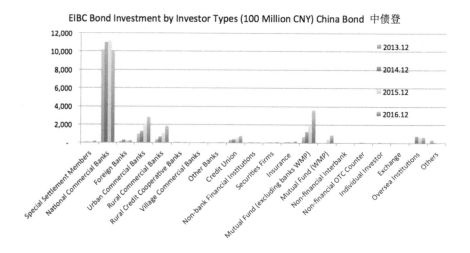

EIBC Bond Investment by Investor Types (100 Million CNY) China Bond 中债登

1.3.1.6 Agricultural Development Bank of China (ADBC)

Similar to the Export-Import Bank of China, Agricultural Development Bank of China is a state bank solely owned by the government, therefore it enjoys the same rating stand as EIBC, and its international credit ratings are the same as China's sovereign ratings. While Export-Import Bank of China focuses on import/export-related projects, ADBC's main focus is to raise funds to support the agricultural sector of the Chinese economy.

Based upon its 2014 annual report, its balance sheet size was 3.14 trillion CNY, 87.6% of which was outstanding loan activities, led by grain reserve and procurement and industrial construction including water circulation systems. Its liability was mostly financed by bond issuance, 70.7, and 15.4% by deposits.

The filing stated that the loan granted was RMB1 430.43 billion, and the loan balance increased 13% to RMB2,831.35 billion, in which, the loans for grains reserve and procurement increased 11.7% to RMB500.04 billion for supporting 473.39 billion Jin (236.695 billion kg) of grains, accounting for 65% of the total grain reserve and procurement amount in the country; the loans for the procurement of cotton amounted to RMB50.14 billion for the purchase of 73.982 million Dan (3699.1 million kg) of cotton, particularly during the cotton settlement year of 2014, supporting 84% of the total procurement amount in Xinjiang and ensuring the smooth reform on target price of cotton; the loans for edible oil reserve and procurement amounted to RMB20.98 billion; the loans for strategic materials reserve, such as sugar, meat and fertilizers amounted to RMB25.95 billion; the loans for leading industrialized enterprises, agricultural science and technology, and the construction of rural circulation system amounted to RMB216.57 billion, by which 4,726 clients and 1,246 projects were supported. The support for irrigation, rural road networks, the new-style urbanization construction had been further enhanced. During the year, the mid and long term loan granted was RMB335.35 billion and the outstanding mid and long term loan reached RMB1.0819 trillion at the end of the year.

The outstanding amount of ADBC bonds is comparable to that of EIBC bonds. So are their investor bases, with the exception of higher presence in ADBC bonds by players from agricultural sector, including village commercial banks, rural credit coop and rural commercial banks.

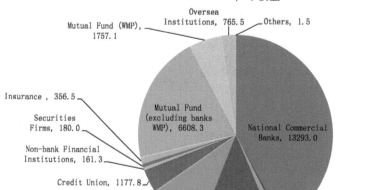

ADBC Bond Held by Investor Types 2016.12 (100 Million CNY) China Bond, 中债登

Urban commercial banks, rural commercial banks and bond funds had increased their purchase of ADBC bonds over the recent years in pursuit of higher yield. National commercial banks also preferred ADBC bonds for their slightly higher yield than CDB bonds.

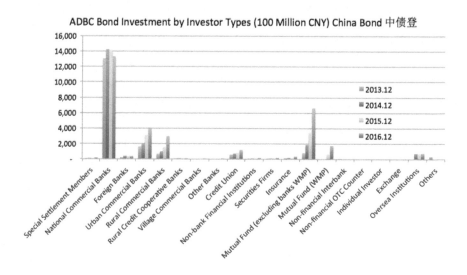

ADBC Bond Investment by Investor Types (100 Million CNY) China Bond 中债登

1.3.1.7 Corporate/MTN

The credit bond sector can be categorized into 3 segments: Corporate, Enterprise, and MTN. Corporate bond is issued and traded on Exchange markets, and its regulatory responsibility falls under CSRC. Different from interbank market, where large banks with their large and stable deposit inflow, participants on the exchange market often use repo to fund leveraged positions and conduct their asset liability management. Though volatile, repo with credit bond collateral is an important financing tool for bond fund. Insurance companies are also important players in corporate bond sector, which they hold to harvest credit premium income.

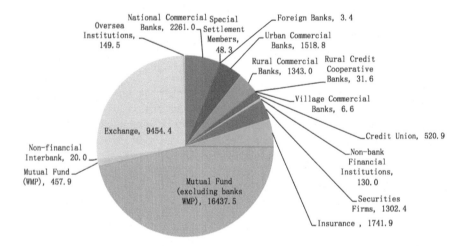

Corporate Bond Held by Investor Types 2016.12 (100 Million CNY)
China Bond, 中债登

Mutual funds have become more active in MTN and corporate bond sector, versus other players. The main reason is that to compete against WMP product, cost of fund for the mutual fund industry is generally much higher than cost of fund for banking industry, hence the urgent need to receive higher return on investment that is only available in the credit sector.

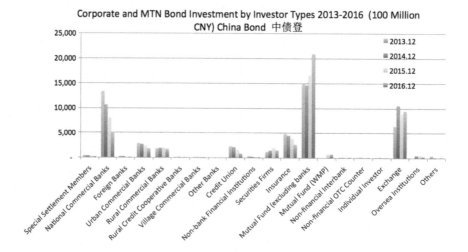

Enterprise bond is issued and traded on both interbank market and exchange market, and its regulatory responsibility falls under National Development and Reform Commission (NDRC). In simple term, only certain state-owned legal entities can be enterprise bond issuers, hence this is an asset class of limited size.

Medium Term Note (MTN) is issued on the interbank market and its regulatory responsibility falls under CBRC. Due to the liquidity depth they need for their large asset size, big banks prefer the interbank market for credit debt investment versus exchange market, this has in turn causes more MTN issuers to issue credit assets on the interbank market.

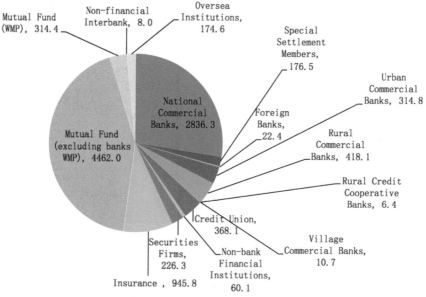

MTN Bond Held by Investor Types 2016.12 (100 Million CNY) China Bond, 中债登

Combined with government cleaning up borrowing by enterprise platform entities, real estate industry growth slowing down and easier issuance of corporate bond on exchanges, MTN issuance shrank. For the still outstanding MTN, the largest amount is held by mutual fund industry, followed by national commercial banks.

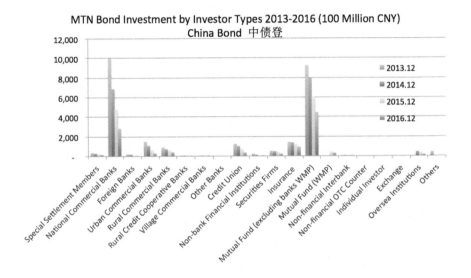

MTN had two large yield spikes in the last 10 years, positively correlated to the interest rate yield movement. The first spike was at the end of 2011, partly for recycling liquidity that was released to counter the global financial crisis, partly for better positioning the domestic return relative to international return to ensure a stable range of exchange rate movement.

The second spike was at the end of 2013, the result of rising yield at the global level as US recovery consolidated. Both yield change later came down as the result of more liquidity being injected into the market to lower borrowing cost.

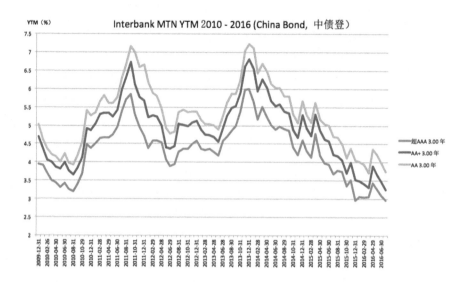

Besides the mutual fund industry, large banks also invest heavily in MTNs. Unlike exchange market-issued corporate bonds, MTNs are issued on the interbank market with larger quantity, thus are traditionally more preferable to large banks with large cashflows. Insurance companies are also active players in MTNs, especially in the longer maturity segment to match their long time horizon liability.

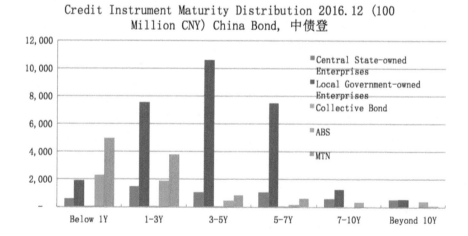

1.3.1.8   Different Assets Issued by Banks

Banks may issue bonds for some of the following reasons: (1) Asset liability mismatch management or balance sheet management. For many banks their main source of funds is deposit, which tends to have short maturities. On the other hand, banks' main asset class is loan, which tends to have much longer maturities than deposit liability. This creates a duration mismatch that can be risky for banks. Loss created by long duration assets is larger than the gain incurred on the short duration liability during a rate rising period. Issuance of longer-dated bonds can mitigate this duration mismatch. (2) As an alternative source of fund that is more stable than deposit, as the competition for cash deposit can be serious especially during end of a regulatory reporting period. (3) To fund leverage during period of fast balance sheet expansion.

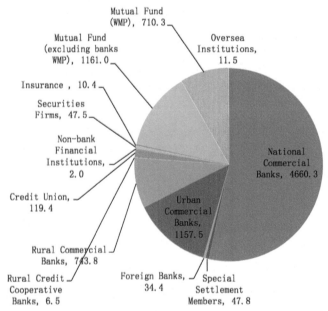

Commercial Bank Bond Held by Investor Types 2016. 12
(100 Million CNY) China Bond, 中债登

Commercial banks also issue subordinated bank bonds, hybrid bonds and tier 2 bank bonds. Subordinated Bank Bonds rank lower than general debt obligation but higher than equities on receiving payments. They were issued with large quantities with the intention to bolster the capital adequacy of commercial banks. As time progressed and risk management practice and capital regulation in China became more stringent, it became evident that previously issued subordinated bonds were not suitable for loss absorption, for its lacking of bond to equity conversion and principal reduction terms during risk event. Thus, regulation was given to stipulate that subordinated bonds issued before 2013.01.01, could still be eligible for being capital instrument, though the amount eligible would be deducted on an annual rate. Insurance companies held large amount of bank-subordinated debt, a lot of which were issued by large banks, thus deemed safe with long maturities and offered decent return. Vice versa, banks bought large quantities of subordinated debt issued by insurance companies. The result is rather small amount of bank investment in the segment of subordinated instrument issued by banks.

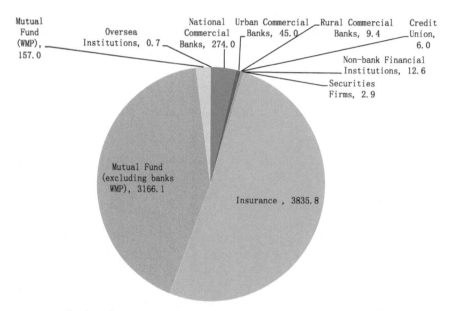

Bank-subordinated Capital Held by Investor Types 2016.12
(100 Million CNY) China Bond, 中债登

Banks also issue hybrid bonds. Lower than general debt obligation and subordinated debt, but higher than equities on debt seniority structure, hybrid bonds exhibit the characteristics of both bonds and equities.

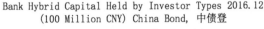
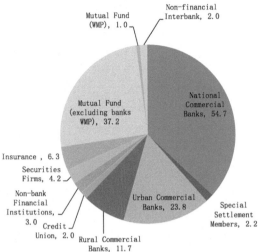

Bank Hybrid Capital Held by Investor Types 2016.12
(100 Million CNY) China Bond, 中债登

The definition of tier 2 capital bonds follows the same global capital structure definition. Banks issue hybrid instruments that are senior tier 2 capital bonds to meet certain BASEL III requirement. For example, it is unsecured, and not callable unless approved by regulators. They are lower than the deposits, bonds and subordinated bonds in terms of seniority during credit events, but higher than equities. Compared to equity dividends, tier 2 capital bonds' interest payment can be deferred and cumulative. For its non-callability, insurance companies are more interested in tier 2 capital bonds than hybrid bonds.

Tier 2 Capital Held by Investor Types 2016.12 (100
Million CNY) China Bond, 中债登

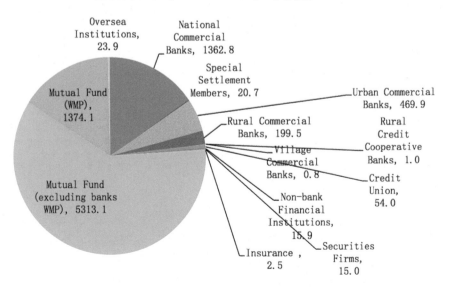

The long tenor distribution of tier 2 capital instrument and subordinated bonds make them very attractive to insurance companies and other investors who are keen to buy and hold investment with relatively higher yield over a long time horizon.

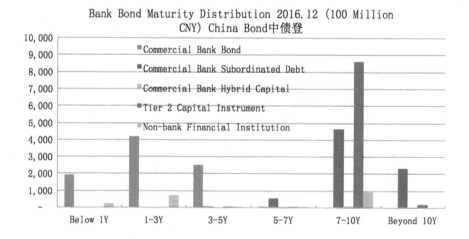

Bank Bond Maturity Distribution 2016.12 (100 Million CNY) China Bond中债登

1.3.1.9   ABS

Banks issue loan-based ABS. As an important asset class it is being pushed forward by multiple regulatory agencies hoping to make bank's balance sheet less dependent on loan while allowing investors direct access to loan-based asset, hence less intermediary transaction cost. This has proved to be a working progress, as legal and financial framework regarding bankruptcy and other important aspects still need further clarification.

Different from traditional bond issuance, ABS is directly tied to the underlying project assets. Some of the typical asset classes include non-standard asset, infrastructure investment, real estate, and others.

Asset-backed Security Types Monthly Trading Volume 2014.03 - 2017.03 (100 Million CNY) China Money, 中国货币网

One type of asset that is heavily linked to ABS is "non-standard asset". Usually a conduit for banks to bypass deposit/loan ratio limit and restriction over investable industry, this type of asset often packages entrusted loan and trust loan, with loan maturity between 1.5 and 3 years.

ABS could also be used to support basic infrastructure project. With duration between 5 and 15 years, and limited liquidity, the return can be much higher than bond.

ABS could also be used to support real estate project via real estate trust or real estate fund. Tied to performance of real estate market, this ABS segment could have significant volatility.

The largest asset management companies and largest commercial companies also issue non-performing loan-based ABS. When this type of asset is structured and analyzed, besides looking into the size of supporting tranche and credit enhancing techniques, it is also important to look into the quality of collateral, and relative allocation of collateralized loan versus pledge loan. Collateralized loan is the most stringent form of loan, for collateral changes hand when a loan is being issued. Collateral quality assessment can also be a complicated process. An example is in general property usage right in a first tier city can be categorized as top quality collateral. This assessment of quality may be questionable when one is to find out later that some owners on the property may refuse to relocate when development plan is to be executed.

1.3.1.10 Foreign Entity-Issued Bonds

Similar to Samurai bond in Japan or Yankee bond in US, these bonds are issued by foreign entities in a domestic market with bonds denominated in local currency. In this case bonds are issued in China interbank bond market and issuances are denominated in CNY. An issuance is often tailored to local projects. Income generated in CNY from local project will be used to cover the bond repayment. Foreign entity-issued bonds alleviate pressure on China's currency reserve. They also help foreign entities in dealing with FX volatilities and currency restrictions.

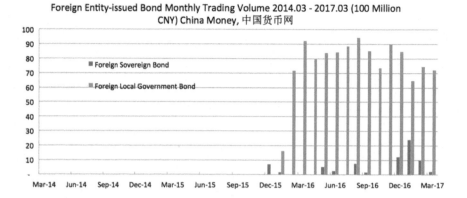

Foreign Entity-issued Bond Monthly Trading Volume 2014.03 - 2017.03 (100 Million CNY) China Money, 中国货币网

1.3.2 Instruments by Cashflow Structures

1.3.2.1 Fixed Rate Bond

Fixed rate bond is by far the most popular cashflow structure for bonds issued in the interbank bond market. Compared with floaters and zero coupon bonds, they resemble multi-year saving deposit that offers return without ambiguity. Fixed rate bond popularity is a reflection that while China's bond market had enjoyed great growth over the recent years, the maturing of monetary policy management practice by financial regulators and various market participants was only a fairly recent phenomenon. As market and interest rate liberalization progress further, more diverse cashflow structure distribution can be expected.

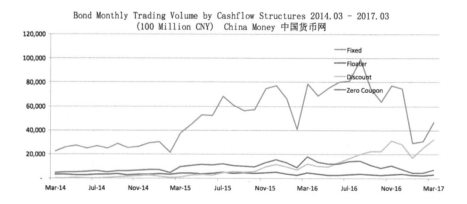

Bond Monthly Trading Volume by Cashflow Structures 2014.03 - 2017.03 (100 Million CNY) China Money 中国货币网

Fixed rate bond is also the most traded cashflow type. While the pricing of floater type has become more sensitive and reliable, its pricing is still not as precise as the fixed rate, especially regarding the liquid sovereign interest rate sector during volatility period. Therefore when short term zero and discount securities are excluded, fixed rate instrument suits investors' need better than float rate instrument.

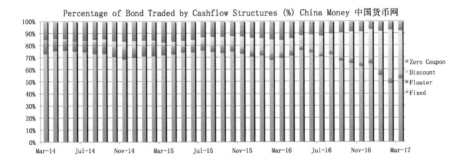

The computation follows ACT/ACT in the interbank market, with Chinese interbank calendar.

1.3.2.2 Zero Coupon, Discount and Floaters

Besides fixed rate bond, interbank market also has floating rate bond, zero coupon bond and discount bond. Regarding floating rate bond, the market has finally settled down on Repo and SHIBOR as the most popular interest rate indices, with SHIBOR strongly correlated with Repo rate. Zero coupon bond and discount bond are similar instruments, with zero coupon making coupon payment with the principal payment at maturity, while discount bond issues at discount and coupon rate is implied in the difference between the face amount and issuing price.

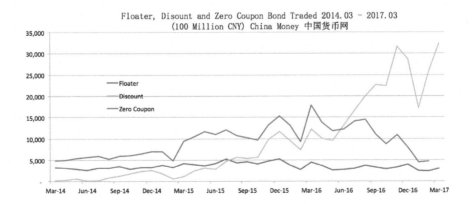

Compared with zero coupon bonds, discount bonds often have shorter maturities. The recent rise of discount bonds for both issuance and trading reflected the need for borrowers to lower their financing cost using term structure during a period of rapid increase of interest rate.

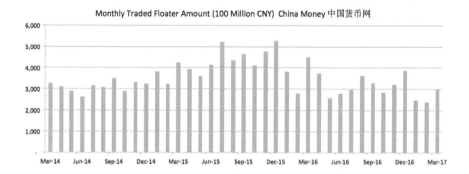

1.3.2.3 Option-Embedded Bonds

Option-embedded bonds are bonds with callable or putable features. Most of these bonds are credit instruments that could have material credit risk. An example is a putable bond issued by an enterprise platform with a 3 + 2 + 2 putable feature. During its life period, issuer may choose to increase coupon payment twice, once at the end of the 3-year period and another at the end of 5-year period. Investor may apply put option when the coupon payment is deemed insufficient when market yield increases.

1.3.2.4 Convertibles

Convertibles bonds are bonds that can be converted to equity shares at certain prices. With embedded stock option, a convertible bond is cheaper for the issuer, in terms of coupon payment financing cost, when compared against other debt instrument in corporate bond market. Its disadvantageous includes complicated clause, its issuance subjected to certain capital ratio limit, longer time for issuance regulatory approval and funds usage restriction.

In Chinese market, beside the fact that as a convertible bond it could be converted to equities at preset prices, it could also have the following main clauses: the bond could be called as a protection for the issuers from large stock price rise hence it usually has a limit for upward potential; a bond put clause an investor can use; a clause for moving down the equity option strike price to avoid the investor put option being exercised. Therefore, in reality, the convertible bond valuation is very complex, and it is often considered more as an equity-financing venue versus a bond with a stock option.

An example is a convertible bond issued by Shanghai Electric 601727.SH. With maturity up to 6 years, its annual coupon is set at 0.2, 0.5, 1.0, 1.5, 1.5 and 1.6% from year 1–6. The equity option strike price is 10.72 CNY and it can be exercised from year half to the end of year 6.

601727.SH also has a bond call option, which can be exercised within the lifetime of equity option. Call option can be exercised if for any 15 days of a continuous 30-day trading period, the stock price is at or above 130% of equity option strike price. The call strike is the face value of bond plus any accrued interest.

601727.SH Equity option's strike price can be adjusted downward, if for any 10 days of a continuous 20-day trading period, the stock price is below 85% of equity option strike price. New equity option strike price should be decided by a shareholder meeting, and the price should be higher of the average trading price of the last 20 trading days and last trading day price, both before the meeting, and it should not be less than the net asset value per share.

601727.SH has a bond put option. Within the last 2 years of bond maturity date, for any continuous 30-day trading period, if the stock price is below 70% of the equity strike price, investor can sell back to the issuer the bond at 103% of its face value, including accrued interest.

The wide application of the bond call option, contributed to the large amount of convertible bond being called by issuer during the early half of 2015, when equity market enjoyed a bull run.

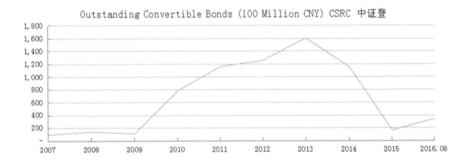

The reason for the wide usage of step up coupon rate is issuer is expecting the equity option or the bond call option to be exercised some time before maturity, and the high coupon payment later in the bond lifetime is not expected to materialize.

The convertible's bond call option is often close to bond face value and this leads the convertibles to be traded mostly at discount price.

1.3.2.5   Small-and-Medium Enterprise Collective Notes (SMECN)

Each SMECN issuance includes multiple legal entities. Credit rating is enhanced by respective agencies to support less established business to enter bond market. This instrument was envisioned to be critical to open the bond market to the small and medium enterprises, in a market that was dominated by blue chip companies and policy institutions.

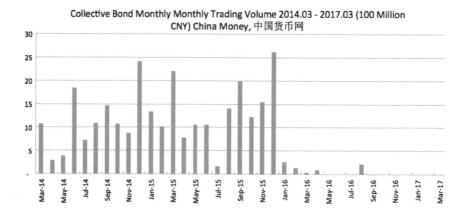

Collective Bond Monthly Monthly Trading Volume 2014.03 - 2017.03 (100 Million CNY) China Money, 中国货币网

The instrument never took off as expected. One of the reason was the difficulty in identifying a good credit entity was the suitable size. Rating for a small and medium enterprise is a difficult issue across the globe, and it was easier to make a loan arrangement with proper collateral arrangement for each specific scenario, versus an unsecured bond issuance.

1.3.2.6   High Yield

High yield bond is referring to a sector of bond with relatively high yield due to lower credit quality. These bonds would have rating below AA+, which is considered to be the threshold for being investment grade. Because AA yield is often unstable due to low trading liquidity, AA yield curve is only used for indicative purpose. Industry often considers high yield specifically for those with yield above 7.5%.

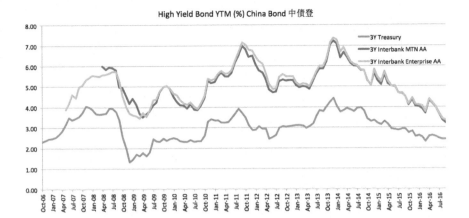

These bonds form an investment sector for fund managers searching for value. They can often be found in low rating enterprise bond issued by county level municipal platform, or MTN often for industry that had built up surplus capacity in metal, coal mining, or paper industry. From time to time the yield or sector criteria used to identify high yield segment may vary after China enters a deeper phase of reform, when liquidity and regulatory condition could change substantially within a short period.

1.3.2.7   Asset-Backed Securities

Asset-backed securities were originally envisioned to reduce the size of banks' balance sheet with enhanced the return on bank equities, and to provide a product with different risk return profile versus more generic fixed income instruments. In reality investors have less confidence in complex securities issued by less established banks or corporations and ABS became relative expensive for them to originate, while well established banks are expected to deliver ABS without significant amount of default, thereby the market reality has defeated the purpose of unloading high yield risk assets from balance sheet that ABS issuance was originally expected to achieve. As China entered deeper stage of economic reform, high yield asset became harder to find amid ample liquidity. Financial organizations were also eager to unload non-performing loan assets from their portfolio during economic upheaval. The increased interest from both demand and supply sides have contributed to regained popularity of ABS.

ABS can have quite a few structure type variations. It possibly involves equity tranche and other credit-enhancing methods including over-collateralization to support more senior high-grade tranche. An example was a Ford ABS issued in 2014. The ABS used car loan as underlying assets and was over-collateralized by 2%. Large Credit ABS securities with underlying loan assets are often issued with somewhat comparable class structure. They tend to have 1 to multiple senior A class tranche, 1 to multiple senior B class tranche, followed by junior class tranche that is unrated. From the perspective of ABS management, yield account is set up to collect interest income and principal account set up to collect principal redemption and recovery. Through a firewall between assets (underlying) and liabilities (ABS investment) and waterfall logic, income from both accounts are funneled into various ABS investment structure.

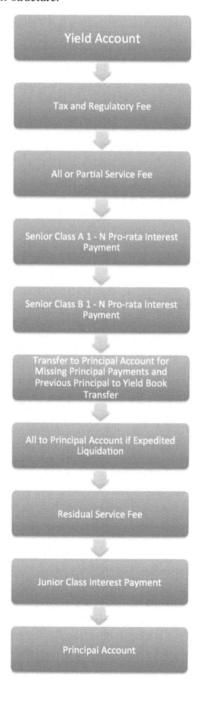

The Yield account pays required tax and service fee and interest on Senior A and Senior B classes. Junior class interest is not paid until missing principal payment or principal payments during expedited liquidation are covered, and previous transfer payments from principal account to yield account to pay for missed senior class interest payment are being compensated for. After junior class interest is paid, the rest of the proceeds will go to principal account.

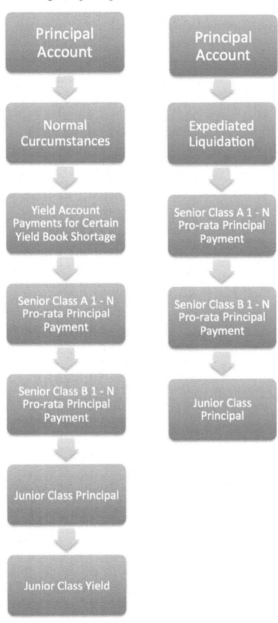

The principal account cashflow payment follows two patterns. Under normal circumstances, principal account will cover missed interest payment for senior classes, and produce senior class A 1—N principal payment until they are paid off, followed by senior class B 1—N principal payment until they are paid off. Junior class principal receives payment next. The rest becomes the yield for junior class. Under the so-called expedited liquidation scenario, for example during a restructuring event that is not a credit event, cashflow received is used to pay down senior class A 1—N first, then senior class B 1—N, and at last junior class principal.

Recovered cashflow after credit events is directly used to pay down interest and principal based upon seniorities. Payment on junior tranche principal or interest rate will not be made, until senior classes are completely paid off.

Versus Credit ABS, the other major type of ABS is the enterprise ABS issued by exchange-listed enterprises and therefore administered by CSRC. They could follow similar cashflow account set up, waterfall logic, and distribution structure of Loan-based ABS.

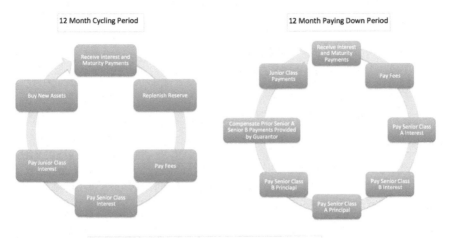

Alibaba Ant Financial Micro Loan Enterprise ABS

An interesting ABS variation is Micro Loan Enterprise ABS, issued by Alibaba Ant Financial. During the first 12 months of so-called cycling period, after paying off interest, and without paying down principals, the received cashflow surplus from the underlying is used to keep buying new underlying assets without exceeding the final maturity of ABS. The next 12 months is so-called paying down period, during which the asset acts as a normal ABS, without buying new assets and standard principal payoff is executed.

1.3.3 The Market Place

1.3.3.1 Exchange, Interbank, and Retail Market

Fixed income products can be traded on three major markets including exchanges, interbank and retail segment. Exchange market under the supervision of CSRC, is much smaller than the interbank market, which is under the supervision of PBOC. Individual customers can purchase OTC bonds from banks. Individuals can also participate in the exchange market, but not directly in the interbank dealer market.

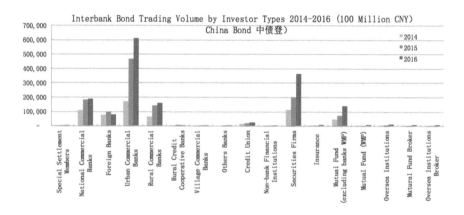

The most active participant in interbank bond trading is urban commercial banks, followed by securities firms, national commercial banks, rural commercial banks and mutual funds. Urban commercial banks, rural commercial banks, securities firms and mutual fund have seen large increase of their share of activities from 2014 to 2016, as they have gradually mastered skillsets required for trading in the fixed income market and sought the opportunity to generate trading revenue.

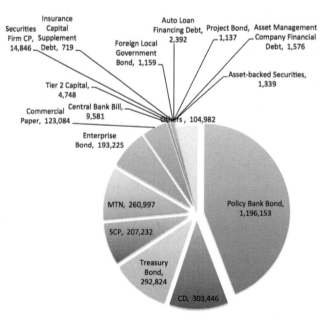

Main Bond Types Traded 2014. 03 - 2017. 03 (100 Million CNY)
China Money, 中国货币网

Policy bank bond is the most actively traded bond type for its sovereign status and its higher yield than Treasury bond. CD, short commercial paper, Treasury bonds are also heavily traded, for their low risk profile. Besides generating return, institutions often hold these liquid instruments for liquidity management. MTN and enterprise bond, issued in the interbank market and exchange market, respectively, can have good liquidity, depending on their rating and whether they can be used as collateral in a repo transaction. Large drop of all trading activities occurred in the end of 2016 partly due to PBOC deleverage effort.

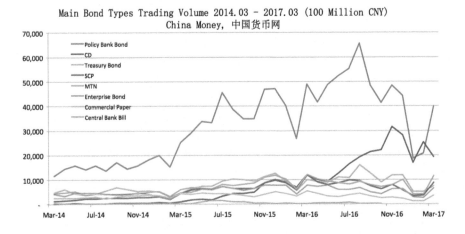

Main Bond Types Trading Volume 2014.03 - 2017.03 (100 Million CNY)
China Money, 中国货币网

When policy bank bond and short term CD instrument are excluded, it becomes apparent that other main instruments, including Treasury bond, MTN, SCP and enterprise bond are quite in sync regarding their respective monthly trading volumes. February tends to produce low monthly trading volume for Spring Festival holiday break.

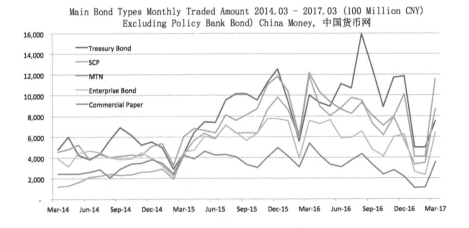

Main Bond Types Monthly Traded Amount 2014.03 - 2017.03 (100 Million CNY)
Excluding Policy Bank Bond) China Money, 中国货币网

While the most actively traded segment within the term structure is within 1 year, the bond market has overall good trading activity distribution among the whole spectrum. Beyond one year, activity either centers on the short to medium space for general trading and investment, or beyond 7 year for investment with long time horizon.

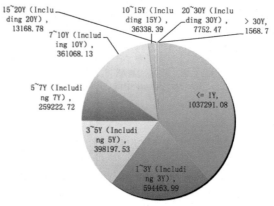

Bonds Traded by Maturities 2014.03 – 2017.03
(100 Million CNY) China Money 中国货币网

The trading behavior for bonds with less than 1Y maturity is different from bonds with longer maturities. Starting from the end of 2016, when PBOC began to focus on deleverage within the financial system, trading of short term maturity instrument, mostly driven by real financing need or active leveraged-arbitrage, fell but quickly rebounded, while longer maturity investment rebounded much slowly for lack of market investment flow and interest.

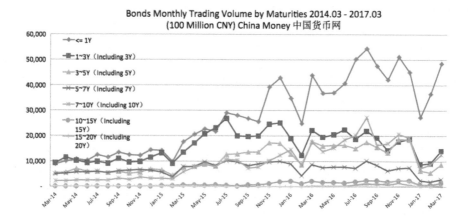

Compared to China Bond, which focuses on bond registration, bond classification on China Money is slightly different, at which interbank trading takes place.

Types of Bonds Traded 2015.07 - 2016.06 (100 Million CNY) China Money 中国货币网

At the retail end, the largest four national commercial banks, including Industrial Commercial Bank of China, Bank of China, China Construction Bank and Agricultural Bank of China are responsible for most of the retail bond trading. Among them, the largest 2 are ICBC and BOC, in terms of value traded on the retail market.

2013-2016 OTC Retail Bond Market Distribution (100 Million CNY) China Bond 中债登

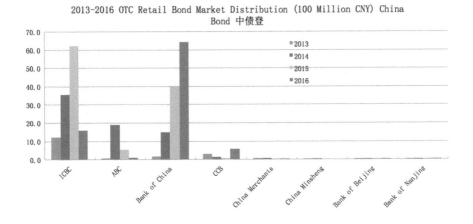

In retail market, it is also important to look into the number of transactions conducted to analyze the relative importance of market distributors. From this perspective, ICBC, CCB and ABC are clearly among the most important, partly because their extensive outlet networks have contributed to their success in the retail market.

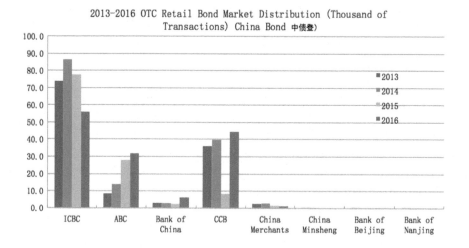

Bond trading is heavily associated with repo execution. Large amount of repo transactions are conducted each day on the interbank market. Vast majority of them are executed using interest rate bonds. Repo transactions have become widely acceptable for financing leveraged positions and balance sheet expansion due to PBOC's stable open market operations in the money market.

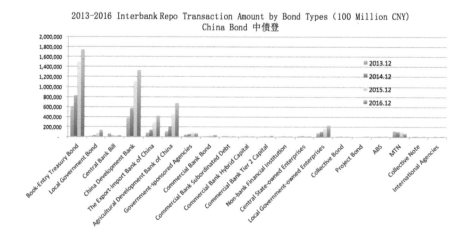

When counterparty credit status is in question, outright repo offers better credit protection than repo. This protection feature makes outright repo a more acceptable instrument to gain yield advantage by motivated players with less credit standing. CDB bond as the high yield instrument among interest rate segment, and enterprise bond and MTN as the high yield credit instrument are preferred as collateral assets underlying outright repo transactions.

2013-2016 Interbank Outright Repo Trade Amount by Bond Types (100 Million CNY) China Bond 中债登

Special settlement members, including PBOC, exchanges and policy banks, are the main lenders in the repo market. Large national banks are overall balanced users in the market with net lending positions. Rural commercial banks and urban commercial banks are very aggressive borrowers, with mutual fund in relatively mild net borrowing position.

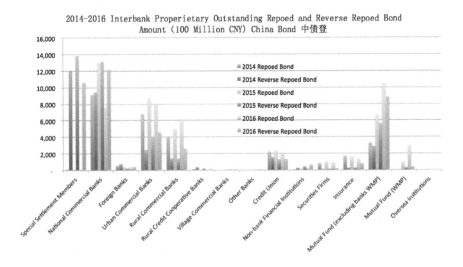

2014-2016 Interbank Proprietary Outstanding Repoed and Reverse Repoed Bond Amount (100 Million CNY) China Bond 中债登

Judging from trading volumes and outstanding bond amount, special settlement members have both conducted lending operations and maintained large lending positions. National commercial banks have acted differently. Since national commercial banks have balanced repo and reverse repo outstanding bond amount but

large reverse repo trade activities versus repo positions, it may be logical to con-
clude that they have provided funding from time to time with surplus cash without
maintaining those lending positions. This role is played by credit union to a less
degree.

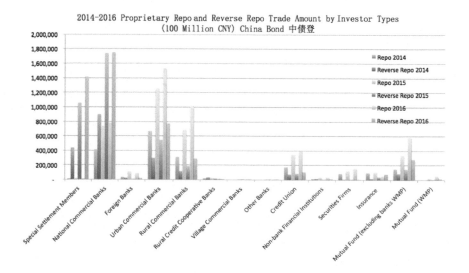

Proprietary outright repo trading volume shows a different pattern. Rural and
urban commercial banks seize these profit-making opportunities to lend to players
with less credit standing and the largest borrowers are securities firms.

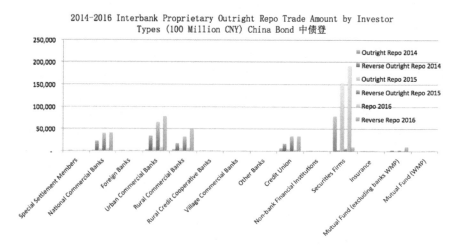

Institutions also engage repo transactions on clients' behalf. Among the commercial players, banks are not major participants in this type of activities. The mutual fund industry is by far the most active in conducting client repo trades.

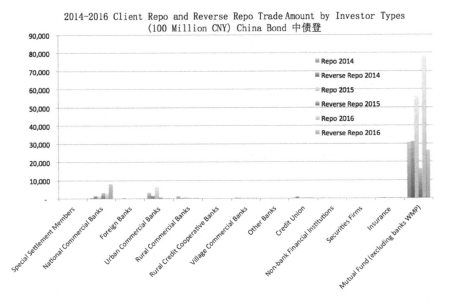

Mutual fund large repo trading volume for client also translates into large for client borrowing amount in the repo market. Due to repo as en effective financing vehicle, large amount of outstanding repo provides substantial amount of saving in terms of borrowing cost.

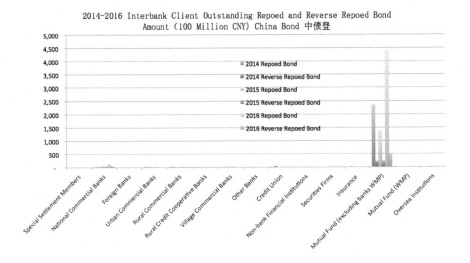

1.3.3.2 Regulatory Regime for the Fixed Income Market Place

Fixed income markets are managed from the perspectives of the markets and the participants. CSRC manages exchange market and PBOC manages interbank dealer market. Fixed income retail market is directly handle by designated banks, under the supervision of PBOC. Based upon the type of fixed income market participants, CBRC manages banks, CSRC manages securities firms listed on exchanges, and CIRC manages mutual fund companies. China Trustee Association manages various trusts. CTA itself is under the management of CBRC.

Among various regulatory agencies, PBOC was especially important in designing and implementing various reforms in the money market and fixed income market. US Federal Reserve for a long period implemented its monetary target via Taylor rule, and more recently carried out three QE programs and set close to zero fed fund rate to help US economy to recover from the 2008 credit crisis. Observing unprecedented global events unfolding, amid difficult domestic economic reform agenda, PBOC manages Chinese fixed income market in unchartered water since 2008 in a different ways, mainly to push forward market reform while manage financial stability after the crisis.

Certain key targets under the close watch by PBOC include: the short end benchmark rate of repo rate; long end benchmark rate of 10 year treasury rate; loan and deposit rate; the loan-to-deposit rate that decides the bank lending amount and the amount of cash banks keep; reserve-to-deposit ratio that decides the amount of reserve bank must keep against deposit; M2 and aggregated social financing amount that are indicative of the amount of economic activities in the country.

CBRC defines, specifies and executes regulatory policies pertaining to the banking industry. The Chinese banking industry's economic importance and the country's nonstop pace of economic reforms together, make banking regulation a very complicated matter. For example, as part of BASIL initiative to strengthen banking risk management using banks' leverage ratio, defined as the tier 1 capital—deductible/on and off balance sheet assets after adjustment, CBRC has to detail exactly what constitutes assets after adjustment. While CBRC manages the BASIL implementation, at the same time it also has to be mindful of anything curtailing the lending activity could have significant consequence in general economy.

CIRC works in a similar capacity as CBRC, except in the insurance industry. The insurance industry has made big transformation in the recent years to relax the regulatory restriction on asset classes, but at the same time strengthen the management practice on overall risk allocation management. Some of this transformation was controversial and had to be called off, especially after the ill-fated push into the equity market.

CSRC provides supervisory role for listed companies and the financial products those companies issue. Corporate bonds listed on exchanges, which create a credit segment different from enterprise bond or MTN, and convertible bonds that have equity component, are under CSRC supervision.

PBOC, CBRC, CSRC and CIRC work together on critical initiatives that may require collaborative effort beyond their respective regulatory areas. An example was regarding the popular interbank repo/trust practice, which was in essence a regulatory capital arbitrage. A company would apply a repo transaction to borrow from interbank money market, and reinvest the proceeds into high yield trust. The risk capital weight for money market repo was set at relatively low ratio, no more than 25%, depending upon the length of repo tenor, versus a 100% capital weight assignment for a standard lending exercise. The repo financing was executed on the interbank market managed by PBOC. The entities executing the repo were banks or insurance companies, many of which are also listed companies. Therefore, on May 16, 2014, to prevent this risk capital arbitrage from distorting the market, the four regulatory bodies together issued a sweeping joint policy announcement to toughen the regulation including repo collateral eligibility and higher risk capital weight.

1.3.3.3 Participant Distribution for Trading

Relative to the moderate size of their balance sheet and bond investment portfolio, urban and rural commercial banks and mutual funds are more aggressive trading participants, when compared with large commercial banks. Yield enhancement generated from both active trading and portfolio reallocation are more important to these relatively medium-sized financial entities. Foreign banks have small presence in domestic fixed income market.

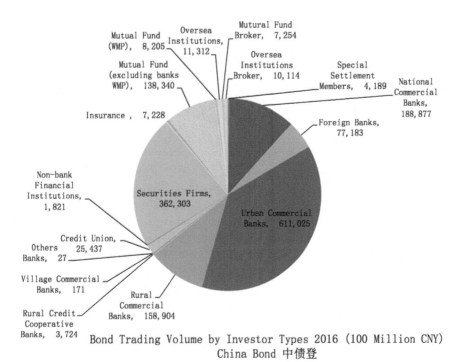

Bond Trading Volume by Investor Types 2016 (100 Million CNY)
China Bond 中债登

Mutual fund's volatile participation in fixed income market is significantly influenced by the performance of the equities market. With a large percentage of fixed income fund invested in money market instrument, the mutual fund is often viewed either as a provider for money market investment, or a temporary safe harbor for funds interested in higher return in the equity market.

1.3.3.4   Investment Community Distribution

Investors include special settlement members, banks, mutual fund, insurance companies, securities firms and individuals. The largest type of participant is national commercial bank. Urban commercial banks and insurance companies are also significant players in the investment community.

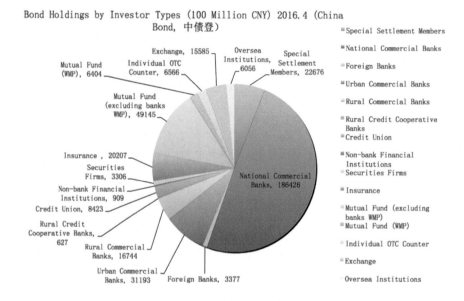

Mutual fund participation rate in fixed income investment is volatile, often as the result of frequent asset reallocation between equity and bond market. Compared with US fund industry, there is no comparable presence of 401K retirement plan equivalent in China and hence a lack of long-term investment objective for both equity or bond markets by the fund companies.

Insurance companies' investment portfolio in fixed income instruments has grown quickly over the recent years, as series of regulatory and industry reforms have made these companies more competitive in the product offering and risk management practice.

1.3.3.5   Specific Interbank Market Versus Exchange Market Differences

There are many differences between the two fixed income markets, the most significant of which are market size and repo execution style. First, the interbank market is much larger than the exchange market. The resulted liquidity difference makes it easier for traders to make market on the interbank market since it is relatively easier to unload positions when needed. It is also easier for bond underwriting and syndication to be arranged.

The second difference is the repo process. In the exchange markets, repo trades are executed against the exchanges, hence a repo with credit collateral can be easily arranged, as long as the credit bond can be accepted as eligible collateral. On the other hand, in the interbank market, repo is executed against other members, a repo with credit collateral is more difficult to arrange due to credit limits especially for companies with lower credit status. Also public listed companies only issue bonds in the exchange market not the interbank market. This causes the exchange to be the focus for corporate bonds issuance, where investors receive lower yields from bond yield but get compensated from repo leverage yield.

1.3.3.6   Liquidity and Issuance

The interbank market is much larger than the exchange market. Most of the offerings on the exchanges are focused on credit instruments, including central state-owned enterprises and local government-owned enterprises, while the interbank market is dominated by interest rate instrument including Treasuries, local government bonds and policy bank bonds.

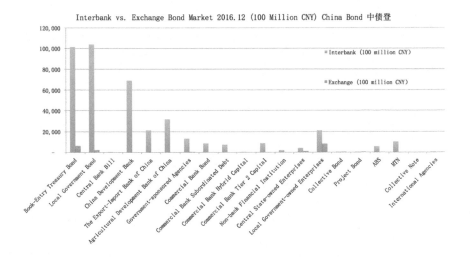

Recently the largest issuance increase on the interbank market was in the interest rate sector, especially in the local government segment. Combined with its size and instant reaction to monetary supply and PBOC monetary policy change, interbank is an important place to understand the Chinese macro and monetary condition.

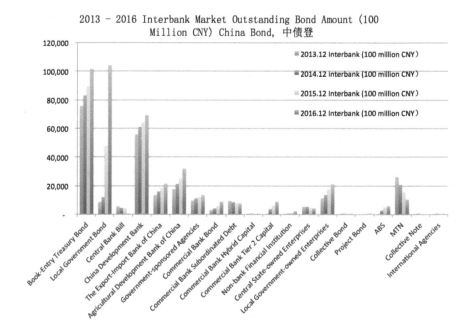

When we look into the exchange market in details, from 2013 to 2016, there were large issuance increases for treasury bonds, local government bond and local government enterprise bond. The issuance of local enterprises bonds on exchange eventually stabilized after central government effort to stabilize local debt amount and local debt cost level with increased usage of local government bond, and measures by the exchanges to control leveraged inter-market arbitrage via more accurately calculated collateral ratio of credit bonds during a repo transaction.

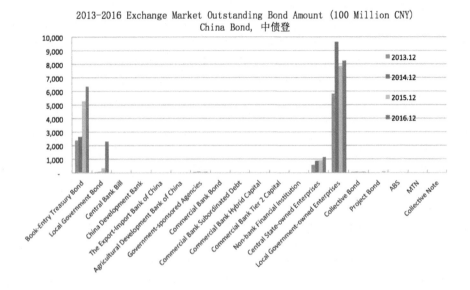

2013-2016 Exchange Market Outstanding Bond Amount (100 Million CNY)
China Bond, 中债登

1.3.3.7 Participants and Risk Appetites

The largest difference between the interbank and exchange markets, in terms of the type of participants engaged, is the presence of banks. Banks are on the interbank market but absent from the exchange markets. The large supply of investment inflow provided by banks has defined the interbank market to be much larger than the exchange market. The largest players on the exchange are various securities firms, which do not have the extensive outlet networks that banks have, therefore they lack the retail investor penetration that could funnel retail assets into bond investment flow.

1.3.3.8 Leverage Usage

Banks on the interbank market do not use leverage to invest for their proprietary accounts. While less so than before, these accounts that mostly adhering to passive investment practice are still the dominant source of investment inflow into China bond market. Leverage usage on the exchange market is very common by securities firms and other financial firms. This phenomenon of frequent leverage usage contributed to low yield of credit instrument and the attractiveness of issuing credits on the exchange market.

1.4   Derivatives

1.4.1   Swaps

1.4.1.1   Instrument Definition, Indices and Application

Swap instrument trading follows international convention. While the swap market does not hold the comparable importance as the bond market, for there is no equivalent of Fannie Mae or Freddie Mac in China's market that actively create market demand for cash flow hedging and market value hedging via interest rate swap, nevertheless, many proprietary trading desks try to use swaps to profit from interest rate swing and the market is active with relative thin spread.

The most actively traded swap index is FR007. It has become the benchmark for money market borrowing cost. This money market rate is also closely followed by PBOC, to monitor interbank money supply condition and inject liquidity when needed. The most important swap types in terms of index and maturity combination are those executed with FR007 and Shibor 3M indices, with most active maturities on 6M, 1Y and 5Y.

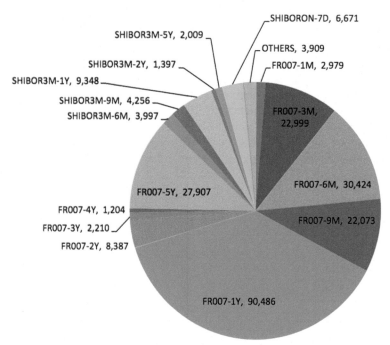

IR Swap Trading Volume Distribution by Index and Maturity 2014.04 - 2017.03 (100 Million CNY) China Money 中国货币网

1.4.1.2 Participants and Trading Liquidity

Banks, especially the large ones that can absorb loss in case the market takes a large disadvantageous turn, trade swaps to make bets on the direction and extent of interest rate change. Therefore the change of monthly trading volume of the most liquid FR007-based swaps on 6M, 1Y and 5Y ladders often coincide with large domestic and international economic events. The volume change also displays a seasonal pattern. There is often a rise of trading activities on March after February low.

1.4.2 Bond Futures

1.4.2.1 Contract Definition and Instrument Application

China Financial Futures Exchange (CFFEX) publishes 5-year Treasury Bond Futures Contract definition. While the definition and trading practice are overall similar to US bond future, there are a few significant differences. 1st is the Treasury bond tax-exempt status in China causing the bond issuances with different age and thus coupon rate differences difficult to dematerialize. 2nd is the difficulty in shorting bonds to hedge long future risk. These two factors combined cause the future's CTD bond IRR to be very low so as to compensate the risk taken by future long positions.

Underlying bond	Nominal medium-term treasury bond with face value of RMB1 million and coupon rate of 3%
Deliverable bond	Treasury coupon bond with the remaining term of 4–5.25 years after the first day of the expiry month
Quotation	RMB100 net price
Tick size	RMB0.005
Contract months	Three recent quarterly months (a cycle of three recent quarterly months among March, June, September and December)
Trading hours	09:15–11:30 a.m., 01:00–03:15 p.m.
Trading hours on last trading day	09:15–11:30 a.m.
Limit up/down	±1.2% of settlement price on the previous trading day
Minimum margin requirement	1% of the contract value
Last trading day	The second Friday of the expiry month of the contract
Last delivery day	The third trading day after the last trading day
Delivery method	Physical delivery
Transaction code	TF
Exchange	China Financial Futures Exchange

China Financial Futures Exchange (CFFEX) also publishes the definition of 10-year Treasury Bond Futures Contract.

Underlying bond	Nominal medium-term treasury bond with face value of RMB1 million and coupon rate of 3%
Deliverable bond	Treasury coupon bond with the remaining term of 6.5–10.25 years after the first day of the expiry month
Quotation	RMB100 net price
Tick size	RMB0.005
Contract months	Three recent quarterly months (a cycle of three recent quarterly months among March, June, September and December)
Trading Hours	09:15–11:30 a.m., 01:00–03:15 p.m.
Trading hours on last trading day	09:15–11:30 a.m.
Limit up/down	±2% of settlement price on the previous trading day
Minimum margin requirement	2% of the contract value
Last trading day	The second Friday of the expiry month of the contract
Last delivery day	The third trading day after the last trading day
Delivery method	Physical delivery
Transaction code	TF
Exchange	China Financial Futures Exchange

1.5   Gold Contract on Shanghai Gold Exchange

1.5.1   Physical Gold

The largest trading place for gold in China is Shanghai Gold Exchange. Physical gold with purity at 99.99% and above or 99.95% are traded with quotation in CNY per gram. Unlike the European style exchange with no large physical presence, or American style exchange with broad commodity coverage unrestricted to precious metals, Shanghai Gold Exchange lists only precious metal, including gold, silver and platinum, with a physical infrastructure. Gradually Au99.99 replaced Au99.95 as the more popular physical gold contract.

Au99.99 contract definition	
Product	Gold
Product code	Au99.99
Trading method	Physical
Product size	10 g/lot
Price quotation	(RMB) Yuan/g
Minimum price fluctuation	0.01 Yuan/g
Daily price limit	30% above or below the closing price of the previous trading day
Minimum quotation size	1 lot
Maximum quotation size	10,000 lots
Trading hours	Morning: 9:00–11:30 a.m.; Afternoon: 13:30–15:30 p.m.; Night: 20:00 p.m. to 02:30 a.m.
Settlement type	Delivery-versus-payment
Product for delivery	Gold ingots with a Standard Weight of 1 kg and a fineness of no lower than 999.9
Delivery type	Physical
Delivery period	T + 0
Grade and quality specifications	Standard physical bullions produced by SGE certified gold producers and meet SGEB1-2002 quality standards, or produced by qualified producers certified by London Bullion Market Association (LBMA)
Delivery venue	SGE certified vaults
Transaction fee	0.035% of the trading value
Delivery fee	0
Listing date	October 30th, 2002

The monthly settled volume of both Au99.99 and Au99.95 hit more than 800 tons in the mid 2015. The actually traded amount can be much larger from time to time. As impressive as the growth of this trading volume is, this monthly amount is close to a daily traded volume in London.

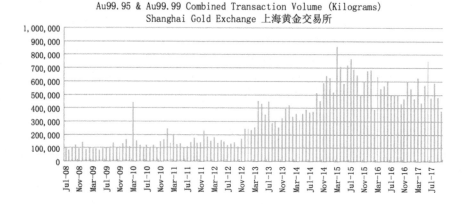

Au99.95 & Au99.99 Combined Transaction Volume (Kilograms)
Shanghai Gold Exchange 上海黄金交易所

1.5.2 Deferred Delivery Gold

Gold is also traded via deferred delivery contract on Shanghai Gold Exchange. Deferred delivery contract can be settled each day or deferred to any future date, hence deferred delivery contract can exhibit both physical contract or forward contract pricing behavior. Also a margin product, deferred delivery contract is a leveraged trading tool to take view on the future movement of gold.

Au (T + D) contract definition	
Product	Gold
Product code	Au (T + D)
Trading method	Deferred
Product size	1 kg/lot
Price quotation	(RMB) Yuan/g
Minimum price fluctuation	0.01 Yuan/g
Daily price limit	5% above or below the closing price of the previous trading day
Minimum quotation size	1 lot
Maximum quotation size	1,000 lots
Product period	Continuous trading
Minimum trading margin	6% of the product value
Trading hours	Morning: 9:00–11:30 a.m.; Afternoon: 13:30–15:30 p.m.; Night: 19:50 p.m. to 02:30 a.m.
Deferred interest payment date	Daily per natural day
Deferred interest	0.02% of the product's market value/day
Minimum tendering for delivery size	1 lot

(continued)

(continued)

Au (T + D) contract definition	
Tendering for delivery period	15:00–15:30
Delivery equalizer tendering period	15:31–15:40
Deferred period	Per the announcement of the exchange
Fee for holding open interest beyond deferred period	Per the announcement of the exchange
Transaction fee	0.02% of the trading value
Default penalty	8% of the value of the product
Settlement type	Daily mark-to-market settlement

The monthly settled volume hit more than 400 billion CNY in the mid of 2016, positions that actually changed hand can be much large.

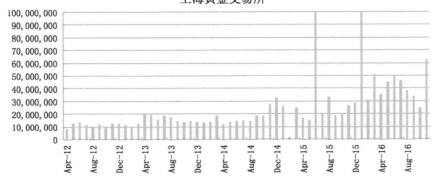

Au(T+D) Transaction Volume (10K CNY) Shanghai Gold Exchange
上海黄金交易所

Chapter 2
Macro Economics, Monetary Cycle, Industry Cycle, Monetary Condition, Supply and Demand

2.1 Traditional Macro Cycle Indicators

2.1.1 GDP and Growth Contribution

Based upon methodology used and data compiled by National Bureau of Statistics of China, there are three main contributors to Chinese economic GDP. Analyzing data published by NBSC for the 4th quarter of 2015, of those three factors the most important is the consumption contributing to domestic GDP at about 60%, followed by investment at about 40%, and net international trade.

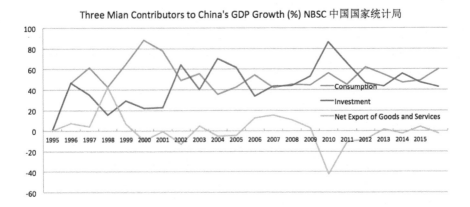

IMF and World Bank used different methodologies in estimating the effect of various drivers on China GDP. Recent World Banks published statistics suggest international trade contribution to Chinese GDP at about 22%, and IMF published statistics suggest investment contribution to Chinese at about 38%.

© Springer Nature Singapore Pte Ltd. 2018
X. Zhang, *Capital Markets Trading and Investment Strategies in China*,
https://doi.org/10.1007/978-981-10-8497-3_2

As Chinese economy evolves, following similar path other industrialized countries have previously taken, it is going through a transformation from massive infrastructure and investment-driven economy towards more advanced manufacturing and service-based economy. During this transitional period, there is a substantial industrial production overcapacity, especially in real estate, steel and coal industry. It was estimated by various public industry reports that the steel and coal industry's overcapacity was above 30% by 2015.

2.1.2 Electricity Generation and Industrial Growth

Comparable to a complex engine in motion, an economy grows with different speed at different time. Different factors underlying economic growth functioning as fired cylinders move and interact with each other in the most complicated pattern. The very large economy of China has large dependence on industrial growth. While PMI was a good indicator for industrial growth, a better precise proxy for its position could be found in the usage of electricity generation. The following figure shows heavy correlation between electricity generation growth and Import/Export growth, and correlation between electricity generation growth and real estate investment growth. Both the real estate and international trade are categorized as main contributing factors to Chinese economic growth.

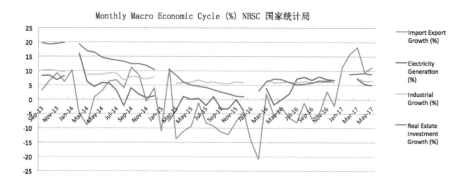

2.1.3 Pork and Copper Price as Growth Indicators

Analysts observed the upward movement of pork price when economic cycle was in its expansion phase in China. There was a clear price increase during the global economic bubble period between 2007 and 2008. The price came down after the bubble burst and later rose again when the massive stimulus package was implemented to counter the global downturn between 2010 and 2011. A relatively mild upward movement between 2015 and 2016 could be related to the state of a stabilizing economy.

Copper has many economic applications including power cable and equipment, a lot of which are linked to real estate and infrastructure sectors. Copper price increases when China's domestic demand is up and copper price sometimes is referred to as Dr. Copper for its sensitivity to China's economic cycle. China imports massive amount of copper-related resources. It consumes more than one third of global copper ore production. In 2015 it produced close to 2 million tons of copper ore and imported about 4.8 million tons of copper ore based upon NBSC data, compared with the global copper ore production of less than 19 million tons.

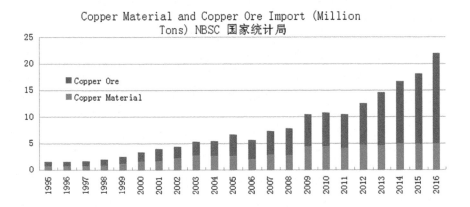

2.1.4   Export Dependency and Market Distribution

Important to China's economic ascendance and overall macro stability, Chinese export industry enjoyed rapid growth in the first decade of 21st century, especially after the entry into WTO. In the aftermath of US 2008 credit crisis, global trade growth lost its momentum and Doha round of world trade talk grinded to a halt. Manufacturing in the labor-intensive segment within China faces competition from low waged countries around the world. East Asian countries' competitive currency devaluation introduces difficulty in tech export segment. Chinese industries are going through a period when various industries are trying to move higher towards research and design within the global supply chain and reorient the production capacity from international trade to internal consumption.

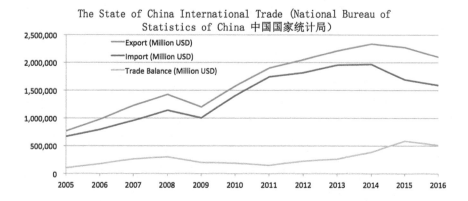

The decrease of export did not result in a large shrinkage of trade surplus, as there was a simultaneous decrease of import. But the loss of speed on export growth engine combined with capital outflow had sizable impact on China FX reserve. The size of the China's currency reserve changed from rapid accumulation increase in early years to more recent stable decrease, when it hit its peak at the end of 2014.

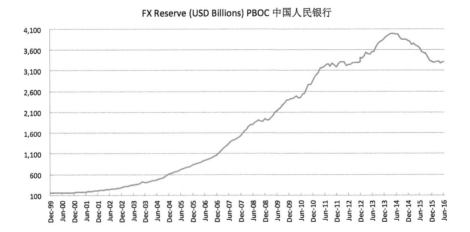

Monthly trade data shows a seasonable pattern of surging import export before international holiday season starts, and a large decline after the holiday season with Chinese Spring Festival holiday kicking in. Monthly trade data is very important for both gauging economic activities and immunize foreign exchange effect on domestic monetary market.

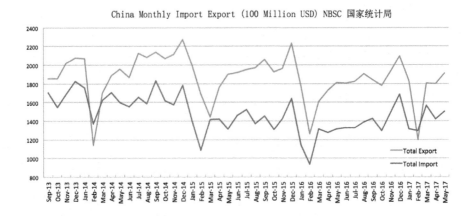

One important FX artifact always being scrutinized by regulatory agencies is the current account versus capital account flow. Capital flows can both contribute to economic growth via investment and introduce monetary volatility via capital flight. The capital account outflow was at its peak in 2008, when credit crisis was in full swing and the global need of capital was dire.

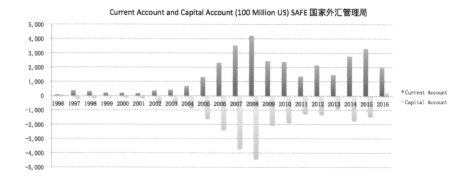

Regarding the current account, General Administration of Customs of China publishes data on international trade breakdown by nation/region. For Jan. to Oct. of 2016, the largest trading partner for China was EU, closely followed by US, ASEAN. Other significant destinations include HK China, Japan and South Korea.

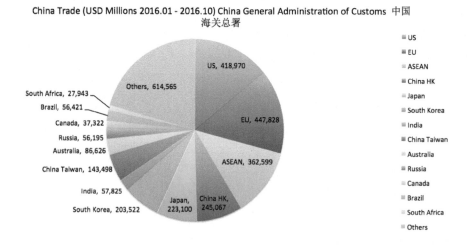

Analyzing the export data from General Administration of Customs and comparing them with the trade data shows China trade surplus with US, EU and trade deficit with China Taiwan, South Korea, Australia and Brazil. The lack of growth in the US export market and Euro zone economy after the global financial crisis had negatively impacted the growth prospect for Chinese export industry. The slowdown of Chinese export industry, with the additional internal economic adjustment in China, caused slowdown in resource export countries including Brazil and Australia, with a severe negative result on global commodity market.

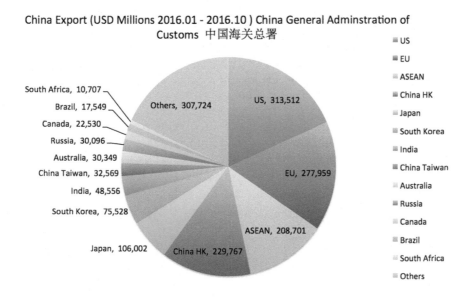

China Export (USD Millions 2016.01 - 2016.10) China General Adminstration of Customs 中国海关总署

2.2   Real Estate Cycle Specificities

2.2.1   New Construction, Sales and Existing Inventory

The long-term prospect of a real estate industry is influenced by the size of population with real demand. As the current low birth rate in China persists, the underlying real demand for real estate has likely peaked, except for largest coastal cities. Nevertheless, real estate is a very important segment of China's economy, and its percentage as of the total fixed investment has stayed around a stable 20% level.

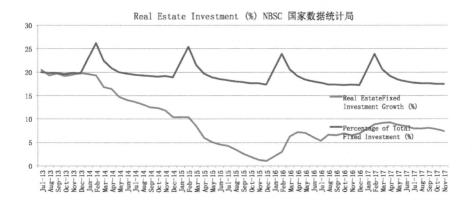

Real Estate Investment (%) NBSC 国家数据统计局

Historically a regular mid term real estate cycle could be observed that was roughly a 2-year period, matching how long a real estate project would normally take to finish, starting from designing phase, to permit approval, construction and ended with sales proceeds received. This pattern is no longer observable as buying is driven both by living and volatile investment requirement.

As the demand peaked and pent-up historical demand was mostly met, inventory started to built up, especially in third tier and forth tier cities around the country. The real estate inventory, including those under construction, has been above 6 billion square meters. Assuming the average price at 7,000 CNY per square meter for those assets, the size of inventory is 42 trillion CNY. By comparison, the GDP of China by NBSC was 64.48 trillion CNY for the year of 2014.

While it is evident that some of these property inventory can take quite some time to clear, the real estate investment, which is represented by new construction, is being processed at a fairly healthy speed. The clearing can be closely tracked by the fairly small difference between newly constructed and sold, numbers published by National Bureau of Statistics of China. A large amount of these new investments are located in the first tier and second tier cities, an indication that the urbanization process in China continues to move people from far-flung regions to places where economies are thriving.

As for the industry itself, most of the companies in this industry are not state-owned. The industry is not concentrated and is geographical dispersed. Heavily leveraged and dependent upon financing to keep afloat in nature, each company's individual's rating, variously obtained regulatory certification, and management capability are all important factors for itself to continuously secure financing resources and thereby keep a healthy balance sheet. The constant need for financing and unpredictable inventory turnover have resulted in the industry being quite sensitive to any regulatory change. In fact, many of the real estate sharp turns in recent history were caused by regulatory policy change, aimed at slowing down the fast price gain pushed up by historical pent-up demand in China's market reform process.

Heavy academic discussion has been presented to make comparison between the Chinese real estate market and real estate market in Japan before and after the bubble period in the early 1990s. While there are many similarities between the real estate markets of the two Asian countries, the conclusion of this type of comparative study is only relative mostly due to (1) the size of China's domestic market and its level of development has produced a much stronger export industry and (2) a very large domestic market of China makes its real state market less subject to international volatility.

Japan Residential Price Index 日本不動産研究所 The Japan Real Estate Institute

2.2.2   Real Estate Dependency

As one of main pillars of current Chinese economy, real estate industry has played a significant role in stabilizing country's economic output after the collapse of international trade market growth. But this economic dependence on real estate industry is quite substantial and some of the historian analysis suggested the 1994 tax reform as the root cause. Before 1994, local government collected business tax revenue, a surplus portion of which was later sent to the central government. Local authorities had the incentive to lower the reported value of revenue surplus collected so as to retaining more funds to support various local initiatives. It became difficult for central government to have enough funds to support countrywide projects. 1994 Tax Reform changed the tax collection from business tax to a new VAT system. 75% of the VAT tax collected will go to central government, while 25% will remain with different levels of local government. Since a substantial amount of civil responsibilities are still carries out by different levels of local government, it became imperative for them to find new sources of funding, and the tax collected on real estate business, a portion of which does not go to central government, became a very critical source of revenue. Volatile in nature, various estimates put the real estate related income at about half the government budget revenue, and 60% of the out-of-budget revenue. As a result, large amount constructions were carried out around the country to meet people's expectation of higher dwelling standard, and also provided funds to many critical local civil projects.

Based upon numbers published by Ministry of Finance, for the fiscal year of 2015, local government received 3955.88 Billion CNY as program revenue. 77.8% of that program revenue was generated from land transfer transactions. This percentage value indicated high dependence by the local government on the real estate industry.

Local Government Program and General Revenue 2016 Fiscal Year (100 Million CNY) China MOF 中国财政部

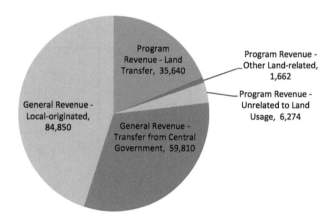

Based upon monthly data published by National Bureau of Statistics China, during the first 9 months of 2016, sales of commercial properties reached 8020.8 billion CNY, and the total value of goods and services sold reached 23848.2 Billion CNY. The sales of commercial properties accounted for about 33.6% of goods and services sold in China. During the same period, real estate fixed investment was 7459.8 billion CNY, and the total fixed investment was 42690.6 Billion CNY, real estate investment account for about 8.1% of total fixed investment. Based upon the estimate that goods and services sold accounts for about 58.4% of GDP, and investment accounts for about 43.4% of GDP, real estate industry alone accounted for about 23.16% of China's GDP. By comparison, numbers by the US Bureau of Economic Analysis indicated the US total residential fixed investment, plus housing services, was in the range of 17.5–19% before the 2008 Great Recession.

The health of real estate industry has broad ramification in Chinese economy. Substantial amount of steel output is being consumed by the real estate industry, hence the stabilization of real estate investment is critical in supporting the steel industry, which is still addressing its oversupply issue.

2.3 Government-Driven Investment

2.3.1 Government Spending and Its History

Based upon fiscal year 2016 expenditure data published by China Ministry of Finance, the largest destination of fund usage include Education (15%), Social Security (11%), Agriculture Forestry and Water (10%), Urban and Rural Neighborhood Services (10%), General Public Expenditure (8%), Medical Services (7%) and Transportation (6%). This order reflected the government priorities in its long list of mandates for a populous country. The largest amount of funds was spent on education at around 2,807 billion CNY, including compulsory 9-year education and other educational services. The amount of funds spent on Medical Services was 1315.9 billion CNY, which translated into close 1,000 CNY per head.

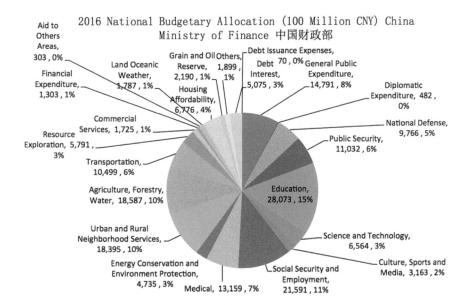

The growth pattern differences within the national budgetary expenditure also reflects China's domestic priority mandate. General public expenditure growth, which supports a large amount administrative activities, has been subdued underlying government effort in reining in bureaucratic cost. On the other hand, education, urban and rural neighborhood services, agriculture and housing affordability received large increases. While China had enjoyed fast growth over the recent years and the budgetary allocation also reflected the coming of a modern country, it will still take substantial effort before its spending levels per person in many sectors are on par with a fully industrialized country.

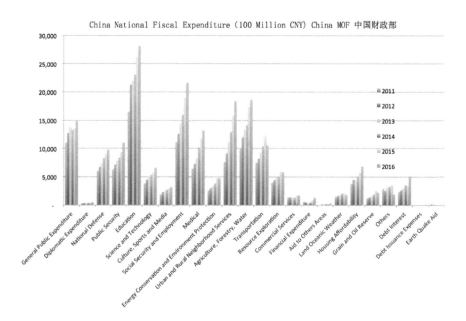

Good understanding of certain government initiatives is important for assessing macro economic settings and compiling a corresponding investment strategy. From 2011 to 2016, budgetary spending on pollution prevention, water-related projects, road construction and housing renovation projects have increased substantially. Spending on railroad transportation had been maintained at about the same level. Affordable housing expenditure came down over the years, reflecting difficulty in administer eligibility assessment and other import technical details.

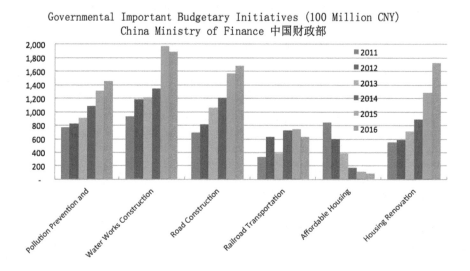

2.3.2 *Budgetary Deficit Constraint*

From historical perspective China had generally observed a conservative budgetary policy at national level. The expenditure growth has mostly kept on pace with the nation's revenue growth. Since 2008, expenditure grew faster than revenue reflecting the need to provide a more stimulative monetary environment in generally weaker global and domestic economic setting. The gap between annual fiscal revenue and fiscal expenditure had been widened from 126 billion CNY in 2008, to 2815 billion CNY in 2016.

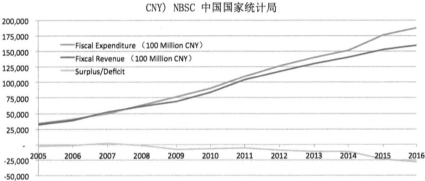

The monthly fiscal data has indicated the slower revenue growth since 2015, when GDP growth has shifted to a more moderate level, and China has entered deeper phase of economic reform for supply side re-engineering. There was a sharp increase of bank loans issued in January and March of 2017 that contributed the increase of both monthly revenue and expenditure, which had fallen back after loan activities returned to their normal level.

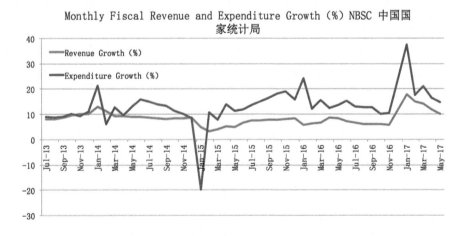

In the beginning of each fiscal year, when the budgetary details are still being compiled and planed out for the rest of year, the spending tends to be slower. Spending then picks up speed through out the rest of the fiscal year. During the end of 2013, there was a crackdown on suspected illicit export trade used to transfer capital into the country to take advantage the relative high financing spread between CNY and USD. The crackdown caused the reduction of so called Funds Outstanding for foreign exchange. Banks receive FX when receipts from export trades are settled and sell FX to PBOC, mostly in USD, to central bank and receive CNY in return. The large sum of USD in the export trade, has always been in the end translated into a significant source of financing to the economies that have large export sector. In this case when lending was impacted, as a result of crackdown on illicit export, government stepped in with larger expenditure to generate more economic activities.

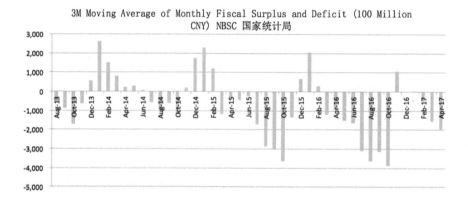

The monthly data at end of 2014 could be partly explained with improving international trade data. From the end of 2013, the trend of US economic growth became clear as it was emerging from the shadow of 2008 credit crisis, and USD also entered a strengthening cycle. Therefore, by the end of 2014, not only China was amassing a large FX reserve with a strong export industry, CNY was also strengthening against many currencies, as its price was mostly linked to USD. Reflecting on this strength, there was a short periodic pullback in terms of fiscal expenditure.

Towards the end of 2015, the assessment on US economy was very positive. During the same time, China export was weakened by both the strength of its currency and anemic global demand, and there was clear difficulty in reducing overcapacity in China's industrial sector. Large fiscal support was provided to buttress the Chinese economy against the economic headwind plus the negative domestic lending environment caused capital outflow from China. The deficit was ever larger in 2016 to maintain a stimulative monetary environment, while progress had been made on the industrial overcapacity reduction.

2.4 USD Cycle

2.4.1 Global Monetary Condition and Funding Cost

Many in the current trading and investment world take USD quotes in foreign exchange domain for granted and often underestimate the significance of dollar influence on global capital flow and investment strategy formulation. US dollar is the most important reserve currency in the world, and its percentage as being part of the central banks' reserve has stayed above 60% since the launch of Euro. There has been no materialistic change on that during the 2008 credit crisis, and its reserve currency status has only strengthened in the recent years, as US economy entered into a stable recovery phase.

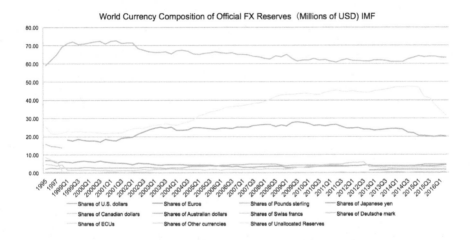

From the perspective of foreign exchange turnover, the importance of USD is no less significant. USD is by far the most used settlement currency in global trade and there is no materialistic change of its share in FX turnover based upon BIS triennial central bank survey. BIS Survey, which takes into consideration of currency pair double counting, out of 100%, would put USD at 43.8% in the global foreign exchange turnover. Euro is a distant second at 15.65%, Japanese Yen at 10.8%, British Pound at 6.4% and Australian Dollar at 3.45%.

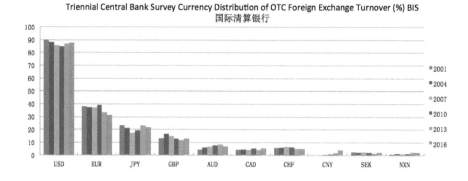

Therefore as the reserve currency of the world and most liquid international currency, the funding rate of USD has large impact beyond US border. From 2008 till the end of 2015, the fed fund rate was maintained at close to 0%, an abnormally low level from historical perspective to tackle the aftermath of 2008 financial crisis. Low level of funding rate, while accommodative during economic crisis, would create distortion in asset prices under normal economic condition. While a central bank may prefer to bring its basic funding rate back to neutral territory when possible, USD fed fund rate hike would raise interest rate in global financial market, therefore could have a huge implication to the world economy.

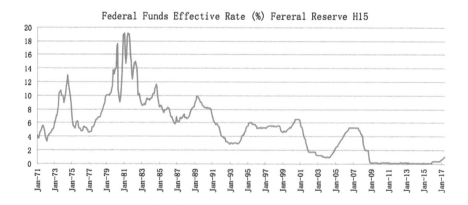

2.4.2   Exchange Rate Fluctuation and Its Impact on Commerce

The US dollar funding rate increase also raises the value of US dollar itself, which brings implications to the world of foreign exchange. Exchange rates are essentially prices of various currencies against the other currencies. Most used exchange rates are those against US dollar. The price of US Dollar can be measured by Broad Dollar Index, which is published by Federal Reserve. This index has strengthened since the end of year 2013, a clear signal that global financial markets mostly concluded that US economy has mended its wound caused by financial crisis.

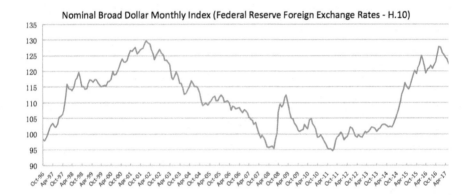

Since an exchange rate is often the price of a non-USD currency against USD, when US dollar gets stronger, without intervening events, other currencies' relative value expressed in USD will become cheaper. If for any reason exchange rates are to be maintained against USD, those countries' domestic base funding rates have to be increased to maintain the interest rate parity, assuming a relative openness of an economy. Partly for that reason and the influence of US economy, funding rates of major economies have come down after the financial crisis and may rise in sync with US rate in the future.

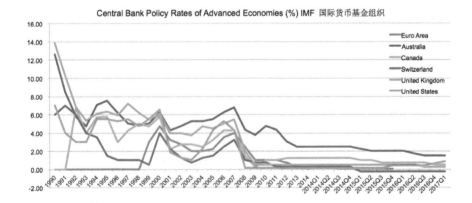

As China moved deeper into financial market reform and interest rate liberalization process, US dollar cycle's impact on China domestic funding rate and CNY exchange rate becomes stronger. If the CNY exchange rate is to be maintained at the current level, China has to increase its domestic funding rate to keep up with the US fed fund rate hike. The rate hike in domestic CNY market would be a concern for China's difficult supply side reform. If China does not increase domestic funding rate correspondingly, capital outflow might increase and CNY will be under devaluation pressure. While this devaluation may increase China's export, but it can also cause competitive devaluation in other export-oriented countries, which may destabilize the current fragile global international trade framework.

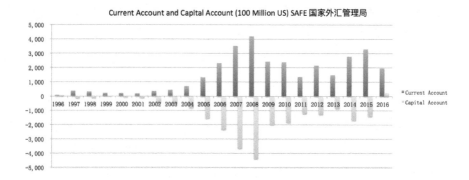

Various measures to counter the volatile USD cycle have been taken, including regulations to tighten capital outflow. Some of the capital outflow is made under the name of international investment with dubious purposes. The regulatory measures have proved to be effective with China capital account flow in 2016 ended with a surplus.

2.5 Industrial Cyclical Specificities

2.5.1 Industry Classification

Manufacturing industries can be broadly classified into three categories based upon their relative positions in the supply chain, including upstream, midstream and downstream industries. Macro economic conditions, influenced by various monetary policy and liquidity condition, drive the demand and performance of downstream industries. The downstream industries pull supply and production of midstream industries, and the midstream industries in turns, pull the upstream supply and production.

【Steel Industry】 One of the important midstream industry in China is the steel industry. Its recent tremendous growth symbolized the industrialization of China. During the first decade of the 21st century the annual production rose from a little over 100 million tons to around 800 million tons.

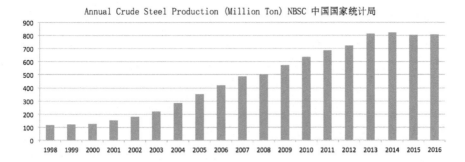

Annual Crude Steel Production (Million Ton) NBSC 中国国家统计局

The largest destinations of the steel output were real estate industry, basic infrastructure, machinery manufacturing and auto industry. China exports less than 100 million ton of crude steel. Steel import is much smaller than it used to be, largely due to improvement in both manufacturing technology and global transportation efficiency that lowered ore shipment cost to China. Iron ore import is very large, for the quality and quantity of iron ore in China make domestic mining not as efficient compared with foreign mining in Australia and Brazil.

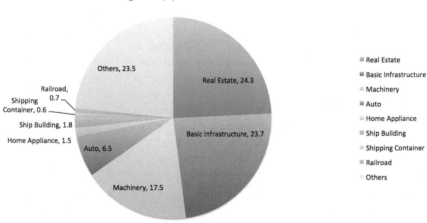

Steel Usage 2014(%) - China United Steel 中钢联

The growth in the downstream real estate industry in the past pulled the growth of the midstream steel industry, which was especially the case after 2008 with the large stimulus package following the global depression. There was certain level of tension between the domestic steel producers and global iron ore suppliers. In 2008, more than half of the global iron ore import was imported into China. The global iron ore suppliers were concentrated in Brazil and Australia, represented by Rio Tinto, BHP Billiton and Vale. The domestic steel industry is on the other hand not concentrated hence the steel producers are in a disadvantageous position during price negotiation. Once the real estate industry is in its own state of slowing down, the steel industry and the ore supplier both receive overcapacity shock. The crude steel production capacity, based upon estimates from China Iron and Steel Association (ChinaISA) and other sources, was at 1100 million tons. Production level at around 800 million would make the utilization ratio at around 70%. The steel production correction also dealt a severe blow to the equity prices of global iron ore producers.

Steel industry is important for both employment and local economic output, therefore making correction to the production overcapacity in China will not be an easy task for the government or the economy to tackle. An analogy can be made to steel overcapacity encountered by the US in the period between 1972 and 1982, and it took about a 10-year period to cut down steel production with massive layoff. By the end of 2017, steel industry production overcapacity was partially addressed.

【Coal Industry】 For its abundance, coal has been and will be an important source of energy for China. The largest usage were electricity generation, steel, construction material, and chemicals production. Steel and infrastructure lead the coal industry in terms of economic cycle. The largest deposit concentrates in certain provinces, the largest being Shan Xi in northern China. The main port for coal imports is Qinhuangdao.

To keep track of coal's supply and demand, analysts focus on its current and future level of production, import amount, and downstream usage especially in electricity generation. Regarding prices, focus is on Datong in Shanxi province for domestic production price on both thermal coal and coking coal, and on Qinhuangdao for import price on thermal coal, and any fluctuation of international thermal coal price index. As far as inventory is concerned, focus is on the level of downstream usage inventory around the country and transport inventory in Qinhuangdao.

The real number level of coal overcapacity is difficult to gather. It typically takes three years to build capacity. The large amount of overbuilt capacity, a lot of which were started before and around 2012, and its associated debt burden have put the coal industry under tremendous stress. The industry as a whole is much less concentrated than the oil industry further worsened the situation. Current supply side reform mandate has required the industry to reduce the capacity.

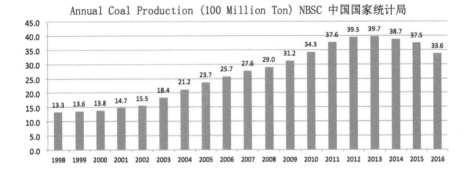

Annual Coal Production (100 Million Ton) NBSC 中国国家统计局

Not being a clean energy source, the wide spread usage of coal also contributed to serious environmental problem. Even though cleaner energy sources, including hydroelectricity, solar power, wind and natural gas, are making large progress in China, coal share of energy produced was still at 72.2% in 2015, versus 77.8% in 2011. Coal will continue to play an important role in China's electricity generation. This is consistent with US Department of Energy's global coal usage forecasting that as the living standard continues to improve in China and in the other parts of the world, the demand for electricity will also increase, and so is the demand for coal used for electricity generation as abundant source of energy.

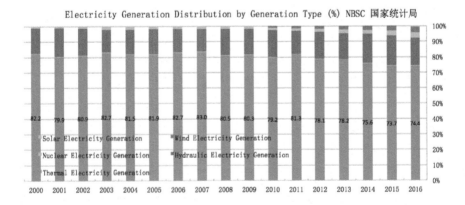

Electricity Generation Distribution by Generation Type (%) NBSC 国家统计局

【Automotive Industry】 One of the largest downstream demands for of both steel sector and coal sector is the car industry. The auto industry includes the following segments: parts, cars, dealership and services. The industry is further downstream versus coal and steel thus less susceptible to the current oversupply problem. It is a large part of the economy and its prospect sheds important light on the state of macro condition.

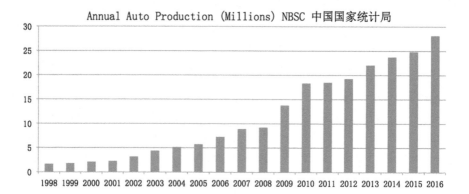

The auto industry had two rapid growth periods. The first was 2001–2003, caused by the rising level of income. Capacity increase followed, and industry relatively slowed down. Capacity became less of an issue during 2005–2007 as increasing demand caught up and margin gradually improved. Starting 2009, with healthier margin and improved liquidity, the industry entered the second phase of rapid growth. More recently certain segments such as the SUV still enjoy relatively higher growth. The high-end segment is dominated by foreign manufacturing or joint venture controlled by foreign manufacturers.

The market is very competitive, with global auto manufactures from Japan, Germany, US, South Korea and to less extent, France dominating the market. Between 2012 and 2016, around 60% of the passenger vehicles sold in China were sold under foreign brands.

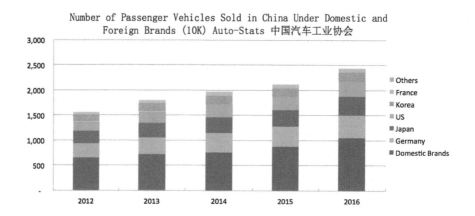

【Mobile Phones and Telecommunication】 The majority of the income for the telecommunication industry is from mobile services, while the lesser amount is from the fixed line services. For the mobile services, the building of 4G networks has mostly completed. The majorities of mobile users are using 3G or 4G services. User migration from lower end of the technology spectrum to higher end 3G and 4G contributed to the bottom line of the service providers as the previous investments started to payoff.

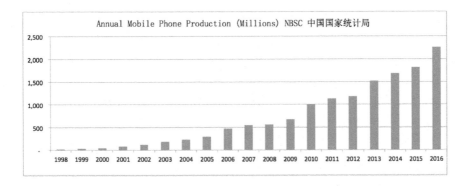

The number of smart phones in services reached more than 1.2 billion some time in 2016, based upon CNNIC stats. Compared with more than 700 million Internet users in China, there are at least 600 million users accessing Internet via their mobile phones. The largest source of business line income for mobile service providers are search engine, electronic commerce and news. Other areas that had enjoyed fast growth include games and movies, commercials, cloud communications. Mobile on-line commercials are expected to hit 6.2 billion USD, the second largest in the world after US market of 9.4 billion USD. Mobile operating system is dominated by Android, while Apple iPhone remains extremely popular.

Built upon the improvement of the mobile services, third party mobile payment became more popular. Dominant service providers in this area include Alipay, Wechat Pay and banks. User acceptance within the younger generation is higher versus the older generation.

【Agricultural Industry】 Analysis of agricultural industry provides domestic economic condition context for macro study and inflation forecast.

Basic understandings of this industry in China have to be centered upon the two essential facts including large domestic demand for food products and scarcity of arable land. First the amount of consumption of certain products such as rice is multiple times of quantity of global export so food security needs to be based upon domestic production and it is a matter of national security. Second, for country's large population, the amount of arable land per person is about half of the world average. For that reason the typical size of farming is small and its operating model has to be different from US and other large countries. Therefore the agricultural industry needs to provide food security to the country, and at the same time, generates stable income for many people working on the land and agriculture-related business. To achieve these two goals, price floor, import/export control, arable land usage regulation policies are put in places. State-owned companies hold important positions in the bulk purchasing and distribution channels hence provide critical price support functions to stabilize agricultural product prices.

Compared against the less efficient mid-stream planting segment, the upstream segments including seeds, pesticides and fertilizers, and downstream segments including processing and food production, are more centralized and efficient.

The agricultural sector's economic performance benefited from global commodity price rise and domestic reform policy support in the past. Current key issues include large amount of import and its impact on domestic producers, and the domination of foreign suppliers in the seed industry.

Changing landscape of Chinese agricultural industry illustrates the transformation that is taking place in the daily life of this large country. The living standard of people has improved substantially and as the result, the production of corn took off to supply enough amount of animal feed. Production of vegetable also increased substantially. Grain production growth percentagewise has been held steady over the years, for the amount of the arable land is limited and real effort has been made to maintain the amount of land for grain production.

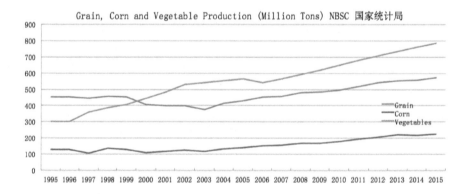

A detailed look into the main domestic crop production over a longer time horizon, illustrates that the rice production had the smallest production growth history and had hit its upper potential limit for its current high acreage yield. Wheat production grew more than rice but also stabilized for the same reason. Corn and soy productions are less efficient than international growers from US and Brazil. For this reason, while corn production increased substantially to satisfy strong need for animal feed, soy import exploded. Imported soy based upon more efficient GM soy production from Brazil and US drove down domestic soy price and forced domestic acreage cutback. Soy domestic production decreased from 17.4 million MT in 2004 to 11.8 million MT in 2015 based upon USDA stats.

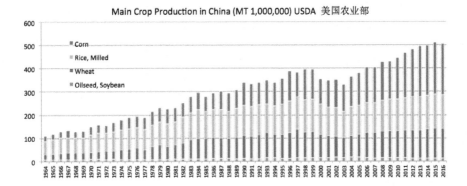

Main Crop Production in China (MT 1,000,000) USDA 美国农业部

Soy is one of the most important traditional food ingredients in Chinese diet. It is also an important source of cooking oil. Soybean meal, a byproduct of soybean oil extraction, serves as an important source for animal feed. As China's living standard improves, it is increasingly hard for domestic soy production to keep up with the increasing soy product demand. The total amount of soy import and domestic production based upon NBSC data was 92.2 million tons for 2015, which includes the domestic production amount of a little more than 10 million tons. In comparison, USDA estimation global soy production for 2015–2016 was 313 million tons.

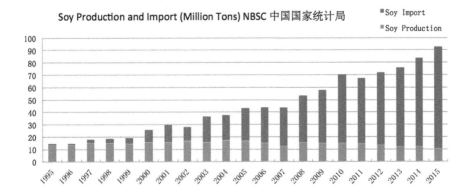

Soy Production and Import (Million Tons) NBSC 中国国家统计局

Meat production saw large growth over the years and its stabilization happened around the same time global financial source hit the shore. Poultry and beef demand grew. Still swine is the main meat source in China's agricultural business.

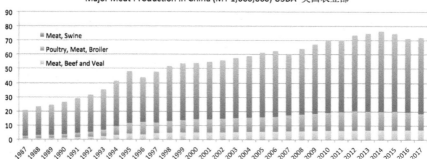

Major Meat Production in China (MT 1,000,000) USDA 美国农业部

Pork and animal husbandry industry observed cyclical price movement embedded within the generally upward trend. For its large quantity, pork price becomes an important part of China CPI index. Upward price movement was often associated with increasing demand for meet diet and more stringent environment regulations. Tougher environment regulation and pork price volatility have made it more difficult for smaller pig farms to compete against large and more efficient pig farms, and the exit by small farms from business further exacerbated pork price and its volatility.

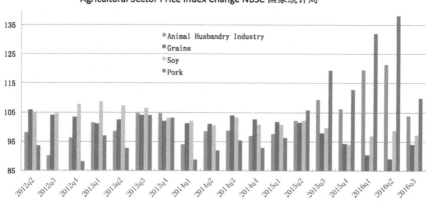

Agricultural Sector Price Index Change NBSC 国家统计局

【Chemical Industry】 Segmented and technology intensive, this industry can be analyzed from the perspectives of its major products, including basic chemical, fertilizer, pesticide, sodium carbonate.

One of the major basic chemical products produced by China's chemical industry, ethylene is used in the manufacturing of many important polymers including polyethylene (PE), polyethylene terephthalate (PET), polyvinyl chloride (PVC) and polystyrene (PS) as well as fibers and other organic chemicals. Ethylene can be made from oil, gas and coal. But for China's general shortage of gas and coal considered as dirty source for chemical production, oil is the main raw material used in ethylene production. For its importance Ethylene's production level is sometimes associated with the level of development of a country's petroleum industry. There is a high concentration of production facilities based in the US and Western Europe, with more recent addition from Middle East and Asia. Also for its wide application and involvement in a variety of economic areas, many analysts use ethylene production level and price level to gauge macro condition. A lot of the production facilities in China are located in the three large river delta areas. Between 2016 and 2020, more production capacity will be added.

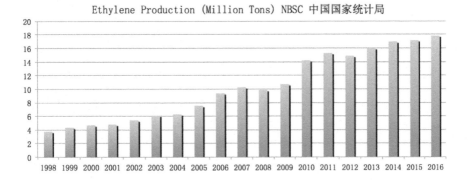

Ethylene Production (Million Tons) NBSC 中国国家统计局

Fertilizer is widely used in China to enhance crop yield. Both nitrogen and phosphates fertilizers can and are mostly produced domestically. The price of nitrogen fertilizer is mostly about manufacturing cost including raw material cost. Nitrogen and phosphate fertilizers are under pressure from both falling international crop price and coming supply from other developing countries. Potash fertilizer price is resource driven and the import percentage is significant.

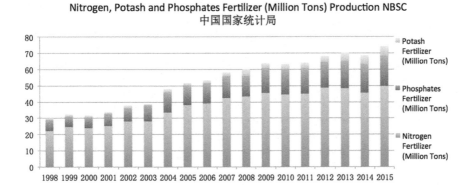

Nitrogen, Potash and Phosphates Fertilizer (Million Tons) Production NBSC 中国国家统计局

Pesticide production data covers a broad category of products including herbicides, bactericides, insecticides and others. A relatively a small sector for upstream chemical agents usage, it had enjoyed healthy growth but now facing a state of its own oversupply, after export market stagnated. The industry also faces scrutiny over environmental irregularities. The investment opportunities in this industry could be those production technologies and products that are more environmental friendly.

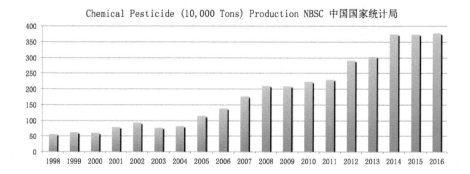

The most important usage for sodium carbonate is to make glass. Hence from the quantity of sodium carbonate, we may infer the level of GDP growth, which is heavily dependent upon real estate.

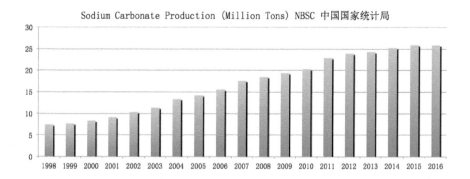

Pharmaceutical and medical product area are going though large changes. In domestic market, for many reasons innovation on the medical front has been a difficult and improving process, tax reform and anti-corruption campaign made prescription market and OTC market that is cost-based more competitive. In the international market, growth based upon basic active ingredients has largely peaked. While future explosive growth is less likely, as China moves forward and living standard continuously improves, steady growth in this area could be expected.

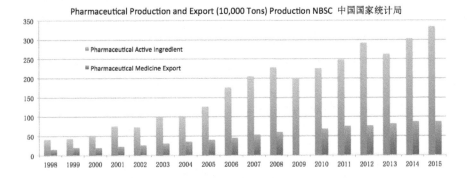

2.5.2 State-Owned Versus Private-Owned

Ownership type is an important factor in the investment decision process. State-owned enterprises are a vital part of China economic activities, for their generally large sizes and a variety of vital functions they provide. Based upon the ownership structure, there are two subcategory, central state-owned enterprises and local government-owned enterprises.

Central state-owned enterprise, when strictly defined, refers to those enterprises that are directly under the management of State-owned Assets Supervision and Administration Commission of the State Council (SASACSC). Examples include China National Petroleum Corporation and State Grid of China. When broadly defined, central state-owned enterprises can also include large banks or policy banks that are under the supervision of CBRC and CSRC. Examples include China Development Bank and Agricultural Development Bank, and other organizations in different areas that are under the management of the State Council. As far as Ministry of Finance revenue contribution on general revenue report is concerned, strict definition for state ownership is applied. By December 2015, they were 106 central state-owned enterprises. If large financial institutions are included, the number was 124.

These large companies tend to be in the business segments that were considered vital and critical, for example, petroleum, coal and shipping building. It is important to remember what is considered critical for a developing country is also an evolving concept. A developing country may consider building an electricity grid to be a daunting task when farmers are emerging from mud huts to become factory workers. Later when developed a government in a modern society might consider that daily economic activities without electricity would cease to exist hence the well being of the electricity grid becomes a national security issue from a different perspective.

In the past these large companies paid considerable amount of taxes and have committed large amount of resources to the development of China. An example was the discovery of oil in China. China was considered to be lacking any significant oil deposit until large reserve was located in Northeastern China. It was carried out by the predecessor of current central state-owned enterprise, and made China self-reliant on oil until economy took off later on. The numbers shown below are from General Public Budget Revenue Report published by Ministry of Finance compiled at both central and local level. The revenue number does not include the total contribution by state-owned enterprises, as taxes including VAT and business income tax are not classified specifically for state-owned enterprises in these general revenue reports. Nevertheless, state-owned enterprises for their large sizes and long history, a lot of which also listed, generally tend to have a much higher level of regulatory oversight and therefore better reporting transparency and data quality. Thus a year-to-year comparison of the state-owned enterprise revenue data shed useful light on the level of their economic activities at both the national level and local level.

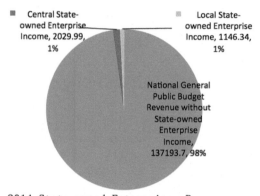

2014 State-owned Enterprises Revenue Contribution (100 Million CNY) China Ministry of Finance 中国财政部

From 2015, China entered supply side economic reform. Government has focused on reducing overcapacity in real estate, steel, coal and cement sector, and redirected more resources towards local economic activities, some of which are through infrastructure building and housing improvement. This has helped to stabilize the general economy. But the less efficient capacity usually got cut was often organized at local level. At the same time, economy at local levels was still saddled with high real estate inventory, especially in the 3rd and 4th tier cities. With these reasons, the performance of central state-owned enterprises was better than local-owned enterprises.

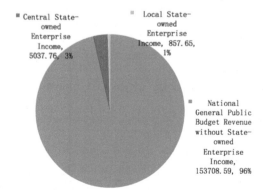

2016 State-owned Enterprises Revenue Contribution (100 Million CNY) China Ministry of Finance 中国财政部

Based upon reports published by Ministry of Finance specifically for state-owned enterprises covering at both central and local level, the stats at sector level are quite indicative of the economic reform that are taking place. Coal industry underperformed for overcapacity reduction, especially in the stream coal segment where coal is being used for electricity generation. Transportation outperformed for various infrastructure-building stimulus initiatives, including high-speed train around the country and urban subway projects and generally healthy state of the car industry. Other areas that have outperformed included machinery, investment services, education and research-generated revenue are all result of the larger reengineering effort to transform the economy into a more self-sustaining growth model less dependent upon old-styled industrialization and export.

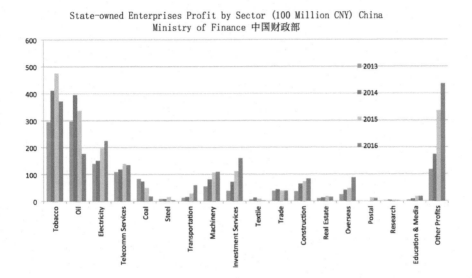

State-owned Enterprises Profit by Sector (100 Million CNY) China
Ministry of Finance 中国财政部

2.5.3 Cycle and Seasonal Patterns

As a country becomes more industrialized, it would demonstrate both business cycle in production and seasonal pattern in consumer spending. While patterns in production business cycle can be subject to many external and internal factors in an evolving economy producing complicated results, consumer spending seasonality can often be clearly analyzed and demonstrated. Within China's consumer spending (excluding real estate), the largest outlay based upon Census Bureau published data, include auto, oil, clothing, food and others. Vehicles are purchased throughout the years. Some consumers find time during the year-end break to finalize their purchase. Auto producers respond to this pattern by producing more vehicles during year-end. Comparatively, July and August tend to be low months.

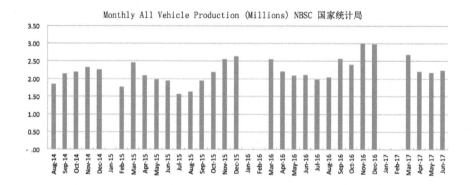

Travel is an important part of people's life and travel spending also demonstrates seasonal pattern. Many families arrange their travel trip during school summer break creating peak travel month in the August of each year. Traveling is also up during year-end and spring festivals for family reunion.

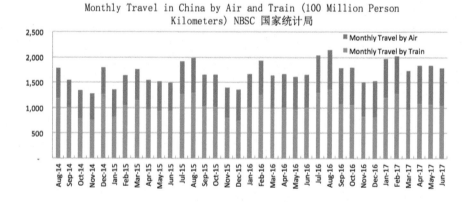

More than half of the electricity generated is used for manufacturing. The combined effects of auto production, year-end travel, winter heating requirement and holiday season production contribute to electricity generation peak during the year-end. Any break of trend and seasonal pattern of consumer spending and electricity generation would demand an update on economic and investment condition assessment.

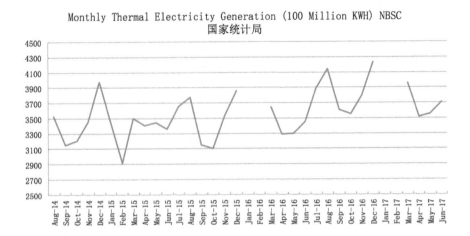

Monthly Thermal Electricity Generation (100 Million KWH) NBSC
国家统计局

2.6 Monetary Cycle

2.6.1 Quantity Versus Price Target

Monetary cycle can be managed either through changing the amount of liquidity in the system, by setting up and trying to achieve a quantitative target, or though the price of liquidity in the system, by setting up and trying to achieve a price target. In the earlier developmental stage of a monetary system, price signal transmission is often not conducive, among different segment, different instruments, or same instrument on different tenors. A yield change in the bond segment may not cause a corresponding yield change in the loan segment. Similarly, a yield change on a 3-year treasury bond may not cause a corresponding yield change on a investment grade 3-year credit bond. Even a change on the 5-year sovereign bond may not cause corresponding prices change of a 3 year sovereign bond of the same sovereign issuance. Therefore a quantity target such as the amount of currency in circulation may be more preferable for accomplishing macro economic goal. As monetary system matures, asset trading becomes efficient and the price discovery among different sectors, different instruments, or different tenors, becomes more transparent. At this stage, using a price target or a selection of price targets can be a more practical choice for its accurate and timely delivery in achieving monetary policy objectives.

2.6.2 Quantity Target, M1, M2, and Total Social Financing

Internationally, policy makers keep close watch on M0, M1 and M2 for quantity management. M0 is defined as cash in circulation, M1 = M0 + checking, M2 = M1 + saving. There is no wide usage of personal checks in China and saving account is not as popular. For those different circumstances, the definition of M1 and M2 are modified for better reflection of liquidity situation in the domestic system. M0 is still defined as cash in circulation. M1 = M0 + enterprise cash deposit, including platform cash deposit, and is influenced by loan and foreign currency adjustment; M2 = M1 + term deposit, resident saving deposit and other deposit, and is influenced by loan and shadow banking. Fast evolving events in the financial world often make these definitions subject to frequent reinterpretation or facing irrelevancy. Comparing sometimes the difficulty task in US to classify certain instruments into either M1 or M2, the problem in China was that M1 and M2 alone are not sufficient enough to explain the level of liquidity that are actually circulating within the economy. This is partly caused by large amount of shadow banking, mostly in the form of Entrusted Loan and Trust Loan.

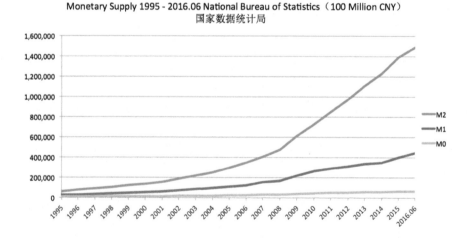

Monetary Supply 1995 - 2016.06 National Bureau of Statistics（100 Million CNY）
国家数据统计局

The large M2 number and its potential implications have caused policy makers and academic concern. Some have argued that the need for ever increasing M2 to sustain an even lower rate of GDP growth, could have been caused by the liquidity inefficiency within the economic structure, therefore both structural and financial regulatory remedies need to be formulated. Others have worried about the potential inflation threat imposed by the large M2, suggesting the only reason M2 was not causing inflation was the real estate asset class's capability in absorbing the excess liquidity. Hence the concern was once the real estate assets including those in 1st tier and 2nd tier cities can no longer support its current rate of absorption, the excess liquidity could pose a large inflation shock that should be managed before hand.

   While M2 measures the amount of financial liquidity from the monetary supply side, the aggregated social financing measures the liquidity from the monetary demand side. As direct financing through bond, equity, and off-balance sheet vehicle through entrusted loan and trust loan become more available, aggregated social financing that covers both direct financing and off-balance sheet financing becomes more relevant for monitoring liquidity sufficiency within the economic system versus M2. From 2012 to 2016, of all the activities forming the aggregated social financing, the largest type of them was CNY bank loans, followed by corporate bonds and entrusted loan. While the capital markets in China had grown substantially over the recent years, it is important to keep in mind that Chinese economy for now has its main financing infrastructure built upon indirect financing methods.

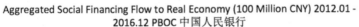

Aggregated Social Financing Flow to Real Economy (100 Million CNY) 2012.01 - 2016.12 PBOC 中国人民银行

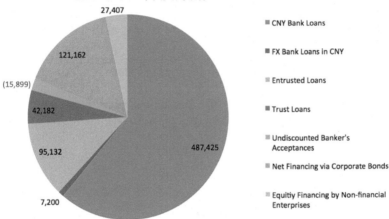

   In the period between 2012 and 2016, within the increasing amount of aggregated social financing, loan growth had been consistent so was its percentage within the group of activities. Bond issuance had rapid growth both in terms of its amount and percentage. Entrusted loans were often tied to local platform hence the local real estate boom and bust cycle. Trust loans were tied to both real estate cycle and regulatory push to make it more transparent to financial regulation, which made trust year over year amount and percentage data volatile.

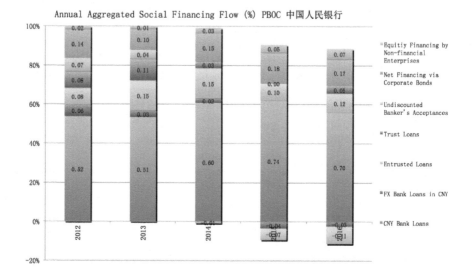

Seasonal patterns exist for different social financing activity types. There generally tended to be more loan activities in March, June, September and December, and those activities partially smoothed out the treasury deposit drain during the end of each quarter. Also typically more loans were administered during the beginning of the year when more credit limits were more available. These observed patterns could be disrupted from time to time by the international capital flow change and other macro economic events.

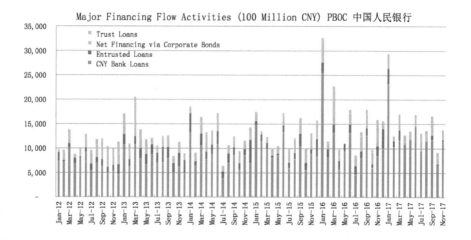

The monthly figure for bonds percentage within the aggregated social financing can be quite volatile, reflecting many factors simultaneously in the play when various market participants are vetting through their perspective decision processes regarding whether bond is the preferred financing resource to act upon for issuance or investment. Generally within each year, more bonds are issued during later half of a year as part of the budgetary cycle. There is also more tax deposit in the later half hence less liquidity in the bond market and investment return could be higher. Bond percentage increased at the end of 2013. There was a need for capital borrowing amid Fed tightening, and a strong search for investment amid asset shortage caused by trust segment deleverage, even when bond yield was at a high point making it disadvantageous for any bond issuers. Bond percentage also increased between 2014 and 2015. The strong need to finance via bond market was heavily driven by the bond for loan swap during the economic growth moderation, even though bond yield was at a low point making it less appealing for bond investors. There was also ample amount of liquidity in the system during economic restructuring. Starting at the end of 2016 bond percentage dropped to negative territory. There was both less willingness to issue and liquidity to invest in the bond market. The circumstance could be partially contributed to a regulatory drive to lower financial leverage within the general economic structure, especially on the local government platform borrowing. China Treasury yield curve became inverted at time, with 5 year yield where investors usually taking position being higher than 10 year yield where traders usually taking positions.

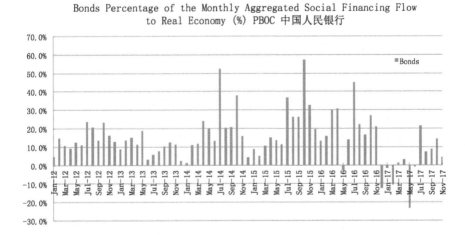

Bonds Percentage of the Monthly Aggregated Social Financing Flow to Real Economy (%) PBOC 中国人民银行

A large percentage of entrusted loans are loans made by one entity to another entity via banks as a conduit. It is the original lender but not the conduit that bears any future default risk. Entrusted loan venue was widely used as financing vehicle by local government to gain financial resource via public listed company that was controlled by State Asset Regulatory Committee at local level. Often entering local sectors including mining, real estate and small enterprises, the listed company acted as funding resource intermediary for the local government and bore potential default risk. For its large quantity, the entrusted loan eventually caught the attention and it was referred to as one of the major pieces forming the current shadow-banking segment.

Trust loan is a loan made by trust. While bank loan is categorized as indirect financing instrument, trust loans is actually categorized as direct financing instrument. A Trust is a legal entity and trusts together as a specific type investment vehicle act with certain economic behaviors. Because of that and also their large quantity, trust activities are grouped together and monitored as one major financing type in PBOC aggregated social financing regulatory report.

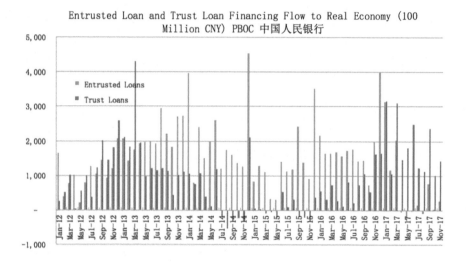

Entrusted loan and trust loan form the majority of the off-balance financial activities in China financial system. From 2012 to 2013, there were large increases of both trust loan and entrusted loan. Banks were setting up large amount of trusts to gain access to off-balance sheet higher yield assets without paying for the corresponding balance sheet capital charge. Lending via trust vehicle lacked standard credit risk management oversight and was outside the scrutiny of banking regulatory regime. Entrusted loan also grew to fund large amount of local real estate projects. The peak of trust loan ended in 2013 when regulatory measures were taken to control banks' off-balance sheet risk. For borrowers, both trust loan and entrusted loan are expensive and risky financing resources, compared to local government bond but they do serve useful purposes within the current economic framework. Entrusted loan continued its growth to provide funding for local project until the end of 2016. Starting from the end of 2016 regulatory effort was made to clean up borrowing irregularity at local government level, causing a significant fall of entrusted loan activities. Since the end of 2017 as both the deleveraging effort and anti-corruption effort were gathering pace, entrusted loan and trust loan activities are under heavy regulatory scrutiny

2.6.3   Regional Distribution of Aggregated Social Financing

Not only is the amount or price of aggregated social financing important, also relevant is their distribution among different regions. The regions in China seeing the largest amount of financing activities include Guangdong, Jiangsu, Beijing, Shanghai, Shandong and Zhejiang. These are coastal provinces and capital city, with vibrant high tech and export industries.

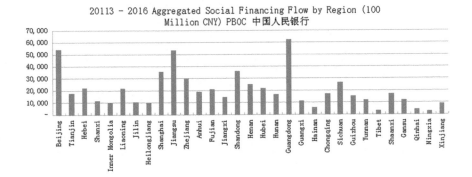

By comparing financing activities originated from different regions, we can make some important observations. For most of these regions loan is the most important method to obtain financial resources, with Beijing being the exception using large amount of bonds to obtain funding possibly because of heavy concentration of large corporate headquarters. Undiscounted banker acceptance is widely used in regions with export supply chain and small medium enterprise financing, which include Jiangsu, Guangdong and Zhejiang.

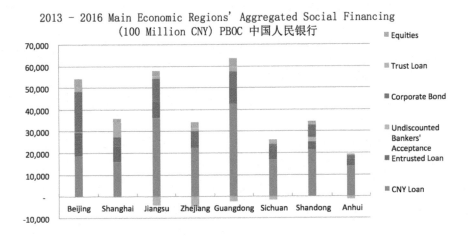

As the capital city of a large nation and an important economic center, Beijing has country's largest concentration of universities, research institutions, large domestic and international corporate headquarters. It obtained large amount of finance via bond issuance, and to a lesser degree, equity issuance and these are cheaper and more liquid sources of funds than credit loan. Its aggregated social financing also enjoyed healthy growth in recent years, an achievement given the overall economic condition.

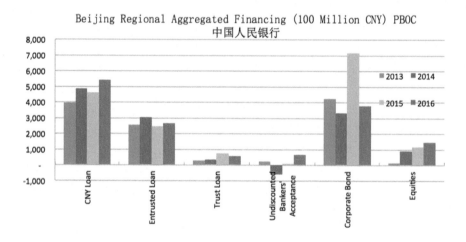

Shanghai also relied heavily on direct financing that included corporate bonds and equities, but to less extent than Beijing. There was larger usage of trust loan than Beijing. Banks often set up trust as conduit heavily associated with real estate projects for convenience. There was also heavy usage of entrusted loan that was historically linked to local projects obtaining financing via public-listed companies.

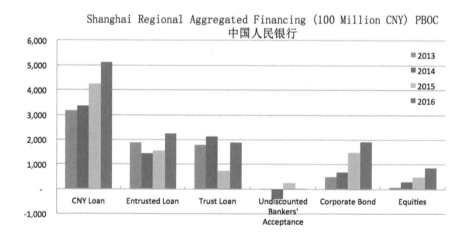

Guangdong obtained most funding via CNY loan, although corporate bonds were also used. BA financing flow turning from positive in 2013 to negative territory in 2016 illustrated difficulty in its export industry.

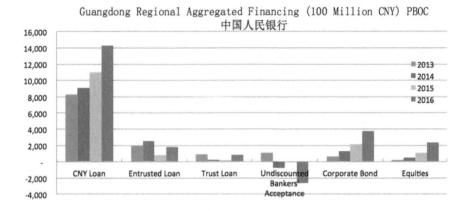

Zhejiang is one of the most active economic regions in China. It actively used capital markets, loan market and trust vehicle to obtain finance. There are a couple of possible reasons for large BA reduction 2013–2016. One was the continuous global trade headwind. The other possible reason was the slowdown of real estate constructions, especially in 3rd and 4th tier cities where oversupply was common. Both of these could dampen the need for small to medium exporters, builders and county level government to obtain finance. BA reduction coincided with the stagnation of loan growth, illustrated Zhejiang economic dependence upon small to medium private enterprises and low level government initiatives.

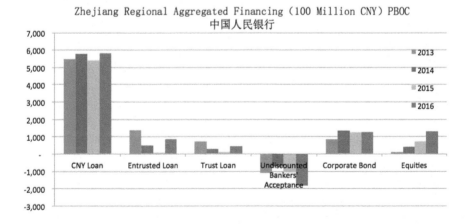

Jiangsu used loan to obtain most of its finance. One observable change over the recent years was the reduction of BA-related financing from 2013 to 2016 when it encountered similar problem as Zhejiang. Export industry in Jiangsu included more oversea companies than Zhejiang and actually felt the slowdown in global trade earlier than the more nimble domestic peers in Zhejiang.

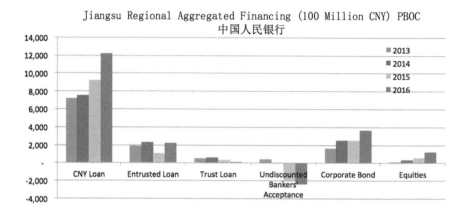

With a long coastal line and fertile landscape, Shandong was performing relatively well in the current economic conditions. Its regional aggregated social financing was relatively smaller when compared with other large coastal regions such as Guangdong and Jiangsu, a reflection of relatively lower cost of living. It also has a large export industrial base, led by companies such as Haier.

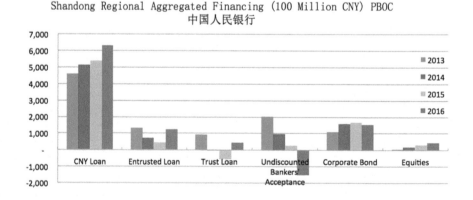

Sichuan is one of the largest provinces in China. Being populous with very fertile land, it is important for both agricultural and industrial capacities. Similar to Shandong, it has much lower cost of living, hence a relatively smaller number of aggregated social financing for its large economic output.

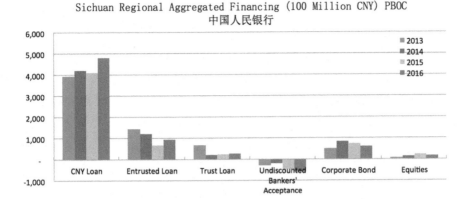

Sichuan Regional Aggregated Financing (100 Million CNY) PBOC
中国人民银行

Anhui had enjoyed good growth over the recent years, represented by its increase in aggregated social financing. Similar to Zhejiang and Jiangsu, its export industry was hit by international trade slowdown.

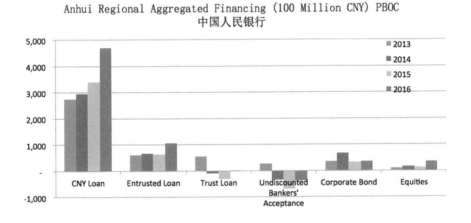

Anhui Regional Aggregated Financing (100 Million CNY) PBOC
中国人民银行

Revenue transfer from central government plays an important role in the growth of economically less developed areas, including agricultural provinces and far-flung regions. By looking at the tax revenue transfer to aggregated social financing ratio, the lower ratio region including Beijing, Shanghai, Tianjin, Zhejiang, Jiangsu and Guangdong were receiving relatively much less revenue transfer. They together were income transfer providers to rest of the nations via the central government budgetary process.

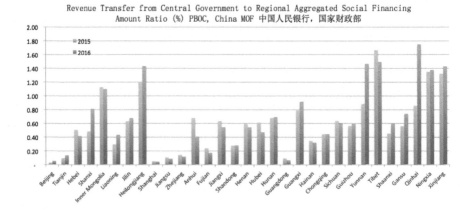

Revenue Transfer from Central Government to Regional Aggregated Social Financing Amount Ratio (%) PBOC, China MOF 中国人民银行，国家财政部

2.6.4 A Distribution Perspective from Financial Intermediary

Financial intermediary institutions hold large importance in aggregated social financing and therefore monetary policy implementation. They obtain credit funds from different sources and distribute them for a variety of usage. The largest destination of financial institutions' credit funds is indirect financing. This includes short term financing in the forms of paper financing and short-term enterprise loan at around 17%, and mid and long financing in the forms of mid and long-term enterprise loan consumption loan at around 35%.

While the level of indirect financing held steady between 2015 and mid 2017, direct financing with bond, increased as the result of capital markets development. Funds usage for direct financing in the form of bond investment grew to be above 14%.

Usage on foreign exchange purchasing gradually come down as China's trade balance reaches a more neutral level and at the same time export of capital has picks up. Shares investment and other instruments to be around 12%.

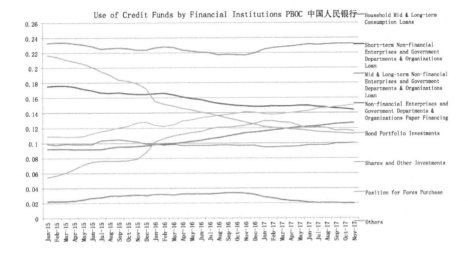

While the monthly percentage of each main credit funding activity out of total funding might seem relatively stable, the month-to-month funding activity change was actually volatile and important. In June of 2015, the high point of Shanghai equity index was reached with significant leverage. Regulation was soon tightened against equity repo transactions and investment was being pulled out from equity markets. Hence the negative change in flows of shares and other investment from July to September in 2015. At the end of 2015, there was large injection of liquidity in the form of mid and long-term enterprise loan, to counter the effect of capital outflow, which drained liquidity from monetary system. Also important were the growth rates of each credit funding activity. A large growth drop, for example in the area of mid and long-term enterprise financing, could indicate a worsening sentiment among the private sectors on future business environment. In January of 2017, loan activity was high to counter a possible capital outflow amid Fed rate hike, but the capital outflow was much smaller than it was in January of 2016, possibly because of both capital control and an economic recovery in the forming. There was an FX surplus in the May of 2017, further alleviating the pressure on the exchange rate.

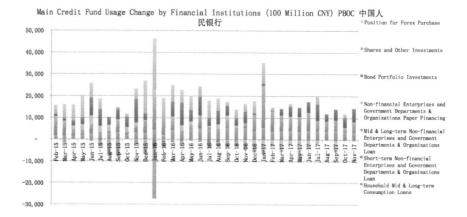

Main Credit Fund Usage Change by Financial Institutions (100 Million CNY) PBOC 中国人民银行

Commercial bank being the most important type within the financial institutions in China determined that loan issued by banks was the most important financing venue. Banks are involved in paper financing, short and long-term bank loan, trust loan, entrusted loan and share investment. The amount of activities within capital markets itself is tilted more towards the bond market, and the bond market is dominated by interbank bond market, versus the exchange bond market.

The largest financial activities carried out by banks are various forms of loans. During the 2-year period between 2015 and 2016, mid and long term loans to household consumption have increased, mostly because of a real estate activities. Both short-term, mid to long term loans to enterprises and government decreased more than expected throughout the year of 2016, even after taking into account the local government bond for loan replacement initiative, causing concern among policy makers that enterprises were refraining from taking on new business initiatives. This concern was alleviated with a large loan activity increase in the first half of 2017. Bond investment increased following both the deregulation reform in the corporate bond market in 2015 and government loan to bond replacement effort, except a large decrease in the end of 2016 that was caused by a regulatory deleverage effort.

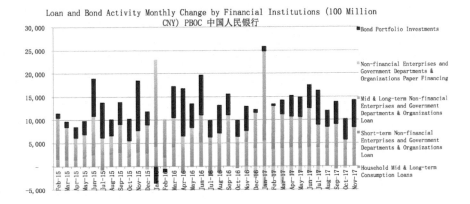

Loan and Bond Activity Monthly Change by Financial Institutions (100 Million CNY) PBOC 中国人民银行

2.6.5 Price Target, 10 Year Bond Yield and 7D Repo Rate

On the short end of the term structure, Repo based upon Treasury bond in the interbank market is becoming the benchmark target. SHIBOR rate closely follows Repo rate in short maturity. The 7D Repo rate level is comparable to Fed Fund overnight rate in signaling the change of liquidity condition in the money market.

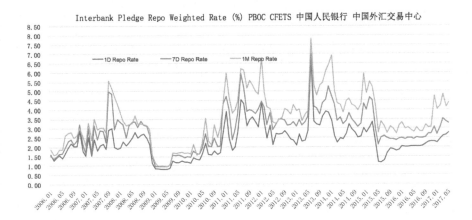

Interbank Pledge Repo Weighted Rate (%) PBOC CFETS 中国人民银行 中国外汇交易中心

Repo rate tends to be quite volatile. The cost of volatility is reflected in the large term spread that existed over the years. Due to the importance of Repo as the benchmark rate for the short end, its stability management improvement is expected as market gains further maturity.

Starting from the end of 2010, repo rate was observing rapid uptick. This could be traced back to the effort by the PBOC to remove yield and liquidity instability that was caused by the asynchronous release of large global and domestic stimulus packages after US credit crisis. The market observed the formation of a relatively stable spread between US and China yield since then.

The pick up of repo rate resumed from the mid of 2013. At that point, the recovery of US economy was firm in place, causing US Dollar to strengthen and the rise of Chinese repo is a reflection of the increase of global funding cost.

China Treasury rate becomes the benchmark rate for fixed income market, mostly for its liquidity, with 1Y for the short end and 10Y for the long end. Sometimes 5Y and 10Y CDB policy bank bond can also be used as yield benchmark. There is a tax spread between treasury and policy bank bond that is subject to the market liquidity. Currently neither treasury nor policy bank bond requires risk capital charge.

Chapter 3
Applied Pricing Curve in the Market and Term Structures

3.1 Curves and Term Structures

3.1.1 FX Curve and FX Swap Points

An FX curve refers to implied interest rate term structure of a specified currency in FX trading, usually the currency other than USD in an FX pair, based upon currency's FX forward rate/forward points in the market.

Within the term structure of CNH FX curve, implied 3M CNH interest rate was computed from USD/CNH 3M swap points using Interest Rate Parity method. This derived implied CNH interest rate closely approximated CNH deposit market rate, which validated Interest Rate Parity as the underlying working mechanism in CNH FX forward market. The fact is worth noting since offshore CNH rate is influenced by the onshore CNY exchange rate, which is a managed float currency, therefore an offshore market-based IRP should not be taken fore granted. The largest difference between CNH FX implied interest rate and CNH deposit rate came during the end of 2013. At the time, after the US economic recovery came into the scene, the expectation was global trade recovery would lead to further CNY appreciation, hence the lowered CNH implied interest rate.

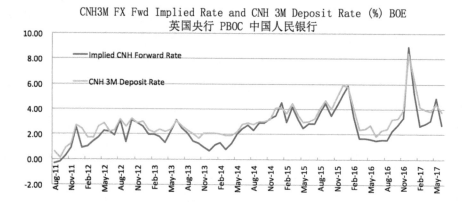

On the other hand, implied CNY rate from onshore CNY 3M FX forward had been mostly unrelated to SHIBOR 3M deposit rate, reflecting a difference in onshore and offshore FX market pricing mechanism.

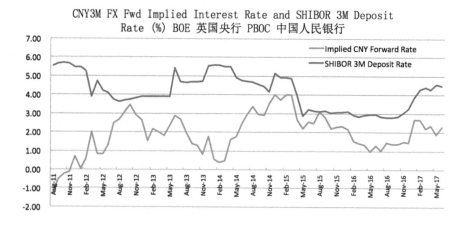

3.1.2   Money Market Curves Across Different MM Segments

Regulators, traders and investors in China have become increasingly sophisticated in domestic money market management. The monthly trading volume for 1D and 7D had been high, as demonstrated below, especially after the 2015 finalization of the interest rate range reform. Among the 6 MM instruments on the short end, 1-Day Repo (R001), 1-Day Outright Repo (OR001), 1-Dday Interbank Deposit, (IBO001), 7-Day Repo (R007), 7-Day Outright Repo (OR007) and 7-Dday

Deposit, (IBO007), 1-Day Repo is the most actively traded and is the main instrument used by PBOC to manage market liquidity.

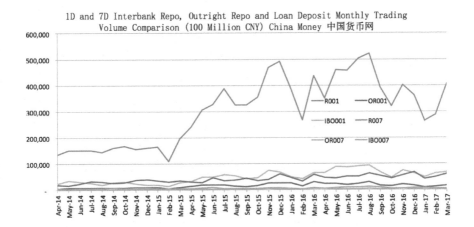

Among the 9 MM instruments with terms from 1 to 4 months, 1-Month Repo is the most actively traded. Their monthly trading volumes can be quite volatile as demonstrated below.

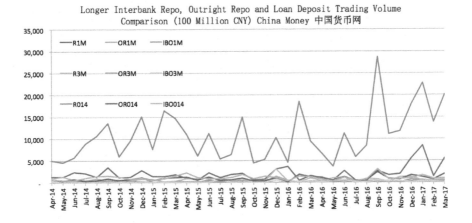

The overall deep liquidity in the money market has resulted in efficient pricing for various money market instruments. As a result, spreads between 1D and 7D, between 7D and 1M are clearly observable for both Repo and Outright Repo to reflect instrument term structure. Spreads between Repos (R001, R007, R1M) and Outright Repo (OR001, OR007, OR1M) are also clearly observable to compensate for the rating and credit risk from risky borrower such as rural commercial banks.

There was a drop of yield in 2015 coincided with the establishment of interest rate range reform.

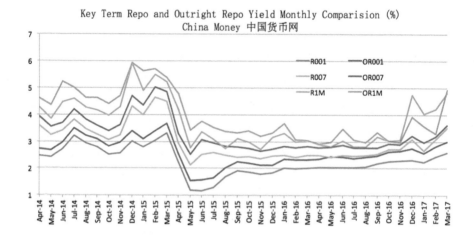

The spreads between repos of 1D, 7D, and respective outright repos of 1D, 7D had been quite stable in the range between 20 and 40 bps. The difference between 7D outright repo and repo decreased and approached 0 in the beginning of 2017, while the spread between 1M OR and 1M Repo went into negative territory amid a deleverage drive during that period.

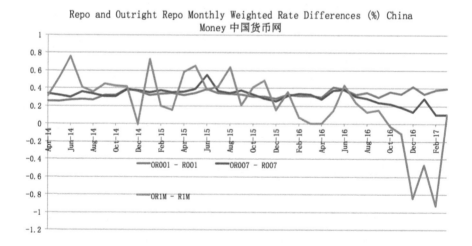

An important observation can be made on how closely loan deposit and outright repo rate are following the very active repo rate. This again indicates the benchmark role played by repo in the interbank money market segment. Among the repo, outright repo and loan deposit, uncollateralized loan deposit requires higher yield versus collateralized outright repo trade. Outright repo requires higher yield versus repo. An outright repo trades often involves a borrower with less credit rating, hence the need to execute an outright repo to minimize counterparty credit exposure. Extra credit premium is required to compensate for that credit risk, even after the changing hand of collateral.

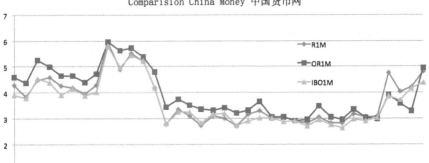

The term structures within money market curves are efficiently priced. For the very short end, led by 1D and 7D repo rates, are the benchmark rates under PBOC's tight watch. 1Y interbank repo rate is closely associated with 1Y treasury rate, since interbank repo mostly uses interest instrument as collateral, therefore both are considered risk free trading instrument. Weighted repo curve moved up from 2012 to 2013 with US recovery, and moved down from in 2014 and 2015 to accommodate domestic growth, and in 2016 rose again with global and domestic economic recovery.

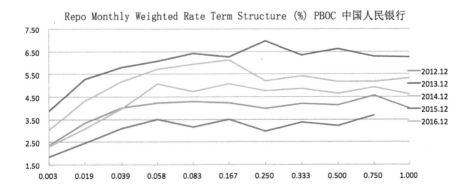

Still ample amount of liquidity was provided until the end of 2016 and the spreads among various money market instruments came down. Carry trade using treasury as repo collateral drew 7D repo and short treasury yield closer, while CD and lower rated CP also kept only small credit spread against the treasury. Many of the CD issuers do not have high ratings. But for CD instruments' generally short maturity advantage, the risk exposure was considered limited.

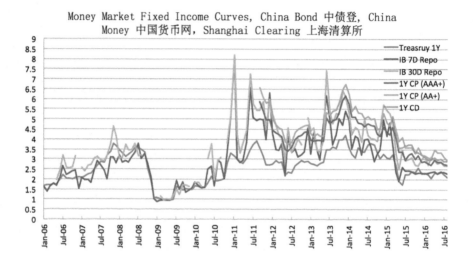

3.1.3 Government Bonds and Interest Rate Term Structure

The level of China's treasury curve moved up in 2010 with a more stable economy in place than 2009. Amid a firmer US economic recovery the treasury curve's level was higher in 2013 than 2010. As China's economic moderation and economic restructuring effort taking over priorities, the curve level decreased during 2015 and 2016.

Different from US treasury market where both the level and the slope of US Treasury curve are indicative of markets condition in terms of financing cost and investment return in fixed income segment, China Treasury on the short end is not as indicative as the repo rate for illuminating on short end market condition. The mid section can be used to measure institutional investment sentiment, and long end for trading condition that is often subject to PBOC effort to set the tone regarding long term borrowing cost. Thus the treasury curve structure in China's bond market is often flat, a reflection of many investors buy-and-hold mentality in this segment.

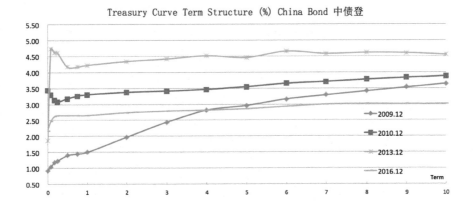

Treasury Curve Term Structure (%) China Bond 中债登

3.1.4 Central Bank Bill Curve

Central bank bill was the benchmark for short end of the risk-free yield curve before the financial crisis, when it was issued in large amount to absorb liquidity generated by large trade surplus. The outstanding amount has decreased due to maturing without reissuance and trading has become much less liquid over the recent years. CB is issued by PBOC so it does not have tax-exempt status. Its value is now benchmarked against treasury with spread includes liquidity premium and tax spread.

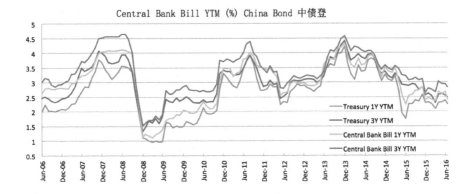

Central Bank Bill YTM (%) China Bond 中债登

3.1.5 Tax Spread Curve and Policy Bank Bonds

Stipulated by CBRC, bonds issued by all three policy banks have zero risk weight under capital adequacy test, and their yield spread difference on top of treasury is regarded as a function of both tax payment and liquidity.

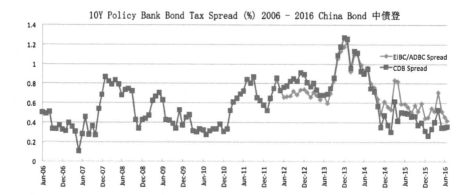

When liquidity is abundant, usually there are more resources readily available from mutual fund and securities firms that often make less reported tax payment for investing into banking accounts. This increased investment flow tends to reduce the tax spread. On the opposite side, when the liquidity is tight, the tax spread tends to widen. The effect of rising and falling nonbanking investment flow makes tax spread moving down and up, in sync with treasury yield movement when liquidity circumstance changes.

3.1.6 Credit Curve by Rating and Industry

China Bond delivers computed credit curves term structure based upon valuation of individual bonds belonging to different rating and instrument classes. Many investors would require a bond rating at or above AA+ as the threshold for investment consideration, similar to the usage of BBB investment grade in US.

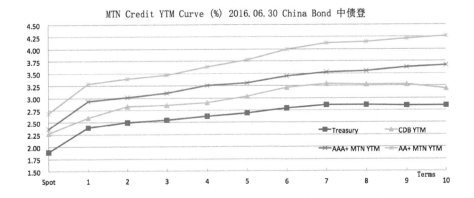

(a) Swaps curve

Even though it is frequently mentioned in a market conversation that practitioners would use swap in combination with the policy bank bonds to bet on the interest rate direction, based upon the spread analysis, the swap and bond cashflow conversion is mostly executed using swap with bonds rated between AAA and AA+. This is reasonable for rating AA+ is often the threshold of bond holding threshold to pass. Even though AA+ is investment grade equivalent, with some of the rating inflated or outdated, between AA+ and AAA would be a rather optimal position for an investors' risk and yield tradeoff.

3.1.7 Bond Future IRR, Contract Spread and Roll-Over

The value of a bond future contract is derived from the value of the underlying Treasury bond, which can be delivered during a cash bond settlement. Many factors together decide the level and shape of a treasury yield curve, and the value of a treasury bond is given by discounting cashflow using the treasury spot curve.

CTD Bond Unlike a gold or a currency future contracts with homogeneous underlying assets, a bond future contract consists of underlying assets that are different issuances of bonds varying from each others by maturity, coupon rate and yield. The reason for this heterogeneous disposition is that a bond future contract is designed to provide feature of a standard future contract for treasury bonds and this feature demands liquidity. To increase the contract liquidity, a list of different treasury bonds are made eligible for delivery during a contract's expiration. The sole preferred choice of bond for delivery, the so-called cheapest-to-delivery bond, or CTD bond, decides the valuation of bond future contract. Which bonds is the CTD bond is not fixed and it may change over the time. A simple rule of thumb is if the yield is above 3% used in conversion factor calculation, the bond that has the highest duration, assuming a positive yield slope, becomes the cheapest-to-deliver for future seller. If the yield is below 3%, the bond that has the lowest duration, assuming a positive yield slope, becomes the cheapest-to-deliver bond.

The value of this particular CTD treasury issuance is also influenced by how long the bond was issued. On the run and off the run treasury, which are issued more recently, will be priced more efficiently and tend to be more expensive. A seasoned bond will have less liquidity and is therefore relatively less valuable.

Implied Repo Rate (IRR) IRR is implied repo rate that is used to finance the bond-equivalent future position. A high IRR against market repo rate suggests overpriced future position, and a low IRR against market repo position suggests undervalued future position.

Contract Spread This is the difference between two future contracts, e.g., 5Y bond future contract and 10Y contract. The value difference is largely a reflection of 5Y treasury and 10Y treasury bonds. The treasury curve may steepen or flatten based upon investor's view of the interest rate bond market and that will change the value difference between the two future contracts.

Calendar Roll When a future contract is close to expiration, investors may close existing future contract positions and open positions on new contract, for example, close an expiring 5 year future contract position and open position on the new 5 year future contract, for hedging purpose or holding on their view of the interest rate market. Spread between two calendar contract could widen or narrow during the life of a contract, depends on a number of factors.

3.2   In-depth Factors Driving Onshore FX and Money Market Curves

For the foreign exchange market in China, the market making mechanism is the combined effect of global players, domestic players and PBOC. The interest rate differential between the spot and maturity date is reflected in the swap points between spot and maturity date.

Most of the time, FX forward points of CNY and CNH are closely tracking each other. But deviations do occur at from time to time. An example of that could be observed around the end of 2015. During that time, CNH 3M forward points were much higher than onshore CNY 3M forward points. There was an offshore currency devaluation expectation for CNY, and a fairly large FX capital outflow, leading to higher CNH swap points. At the same time, PBOC managed expectation of onshore CNY, which eventually led to CNH back to the CNY level.

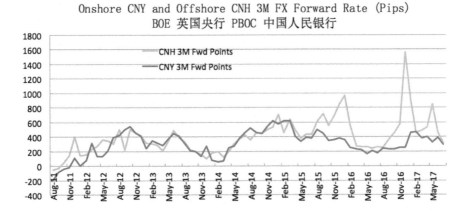

Onshore CNY and Offshore CNH 3M FX Forward Rate (Pips)
BOE 英国央行 PBOC 中国人民银行

CNH forward points matched IRP triangulation computation based upon CNH deposit. CNY forward points did not match IRP triangulation computation based upon SHIBOR and USD LIBOR deposit. The CNY/CNH forward points and deposit rate history pattern and 2015 year-end deviation suggested that (1) The offshore CNH forward market was most of the time driven by the onshore CNY forward market; (2) From time to time the offshore forward rates can deviate when market expectation differs between the managed float onshore market and free floating offshore market; (3) The offshore market observes USD LIBOR and CNH IRP triangulation but the onshore triangulation does not.

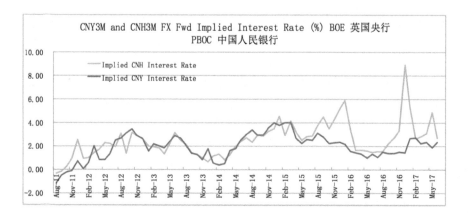

Many of the global traders use standard US dollar curve during currency pair triangulation to derive the non-USD currency interest rate in FX market. This is applicable assuming open capital account, especially regarding US dollar flows. In the case of Chinese FX market, both US dollar and CNY interest rates are domestic in nature, therefore implied CNY forward rate without US dollar adjustment can be quite off from real CNY domestic interest rate.

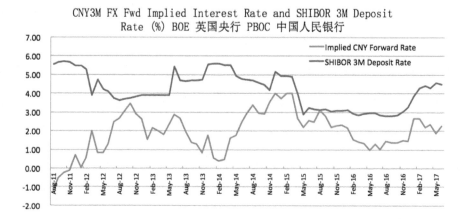

3.3 Monetary Policy-Driven Supply Policy Factors

3.3.1 Deposit Reserve Ratio

For the important roles played by banks in China's financial industry, one of the instruments applicable for changing the quantity of monetary liquidity is the deposit reserve ratio used on banks. The deposit reserve ratio regulates the percentage of reserve a bank must keep for deposits held. At the end of 2016, banking balance sheet stood at 232 trillion CNY. A 0.5% cut would be more than 1-trillion equivalent CNY direct liquidity released into market, and with multiplier factor, the amount of total liquidity released would be much larger. Hence this is a blunt instrument that has to be dealt with care. Still it is an important and effective tool to achieve desirable monetary policy objective. As China's economy evolved over the time, monetary authority has tried to move from quantity target such as deposit reserve ratio to the more sophisticated pricing targets. This task is not trivial, as it requires different asset classes in the financial markets to be more or less fungible. A yield change in treasury market for a benchmark on-the-run 10-year Treasury bonds, needs to have corresponding yield change on different types of credit loan market including collateralized loan, pledge loan, bridge lone and credit loan. It also needs to have corresponding yield change on different types of credit bond instruments, including fixed rate bond, floating rate bond, convertible bond and asset-backed securities.

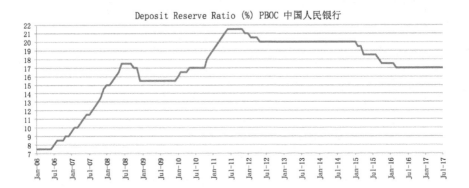

3.3.2 Open Market Operation

PBOC conducts open market operation in pursuit of stable money market funding level. Over the last several tumultuous years those open market operations have been generally successful in achieving monetary policy goals. Liquidity is released and recycled back via repo and reverse transactions. Longer and less volatile 7D Repo rate gradually becomes the short-term benchmark used in both swap trade and floaters. While the Fed was searching for a pricing mechanism to replace LIBOR indices with better transparency, PBOC and domestic market in China have settled down on the 7D Repo rate as short-term anchor rate.

3.3.3   Discount Window

Rediscount instrument used by PBOC is the equivalent of Federal Reserve's discount window. Banks use commercial bill as collateral to obtain funds from central bank. It is a passive monetary tool not to be used for direct monetary supply management, as initiators are banks rather than the central bank. Central bank uses the rate on rediscount to increase or lower cost on banks' funding to influence the broader market. Its decision on what bill from which industry is acceptable in discount window operations can also guide financial resources towards an intended industry target.

3.3.4   Short-Term Liquidity Operations

SLOs have maturities within 7 days. The participants are first tier market dealers. PBOC will initiate the bidding for SLO operations in the forms of repo or reverse repo. The types of collaterals include Chinese government bonds, policy institutional bonds and bank bonds. The objective is to provide stability during temporary market volatility. Different from open market operation that has a fixed operational schedule, SLO can be initiated by PBOC at any time, thus considered an important supplement to open market operations.

3.3.5   Standing Lending Facility

Comparable to Federal Reserve's Discount Window, ECB's Marginal Lending Facility, SLF was created in 2013, to manage financial institutions longer-term liquidity requirement with substantial quantity, thus achieve the short-term interest rate objective.

During an SLO operation PBOC is the initiator. On the other hand, during an SLF operation a bank is the initiator to PBOC on a one-to-one basis. When funding is required, large commercial banks or policy banks will try to enter an SLF transaction in a one-to-one transaction with PBOC. The maturity is within 1–3 months. Collaterals include high rating credit bond and high grade lending assets.

3.3.6 Mid-term Lending Facility

The objectives of PBOC liquidity management is not limited to smooth out the fluctuation of capital flow, fiscal expenditure and the effect of IPO on capital market, it also needs to set the market interest rate, maintain the appropriate level of total liquidity in the banking system, support and direct the healthy growth of credit lending activity.

In 2014, MLF was created by PBOC to issue loans to commercial banks and policy banks aimed at supporting certain agricultural sectors and small business. It is used to set interest rate and release liquidity into the targeted or broader areas. The maturity is 3 months and a trade can be done on a renewable basis. The collateral is interest rate bond and high-grade credit bond.

3.3.7 Pledged Supplementary Lending

PSL was created in 2014, to support developmental agency such as National Development Bank, Agricultural Development Bank and Import Export Bank, to facilitate the development of certain economic sectors that are relatively weak nevertheless have social and economic significance. It has the effects of both injecting monetary supply and lowering the long term borrowing cost of a targeted sector.

The maturity is from 3 months to 5 years. The fund is delivered as an interbank loan. Different from relending, collateral is required and both high-grade bond and high quality loan assets can be used as collateral.

3.3.8 Non-monetary Policy-Driven Supply Factors

3.3.8.1 Funds Outstanding for Foreign Exchange

Trade-related currency flows change funds outstanding for foreign exchange. Exporter sells foreign currencies to banks to receive CNY and banks in turn will sell foreign currencies to PBOC to receive CNY. The amount of CNY released by PBOC as the result of buying foreign currencies is the funds outstanding for foreign exchange. Its monthly change can be quite volatile for a large trade nation caused by unpredictable export/import trade number. Large amount of released CNY from trade surplus could quickly become inflationary if proper management is not given in time.

Capital flows also change funds outstanding for foreign exchange. During the end of 2015, as US economy was picking up speed and the expectation for Fed rate increase was high, there was very large capital outflow from China, at the estimated monthly rate of 100 billion from various sources. The outflow stopped when it became clear that Fed was concerned about the impact of rate increase on weak global economy. Capital outflow reduces funds outstanding for FX.

This funds outstanding number is important for understanding both general market liquidity condition and cost of funding in the broad monetary system. Liquidity is released when PBOC sells CNY into the market in exchange for foreign currencies and the CNY selling expands the monetary base. Liquidity could become tighter when the release of CNY into the money supply is slower than average. When the US dollar funding rate goes lower during a period of trade surplus, the large FX to CNY conversion actually reduces the cost of funding of the China monetary base. When US dollar rate goes up with smaller trade surplus, the capital outflow combined with higher base rate could generate quite negative monetary conditions.

3.3.8.2 Treasury Deposit

Institutions pays taxes each quarter and the taxes collected become fiscal deposit before they are spent. The amount of fiscal deposit reported by PBOC is the tax amount collected by Ministry of Finance and deposited at its central bank account. Fiscal deposit drains funds available in the interbank market. When spent, funds are released back into the market. The fluctuation of the fiscal deposit amount, together with the funds outstanding and open market operations, are the main deciding factors to the Chinese money market liquidity equilibrium.

The amount of fiscal deposit often rises in the middle of each quarter, and falls towards the end of each quarter. The fall is especially pronounced towards the end of the year. Within each month, tax must be paid by 7th or 15th, and be dispersed by 25th for the next month fiscal expenditure. These specific payment and disperse dates cause the deposit amount to rise in the middle of each month and to fall towards the end of each month.

The amount of treasury deposit rose over the years together with China's economic growth. But since 2015, as the result by the government to increase the usage efficiency of funds available in the monetary system, the outstanding deposit amount has gradually come down. Still, the rise and fall pattern persists, and it is important to manage the tighter liquidity condition in the middle of each quarter especially of the first quarter and 2nd quarter, and the likely fall of yield towards the year end.

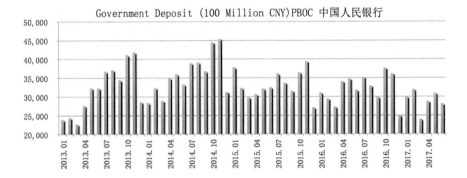

3.3.9 Structural Factors

3.3.9.1 IPO and Other Investment Flows

In terms of funding destination among sectors within China's capital markets structure, large amount of funds could flow out of money market and wealth management products during a busy IPO season, drying up liquidity and pushing up yields in the money market and fixed income market. The active players behind these equity-related fund flows include retail investors, type-1 bond funds, insurance companies and securities firms. Investors bidding in the IPO first need to set aside their funds readily available in the IPO bidding process, hence have their fund taken out of money market and fixed income market. During the stock market boom year of 2007, the amount of funds taken out could be amounted to 3.5 trillion CNY on a single day, pushing repo rate to mid 30%.

Many steps were taken since then, including more dispersed IPO schedules to avoid concentrated stock purchase funding demand and better targeted stock issuing dates to avoid any overlapping with treasury fiscal deposit collection dates. A lower bidding success ratio and most importantly a more tepid secondary stock market have also driven down the amount of fund dedicated to pursue IPO issuance. Still, hundreds of billions of CNY could be set aside before an IPO bidding in 2015. This usually leads to the rise of 1-day and 7 day-repo rates. The liquidity dearth caused by IPO can be felt earlier on 7-day repo than on 1-day repo.

The spread between bonds that can be repoed versus those that cannot be repoed from time to time can be estimated via the following logic on the exchange market during IPO event:

$$\text{Yield of bond not eligible for repo} - \text{Yield of bond eligible for repo}$$
$$= (\text{Leverage ratio} - 1) * (\text{IPO return} - \text{Funding cost})$$

3.3.9.2 Bank Fund Volatility

In terms of source of funding within China's capital markets structure, banks are the most important funding providers and the amount of funds banks have available for investment has direct influence on the performance of fixed income market. The level of bank funds is influenced by a list of factors, including M0, M1, M2 and funds outstanding in foreign exchange, which change the size of banks' balance sheet and the size of their fixed income portfolios. PBOC manages the banks liquidity level using loan-to-deposit ratio, capital requirement, open market operation and specific market operations. In the last couple of years, due to local government bond purchase initiative, large banks have had less funds available for traditional government and credit bond investment, and the further usage of MLF by PBOC encouraged some 2nd tier banks to redirect their resources towards loan lending in agricultural and micro lending sectors that are less speculative in nature.

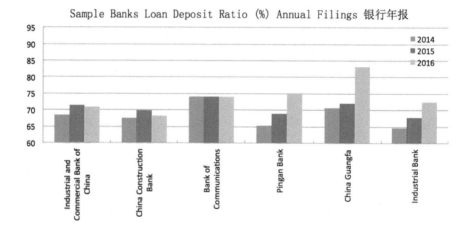

Besides shifting their funds between lending and investment, banks also shift resources between on-balance sheet investment and off-balance sheet investment. On-balance sheet investment is more focused on the interbank fixed income market with transparent risk management procedure while off-balance sheet investment has more diversified investment instruments to select from and less transparent risk management procedure in place. Off-balance sheet investment drives wealth management products, entrusted loan and trust loan growth that offer higher yield than more traditional fixed income market.

Banks also shift their resources between equities and bond market. IPO and other equity-related activities divert funds away from traditional fixed income market. Bank can not directly invest in equities but can invest in certain wealth management product derived from equities products. Whether banks have enough funds for fixed income market around the time of those events can be deciphered via the level of 7D repo and the bidding yield on various fixed income instruments.

3.3.10   Seasonal Issues and Market Expectation

Financial markets respond to changing condition of economy that from time to time displays seasonal characteristics. The level of certain consumer spending and industrial production change with seasonal patterns including peak travels during holiday and summer break, and auto production and electricity generation in year-end hike. Many economic statistics are also gathered and published on scheduled quarterly and yearly dates. Policy makers and investment community will react to the updated information on economic activities and general data publication result, and in their responsive process create financial market season patterns.

   Financial market has also to respond to and handle seasonal issue created by the working mechanism within financial market community itself. Many financial houses need to fund their positions with repo. Repos tend to have short maturities. Enough liquidity has to be provided before the Spring Festival and other long holiday break to avoid pre-holiday market liquidity stress. Some of the investors may try to take advantage of any perceived liquidity stress by executing long-term investment before the holiday to lock in higher investment return.

3.4   In-depth Factors Driving Fixed Income Portfolio Return and Risk Curve Parameters

3.4.1   Cross-Border Monetary Flow and Pricing Transmission

Compared with the onshore managed-float CNY currency system, offshore CNH market is a free-floating market. Both wholesale and retail offshore markets are fairly efficient with retail spot CNH market bid ask spread around 50 pips in 2015. Conversion from offshore CNH to onshore CNY has to be settled via one of the CNY clearing banks designated by PBOC, therefore the ultimate CNH price and yield are decided by PBOC, based upon its perspective on mainland China's macro economic and global macro factors, trade flows, etc.

   Under normal conditions, with CNH liquidity is sufficient and global financial market stable for arbitrage, certain amount of CNH will be recycled back into the onshore market to take advantage of higher interest rate in the onshore CNY market. The stable financial condition includes high CNY versus CNH short-term interest rate differential and stable or appreciating CNY exchange rate. When those conditions are met, from time to time, large cross-border CNH inflow impacts domestic fixed income and other parts of the capital market.

   Non-CNY monetary flows are those related to capital account flows mostly in US dollars that come and leave China capital market depending upon the changing assessment on China yield risk condition by global investment community. FX capital accounts flows have to be neutralized by PBOC FX transaction with further corresponding domestic CNY liquidity release or withdrawal, hence change the level and shape of fixed income market curves.

3.4.2 Domestic Monetary Supply

Monetary supply is fundamental to the level and shape for fixed income market curves. M0, M1 and M2 and aggregated social financing are liquidity factors that need to be analyzed. M2 is a liquidity measure from the perspective of the lender, while the aggregated social financing is a liquidity measure from the perspective of the borrower.

Macro economic change can cause M1 and M2 growth to change and diverge from each other from time to time. If economy cools down and companies reduce their investment activities, M1 could outgrow M2. Vice versa, if economy accelerates, M2 could outgrow M1. International trade flow and capital flow can also increase or decrease the fund outstanding for foreign exchange, and substantially change M1 and M2.

Different central bank policy events could also change the monetary supply condition. Central bank could engage open market operations, and other market operations including MLF and PSL to change both the short-term and long-term supply. It could also use reserve rate and loan-to-deposit ratio to release or withdraw liquidity from the monetary system.

Certain financial practices also change the pattern of monetary supply. Shadow banking activities were sometimes criticized for being a regulatory arbitrage that amplifies the amount of money circulation in the monetary system represented by M2 indicator without generating real economic benefit. On the other hand, more shadow banking does generate additional monetary supply measured in aggregated social financing that help local government enterprise to create economic growth.

Without macro monetary supply change, monetary flow into investment can still change. Large concentrated IPO events could freeze the money available in the system, and so it the amount of treasury fiscal deposit. Money flow into trust and other high yield vehicles can leave less money for traditional fixed income market.

3.4.3 Product Supply and Demand

Because of the large quantity to be issued every year, the supply of interest rate product often has large influence on the pricing and return of this asset class.

For Treasury bond, Department of Treasury creates annual fiscal budget plan that estimates the amount of budgetary surplus or deficit for each coming year. Fiscal deficit is financed by Treasury bond issuance, with a debt limit set by the department to stipulate the additional amount of treasury that can be issued. The amount of bonds to mature next year, combined with the amount to be issued to cover the fiscal deficit, is the estimated issuing amount of Treasury bond for next year. Department of Treasury will also publish bond issuance plan, including issuing date, coupon frequency and the maturity of bond to be issued.

For fiscal year 2016, in published outstanding treasury report MOF set the increase to be at 1.4 trillion CNY. China Bond also reported at the end of 2015 that the amount of treasury to mature within a year around 1.4353 trillion. Taken into account that some of the treasury will be issued overseas, total amount of treasury to be issued domestically was estimated to be around 2.7 trillion CNY.

For policy bank bond, PBOC issues annual quotas to three policy banks. These are the upper limits of increases they can have for their outstanding bond amount. For the year of 2016, 500 billion CNY was given to China Development Bank, 650 billion to Agricultural Development Bank and 350 billion to Import Export Bank. China Bond published data showed that CDB, ADBC and EIBC each had 943.3, 597.1 and 357 billion bonds to mature in 2016 respectively. The increased outstanding amount plus the quantity of maturing bonds in 2016 are the newly issued policy bank bonds to the market. That put the estimated new bond issuance of three policy banks at 1.443 trillion, 1.247 trillion, and 0.707 trillion CNY, respectively.

For local government bond, in published outstanding local government debt report, MOF sets the limit on additional amount of debt local government can issue to finance its growth and stipulate the amount local government can issue to replace maturing local government debt. For the year of 2016, the amount of issuance was 3.5 trillion CNY.

Credit instruments supply is relatively small and yield is higher. For credit products with short maturity or high credit rating, their prices are driven more by the amount of supply. Lower supply will lead to lower yield requirement by investors. On the other hand, for credit products with longer maturity or lower credit rating, their demand is driven more by risk appetite of investors at the specific time, and their supply more by level of yield at the specific time. In a boom market when investor is less risk-averse, yield on lower rated product can be lower than historical average. The lower yield could in turn make borrowers more willing to issue additional amount of debt.

3.4.4   Tax Consideration

Tax system in China is relatively simple. Ministry of Finance and Sate Administration of Taxation publish tax guidelines. Tax rate for capital gain is set at 25% for institution, 20% for individual investor. Value-added tax put in place in 2016 is set at 6%, replacing Business Tax, which was at 5%.

In the Chinese bond market, there is no VAT tax or Capital Gain tax on Treasury and local government bond, regardless trading or banking accounts; while VAT and Capital Gain tax are applicable for both policy bank bonds and credit bonds. This is different from the US bond market, where there is no distinction in terms of tax treatment between treasury and credit debt instrument. For that reason, yield spread is expected for bonds that require interest tax payment.

The tax spread changes over time, not only as a function of the yield, but also as a function of the amount of resources available for banking account investment and non-bank trading accounts. Banking accounts book's accounting practice combine discount price appreciation and coupon into interest payment entries. This eliminates capital gain for price appreciation when held to maturity and the business tax or VAT tax on interest payment is rather small. Therefore banking accounts investment takes less consideration regarding the tax spread on policy bond and credit bond if assets are held to maturity.

Trading accounts owning policy bank bonds and credit bonds need to pay both capital gain tax and VAT tax. In buy and sell transactions price appreciation is reflected as capital gain hence the tax impact cannot be ignored. Non-bank trading accounts pay tax based upon entity P&L hence there is less concern on tax.

Therefore when liquidity is ample, bank banking account and non-bank trading account investors drive the market tax spread to be within a narrower range. When liquidity dries up, the reverse happens. At this time trading accounts' relative size when compared to banking accounts is rather small. As market liberalization moves forward, this pattern may change.

3.4.5   Cost of Funds and Risk Appetite

Cost of funds is critical in formulating investment decision. For each type of major financial institutions, we can derive a cost estimation:

$$\text{Cost of deposit} = \text{Percentage of cash deposit} * \text{Cash deposit interest rate}$$
$$+ \text{Percentage of term deposit} * \text{1Y deposit interest rate}$$
$$\text{Cost of interbank borrowing} = \text{3M Shibor}$$
$$\text{WMP} = 1{-}3\text{M WMP expected return}$$

For a large bank, assuming the date as of July 1st, 2016, following the above equations, the cost of deposit = 50% * 0.35% + 50% * 2% = 1.175%; 3M Shibor = 2.82, 1–3M WMP cost = 4.6%. The mixture of funding liability is 80% deposit, 5% interbank borrowing, 15% WMP. The cost of fund = 0.94 + 0.14 + 0.69 = 1.77. The real number could be slightly higher, close to 2%, for the cost of deposit coming from corporations could be higher than cost of deposit from retail individuals, and also the cost number needs to have a term adjustment to compensate for term difference between asset and liability.

For a share-holding commercial bank, its cost of funding would be higher due to higher percentage of WMP and interbank borrowing. Its cost of funding is often between 0.5 and 1% higher than a large commercial bank.

Mutual funds can be mainly divided into equity fund, bond fund, hybrid bund and MM fund. For bond fund, the funding cost is the return to the client in addition to management cost. Current MM fund mainly invests into interbank deposit. Since the management cost is fairly small, MM cost of fund can be approximated by Shibor rate, with significant amount of day-to-day volatility.

For insurance companies, the starting cost of fund is close to WMP. The industry in general sets fee charged by sales channel to between 1 and 1.5% and employee, traveling and other overhead between 1 and 1.5%. Therefore insurance company's cost of fund, assuming WMP yield to be at 4.6%, when all are taking into account, will be 4.6% + 2.5% = 7.1%.

For trusts and other borrowing channel, their expected return is their cost of fund plus management fee. Trusts usually demand return above 7% and often close to a historical 9%. The return expectation for a more complicated channel is often 1% higher than that of a trust.

3.4.6 Credit Allocation Limits and Industry Policy Issued by Government

Credit policy application is part of the investment decision formulation. From time to time, banks will adjust their credit allocation policies that reflect their risk perspective on total credit, industry credit and single issuer credit condition. Often credit limits for industries and particular legal entities are unified for both lending and investment across the board on the whole balance sheet. Under the regulatory policy guidelines and with market incentives, bank industry credit policies can be very stringent for industries with over capacity including steel, cement and steam coal, while credit policies for agriculture and micro lending are more accommodating for economic transformation.

Since on balance sheet credit policy can be very explicit and stringent, sometimes the strong need for investment in overcapacity industry or local enterprise platform causes lending to be executed via off-balance sheet financing including wealth management product, entrusted loan and trust loan. Due to this concern government continuously try to guide off-balance sheet financing back to on-balance sheet financing without causing market disruption.

3.4.7 Bond Future Net Basis, Implied Repo Rate and Cheapest-to-Deliver Optionality

Gross Basis A bond future contract derives its fundamental value from treasury bonds. Traders monitor the difference between cash bond and the bond future contract, defined as gross basis. Any perceived divergence, could signal that the value of the future contract is out of line with cash bond and a profit trade can be executed.

$$\text{Gross Basis} = \text{Cash Bond Value} \ - \text{Bond Future Value}$$
$$= \text{Cash Bond Value} - (\text{Bond Future Price} * \text{Conversion Factor})$$

Net Basis The holder of cash bond position gains accrued interest over time, which is not included in the value of a future bond. Repo rate is the financing cost of that position. Hence, a spot cash bond price, minus accrued interest rate from spot time to future contract settlement time, and plus repo financing cost over the same period, should be the theoretical value of the future contract. The difference between cash theoretical future price after taking into account the accrued interest and repo cost, and traded future price, is defined as net basis. The net basis is therefore a more accurate measurement for bond future relative value analysis than gross basis.

$$\text{Net Basis} = \text{Gross Basis} \ - \text{Coupon Income} + \text{Repo Cost}$$
$$= \ \text{Cash Bond Value} - (\text{Bond Future Price} * \text{Conversion Factor})$$
$$- \ (\text{Future Date Accrued Interest} - \text{Spot Date Accrued Interest})$$
$$+ \ \text{Spot Date Dirty Price} * \text{Repo Rate} * \text{Number of Days}/360$$

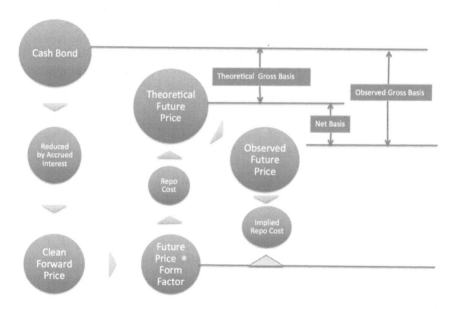

Implied Repo Rate (IRR) For each future contract, from the pool of the bonds eligible for delivery during the cash bond settlement, the one with the highest implied repo rate, will yield the smallest observed gross basis, and is therefore the cheapest-to-deliver bond CTD during a cash bond settlement. This CTD bond is used in gross basis and net basis for relative value analysis.

A minor rearrangement of the net basis equation will give the following calculation for implied repo rate. Implied Repo Rate (IRR) = (Future Settlement Amount/Spot Dirty Price − 1) * 360/Holding Period

For the CTD bond which has the highest IRR, when its IRR moves lower, net basis becomes higher, which indicates the possible undervaluation of bond future. But in reality IRR is often lower than observed treasury repo rate, as the long future positions need to be compensated for optionality embedded in the future contract, including which treasury bond will be delivered and the date of the bond delivery. Due to the fact old treasury issuance when delivered can have low liquidity and thus difficult for the long future side to close the bond position without a loss, future IRR can be substantially different from actual repo rate observed in the interest rate bond market.

3.5 MTM Basics for Listed Capital Markets Products

Mark-to-market process execution follows international norm. For banking account, interest income includes both coupon and any price appreciation. Realized gain includes interest income and any possible trading gain. Total gain includes realized gain and unrealized gain. Trading account differs from banking account by having interest income covering only coupon income but not the price appreciation.

For bond in the last payment period, Yield to maturity = (Future value − Present value)/Present value * (Current year day count)/(Days to maturity). For bond not in the last period, the YTM computation uses the same ACT/ACT US treasury convention. Accrued interest is computed with a standard ACT/ACT ISMA convention: AI = (Coupon rate/Coupon frequency) * (Number of accrual days)/(Current accrual period days). China bond as a third party provides reference bond price for interbank bond.

Chapter 4
Regulatory Regime and Some Policies in Focus

4.1 Central Bank Objectives and Its Balance Sheet Analysis

PBOC regulates China's financial markets, including the inter-bank money market, the inter-bank bond market, domestic foreign exchange market and gold market in collaboration with other regulatory agencies. Due to the rapid international trade growth in the first decade of 21st century and steady capital investment inflow, an important task for PBOC was to absorb large amount of incoming foreign exchange and manage subsequent liquidity associated with central bank's foreign exchange conversion operation. In this conversion process, PBOC accumulated large amount of foreign exchange with its peak percentage at 83.3% on PBOC total balance sheet. The percentage decreased to a more manageable 62.4% in the mid of 2017 with a combination of global export market slowdown and US recovery drawing capital flow away from emerging markets. With decreased foreign exchange conversion since 2015 that reduced monetary supply, PBOC replenished domestic liquidity with large increase on Claims on Other Depository Corporations, which can be considered as lending to the banking industry.

© Springer Nature Singapore Pte Ltd. 2018
X. Zhang, *Capital Markets Trading and Investment Strategies in China*,
https://doi.org/10.1007/978-981-10-8497-3_4

To reduce the inflationary pressure brought by foreign exchange inflow and conversion, large amount of liquidity was taking out of the circulation by increasing the bank reserve requirement at central bank. The Deposits of Other Depository Institutions first increased and subsequent decrease on PBOC balance sheet liability side corresponded to the Foreign Exchange change on its asset side. Since 2015 currency issue also increased corresponding to PBOC funding supply to banks.

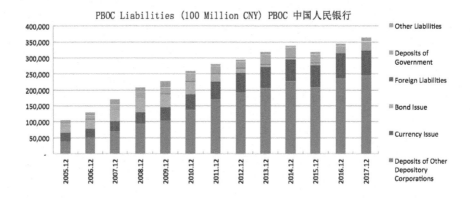

PBOC uses a list of monetary tools including open market operation, loan rate, SLO, MLF, PSL, deposit reserve requirement and others to achieve domestic economic management agenda. Open Market Operations are important tools to manage the amount of currency in circulation and market liquidity, via buying and selling securities and foreign exchange between central bank and various counterparties, to achieve desired monetary objectives. China's Open Market Operations were put into practice in 1994 to manage foreign exchange liquidity, and in 1996 to manage domestic market liquidity, have since then become instrumental in managing liquidity in the banking system, setting up expectation of interest rate movement, and introducing stable monetary growth.

In its open market operations, PBOC deals with a list of selected counterparties that are capable of handling the large quantity required, which includes some large banks such as ICBC, BOC and some other non-banking institutions. Main applicable instruments include Repo, securities buying selling and issuance of central bank bill. For different type of Repos, regarding the directions, both Repo and Reverse Repo are applicable. Regarding the ownership of the underlying bonds, both Pledge Repo and Outright Repo are applicable. For Outright Repos, the underlying bonds are purchased on the secondary market. Central bank bills are issued to absorb excessive liquidity from the market from time to time, and upon their maturity liquidity would be released back into the market.

More recently, since 2013, to supplement the traditional open market operations instruments, People's Bank of China implemented SLO (Short-term Liquidity Operations), to meet the temporary demand of capital requirement in the market, smoothen capital markets operation and help to stabilize market expectation. Later, three more instruments, SLF (Standing Lending Facility), MLF (Mid-term Lending Facility), and PSL (Pledged Supplementary Lending) were implemented.

Published by PBOC's Monetary Policy Department, the following were examples of SLO, SLF, MLF and PSL operations. (1) For SLO, on May 23rd, 2016, PBOC conducted an SLO operation, in the amount of 65 billion CNY, with 7 day maturity, at the rate of 2.25%. (2) For SLF, in April of 2016, PBOC conducted SLF operation in the amount of 760 million CNY. Out of those, 750 million was for overnight fund, with rate at 2.75%, and 10 million was for 7-day maturity fund, with rate at 3.25%. SLF achieved setting the upper boundary of interest rate tunnel, thus maintained the stability of money market interest rate. (3) For MLF, in April of 2016, PBOC conducted MLF operation in the amount of 715 billion CNY. Out of those, 311.5 billion was released for 3-month maturity, at the rate of 2.75%. 403.5 billion was released for 6-month maturity, at the rate of 2.85%. In the same month, 551 billion was recovered. (4) For PSL, in April, 2016, due to progress of fund release and fund recycle for Housing Improvement Project, 3.6 billion loan was returned to PBOC by China Development Bank. PBOC conducts PSL operations in the beginning of each month to China Development Bank, China Agricultural Development Bank, and China Import Export Bank, to support the three institutions for Housing Improvement Loan, Critical Water Project Loan, and CNY internationalization Project Loan.

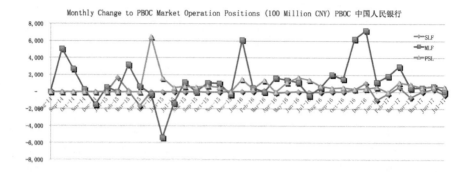

The total outstanding amount of SLF, MLF and PSL reflects regulatory effort in providing financial support to economic growth. The month-to-month change reflects the type of instrument and amount of involvement at particular time point. MLF was used during the end of 2015 and 2016 to counter the effect of fed fund increase and capital outflow. PSL in the mid of 2015 was used to provide economic stimulus to mitigate the consequence of bursting equity bubble.

4.2   Foreign Exchange Trading Regulation and Mid Pricing Guideline

The regulatory article No. 188, published on PBOC site on Jul. 2, 2014, laid out the basic rules for the pricing mechanism of CNY. For the on shore CNY foreign exchange market, each day before the market open, CFECS will get a price quote from each market maker. Within gathered quotes population, the highest and lowest will be eliminated, and the rest weighted, to reach the mid price of CNY of that day. Weight of the quote from each market maker is decided by CFECS based upon the trading volume of each market maker plus other criteria.

The CNY mid price quote against Euro, HKD, and CAD are derived based upon CNY versus USD, EURO versus USD, HKD versus USD, CAD versus USD, at 9:00 a.m. each money. The CNY mid price quote against JPY, GBP, AUD, NZD, MYR, RUB are based upon the quote gathered from each market maker before the market open.

Each day, the USD CNY price movement should be within −2 to +2% range of the published mid price. CNY quote against EUO, JPY, HKD, GBP, AUD, CAD, NZD movement should be within −3 to +3% range of the published mid price. CNY quote against MYR, RUB movement should be within −5 to +5% range of the published mid price.

On Aug 11, 2015, PBOC made an announcement to further improve USD CNY mid price mechanism. Starting on that day, 14 market makers would submit their open quotes mainly based upon the prior day market closing price, in addition to prior exchange rate change and supply demand. This announcement was very significant. On that day, the CNY fell for more than 1,000 points, and it was the largest in 20 years. It was a clear attempt to create an alternative pricing mechanism by having market input other than simply following central bank's expectation.

4.3 Leverage Regulatory Requirement

Leverage regulatory requirement is enforced at 4 levels. At the 1st level, from the country perspective, the size of combined banking balance sheet, above 230 trillion CNY by 2016 year end versus China GDP, and government determination to drive down systematic leverage, can be considered leverage regulatory requirement that sets limits upon the monetary growth and creates impact over capital markets. The 2nd level is the global financial industry level requirement, which is codified by Basil requirement including tier 1 leverage ratio and NCR, in progressive stage of implementation. 3rd level is the domestic financial industry leverage requirement, which can be further segmented into banking, insurance, mutual fund and off-balance sheet financing such as trust. Trusts have much higher asset to equity ratio than banks and mutual funds. 4th level is the sub-industry leverage management practice that changes over time. Large commercial banks often have much less leverage versus urban commercial banks in terms of total liabilities including off-balance sheet liabilities relative to their equities.

Specifically for fixed income trading, banking's large prop investment desks have very low leverage ratio in general. So do their comparatively smaller trading operations due to shorting difficulties. Publicly traded bond fund leverage ratio is required to be no more than 140%. Trusts have high leverage ratio but are often considered less risk for their banking association. One particular product that was popular during the 2015 equity bubble period was the equity-backed CDO that offered fixed interest income for the senior tranche with mandatory stop loss requirement that are often purchased by banks. The equity tranche is often setbatb 10% of the total face value, which makes its leverage ratio at 10.

4.4 ABS and Its Related Regulation

There are three types of ABS based upon regulatory framework. Loan-based ABS is under the supervision of PBOC and CBRC. Issued by banks, the original owners of the underlying assets are banks. The underlying assets are credit loans and financial leasing assets. LABS are traded in the interbank market. It requires dual rating. The issuer needs to keep 5% of the underlying asset risk.

Corporate ABS is under the supervision of CSRC. Issued by securities firms and fund subsidiaries, the original owners of the underlying assets are corporates. The underlying assets are receivables, credit loans, BOT buyback, rights and real estate assets. They are traded on exchange, securities firms OTC counter, AMAC Bidding and Transferring System. The issuers often keep the equity tranche.

Asset-backed Note is not a real ABS as the asset is not removed from originator's balance sheet. It is under the supervision of National Association of Financial Market Institutional Investor (NAFMII). Issued by corporates, the original owners of the underlying assets are corporates. The underlying assets are usually fee generated by public utility. ABNs are traded in the interbank market. It requires dual rating. Not required to keep the underlying risk, the issuers need to keep the contractual investor protection promise it made during issuance.

4.5 Currency Account and Capital Account Market Liberalization

Market liberalization process is a worthy topic since it provides a broad context within which China regulatory framework reform took place. Following the path of other major trading nations and learning from their experiences, China embarked on current account and capital account market liberalization.

US started the critical process of market liberalization by first setting up Federal Reserve to conduct independent interest rate policy during World War I. The US dollar briefly achieved the reserve currency status during the war period and lost it to British Pound after the war. In 1925, US dollar regained the status of reserve currency and have kept that status ever since. 1970s was tumultuous period for US dollar. Fight against poverty, war in Vietnam, oil crisis and certain policies by Fed were in motion and Inflationary pressure was building up. Interest rate regulations that were put in places in the aftermath of 1929 great depression to protect deposit institutions from over competing for customers started to cause interest rate disparity between US domestic market and the Euro Dollar market, thus the capital flight from US domestic financial institutions to international market. To deal with this problem, between 1970 and 1986 various reform steps were introduced to eliminate those archaic interest rate regulations. Rate ceilings were lifted carefully starting from long-term deposit to short term deposit and from large notional to small notional.

As a result, a pricing mechanism was set up and continuously refined over the time, using a set of monetary policy tools, including federal reserve fund, discount rate, open market operations, to reach intermediary monetary objectives including reserve amount, short term and long term interest rate, fed fund rate, treasury bond yield, with the eventual objectives in achieving economic growth, sufficient employment and the financial markets stability.

UK started to eliminate the restriction on foreign exchange purchase in 1973. In 1979 it eliminated control on capital accounts. Between 1980 and 1986, UK removed credit control and highest lending and mortgage rate control.

Japan set the legal groundwork in 1949 so foreign currencies earned from export were centralized for purchasing items important for nation's rebuilding. As the country started to gain strength on export, in 1964, currency account was opened with a managed float FX regime. Japan's export surplus resulted the strong need for JPY in international trade and the currency's appreciation was in order. Capital account control gradual liberalization was started in 1967. Following Vietnam War and Oil Crisis, Bretton Woods System collapsed and JPY became a free-floating currency. As an OECD principal requirement and under the US pressure, Japan opened capital accounts in 1980. In 1984 Japan started the interest rate liberalization, specifically under the guidance of US-Japan Yen-Dollar Committee. Due to the fact that US Dollar's was under large pressure, the Plaza Accord was reached and a coordinated effort by the industrialized countries was made to weaken US dollar.

Important to Japan interest rate liberalization was the allowing JPY Treasury bond trading in 1977. Between 1978 and 1991, from large notional to smaller notional, interest rate control was eliminated, until all interest rates was set free in 1994.

Germany's emergency decree designed to deal with the Great Depression was expanded into 1934 Credit Act. After the WWII, US pushed for financial legislation aimed at decentralized financial supervision. In 1955 Germany regained the right of independent legislation and capital control was liberalized. New German Credit Act came into effect in 1961. In 1972, the weakness of US Dollar and Mark's appreciation pressure caused the reintroduction capital control of FX. 1973 collapse of Bretton Woods caused the free floating of Mark, and in 1974, capital account control was eliminated. Specifically for interest rate policy, historically coordination was done via the establishment of Central Credit Committee. The critical step was taken to eliminate this interest rate coordination mechanism in 1965. Between 1965 and 1967 interest rate control was loosened. Credit control was complete eliminated in 1973.

Market liberalization is a complex reform process unique and significant for every country involved. Learning from international experience and trying to apply it to domestic economic and financial systems, China's market liberalization process was proceeding over a long period of time. In 1993, market liberalization objective was announced. The process was started in 1996 with the liberalization of interbank borrowing rate. Repo rate was the next in 1997. In 1999 MOF began to be issue bonds via open market bidding process. In 2000, rate for large notional foreign exchange deposit was decided by market. In 2004, rate for small notional foreign exchange deposit was liberalized. 2004 also saw loosening of deposit rate upper limit and loan's lower limit. The loan's lower limit was set to be 0.9 of the benchmark loan rate. In 2005, interbank deposit rate was set free. 2007 was the year for interbank Shibor rate. In 2012 deposit upper limit was loosened to 1.1 of benchmark deposit rate, loan rate lower limit was loosened to 0.7 of the benchmark loan rate. In 2015, deposit upper limit was set free.

While the US experience provided useful insight into complex handling of interaction between regulators and markets, the German and Japan lessons showed the difficulty in market liberalization without a reserve currency status. CNY does not have the reserve currency status that US dollar had during the 1980s US market liberalization process, and it has to always consider the tradeoff between interest rate independence and the stability of exchange rate, an issue of concern also for Germany and Japan central banks. After the free floating of their currencies, Japan was concerned with the negative impact of JPY appreciation on export and low interest rate was set to help corporations to handle the pressure. Germany on the other hand maintained relative high interest rate, which had caused long period of high unemployment. Japan gained on employment, but the low interest rate distorted asset price eventually leading to asset bubble. This was a huge problem and the government eventually decided to deflate it. There was a lot of academic discussion on the appropriateness of the speed or the timing of the bubble piercing. But the consequence of bursting of asset bubble was severe. On the other hand German export industry remained competitive without asset bubble, but the loss of employment caused social upheaval, a problem a government would strive to avoid. Therefore, a relative stable exchange rate, with an interest rate not too high to cause social instability and not too low to cause an unmanageable asset bubble, would be an optimal path for China's interest rate market liberalization.

4.6   CFETS (China Foreign Exchange Trade System)

The interbank market is the largest segment of capital markets in China and it is under the supervision of PBOC. There are three intermediary agencies in this market. China Foreign Exchange Trading System (CFETS), China Central Depository & Clearing Co., Ltd (CCDC) and Shanghai Clearing House (SHSH). National Association of Financial Market Institutional Investor (NAFMII) is a self-regulatory body for institutional investors.

Members of the interbank market trade via CFETS to reach a deal. Non-financial members need to sign documents to reach deal. CNY and non-CNY FX spot deals can be executed in anonymous mode with CFETS in the middle taking over credit risk. All FX instruments can be executed in bilateral mode. Standardized CNY FX swap and CNY FX forward can be specifically executed on CFETS platform in C-Swap and C-Forward format, via anonymous mode with pre-arranged bilateral credit limit agreement when buy sell prices match, or via one click when buy sell prices do not match. Market making effort drives FX trade flow. There are three types of FX participants on CFETS: pricing dealers that can make market, post and reply to RFQ and trade; dealers that can post and reply to RFQ and trade; trader that can post RFQ and trade.

Bond trades can be executed on CFETS via market maker one click mode or bilateral RFQ mode. The FX C-Swap and C-Forward equivalent in bond world is X-series, i.e., X-bond, X-Swap, that can be executed anonymously when price match with pre-arranged bilateral credit limit agreement. Bond trades are settled via CCDC and SHSC. CCDC is the custodial agency for interbank bonds and SHSC is the custodial agency for interbank SCP and CP. There are three types of interbank market participating members. Type A, deposit-taking institutions that can both directly trade in the interbank market and act as an agent for Type C members; type B, non-banking financial institutions that can directly trade but can not act as an agent for Type C members; type C members that can only trade via Type A members. Type C includes small to medium financial institutions, non-financial institutions, non-legal entity and some foreign institutions. Alternatively speaking, financial institutions can either become direct settlement member, or indirect settlement member. Non-financials can only be an indirect settlement member, and execute bond trade and bond repo trade via type A members or market makers.

Transaction payments are mostly cleared via China National Advanced Payment System (CNAPS). CNAPS is composed of two large systems, HVPS (High Value Payment System), and Bulk Electronic Payment System (BEPS). HVPS handles bonds-related transaction clearing on a real time, deal by deal, full amount basis. Some of the clearing is handle by commercial banks' own clearing system. BEPS provides clearing services for small notional debit credit transaction settlement 24×7 in large volume, by net amount using batch mode.

4.7 China Banking Regulatory Commission and Interbank Market

CBRC formulates supervisory rules and regulations governing the banking institutions, promotes the financial stability and facilitates financial innovation at the same time. It often works with PBOC to improve the financial market practice in terms of fairness, transparency and financial stability. For example it issued a mandate in October of 2016 to forbid bank WMP funds from going into real estate, a sector with inflated value that could pose substantial risk for incoming funds. It was also directly involved in cracking down on shadow banking regarding off-balance sheet financing.

4.8 China Securities Regulatory Commission and Exchange Markets

CSRC manages exchange markets and the fixed income trading on those exchanges, including interest rate bond, enterprise bond and corporate bond. Over the years corporate bonds that are exclusively traded on exchanges have become an important source of funding for corporations. On exchange market, corporate bond are frequently repoed when eligible, this leverage practice makes holding corporate bond on exchange more advantageous to investors, which causes corporate bond yield on exchange to be much lower than those credit instruments of comparable quality in the interbank market. The regulatory arbitrage between exchange bond market and interbank bond market is one of the key drivers behind the coordination working mechanism reform of PBOC, CBRC, CSRC and CIRC.

Chapter 5
Market Participants

5.1 Fixed Income Institution Players, Market Making Participation

The most important fixed income players in China are banks. While banks started to appear in China the mid 19th century, modern banking system started to form in 1979 when China Construction Bank, Bank of China and Agricultural Bank of China were set up to address the need of financial services in basic infrastructure development, foreign exchange and agricultural development respectively. In 1984, three policy banks, China Development bank, Agricultural Development Bank of China and Export Import Bank of China were set up to free CCB, ABC and BOC from policy-related tasks in agriculture and other areas. ICBC was set to free commercial functions from the central bank, People's Bank of China. ICBC, CCB, ABC and BOC together formed the backbone of current China financial systems. Later, share-holding banks appeared, led by Bank of Communications. Smaller banks include urban and rural commercial banks. Urban commercial banks were formed based upon urban credit cooperatives and rural commercial banks were formed based upon rural credit cooperatives.

Compared with banks, other segments within China financial industry emerged later. Securities firm started to form in 1987 and the industry took off after the introduction of sponsorship system in 2004. Mutual fund industry started to form in 1991 became a more structured industry after regulatory implementation in 1997. One large difference with the US capital market is that non-banking institutions such as mutual funds or securities firms do not have the comparable market sway as the US non-banking institutions, and their fixed income holdings are relatively small when compared against banks. Non-banking institutional domination in capital markets especially regarding fixed income is rather a US exception that does not exist in other large economies including China, Japan and Germany.

© Springer Nature Singapore Pte Ltd. 2018
X. Zhang, *Capital Markets Trading and Investment Strategies in China*,
https://doi.org/10.1007/978-981-10-8497-3_5

Amid progressing market liberalization, even though urban commercial banks and rural commercial banks do not possess the amount of funds that large national commercial banks have for investment, they are nimble players looking for higher yield and trading income. Securities firms, mutual fund companies and foreign banks are also quite active. Therefore even though national commercial banks held about half of the total bond inventory in 2016 and still important in the fixed income space, smaller peers are gaining measured by growing trading volume.

Special settlement member is one type of investor that includes People's Bank of China, Department of Treasury, Policy Banks, main exchanges, China Bond and China Clearing.

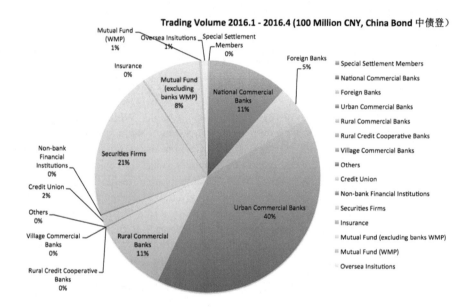

While the relative rise of smaller banks is significant and welcoming news in terms of providing more market diversity, it has also contributed to more volatility during period of illiquidity and had its own inherent risk. Many of the smaller banks trading volume are related to off-balance sheet financing, part of the shadow banking activities that China's deleveraging effort is focusing upon. Deleveraging took its toll on urban commercial banking bond trading volume in the beginning of 2017.

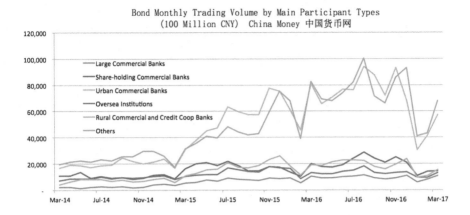

Bond Monthly Trading Volume by Main Participant Types
(100 Million CNY)   China Money 中国货币网

5.1.1   Interbank Money Market Activities by Bank Types

A quality starting point for analyzing banks' trading and investment behavior is money market when banks of different types and sizes would actively engage in lending surplus fund and borrowing in fund shortage based upon their specific balance sheet characteristics. Among Repo, Outright Repo and Loan deposit, Repo is the by far the most important type of MM activities banks engaged in. In terms of open positions relative to their balance sheet size, urban commercial banks are the largest users followed by rural financial institutions.

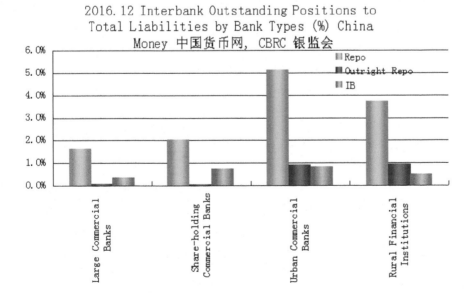

2016.12 Interbank Outstanding Positions to Total Liabilities by Bank Types (%) China Money 中国货币网, CBRC 银监会

The general application of money market funding has been on the rise for all banks. For their relatively moderate balance sheet size, urban and rural commercial banks have been disproportional large repo users to access money market quite volatile but cheap funding source.

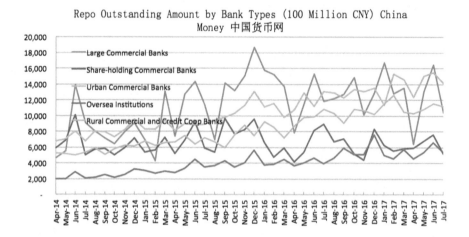

Urban commercial banks participation in the repo market is even more striking from the perspective of repo trading volume. Rural commercial banks are also quite active. Combining open positions and trading volumes, both urban and rural commercial banks possibly engage more than other bank types in short-term repo to access the cheapest source of funding possible to gain higher yield.

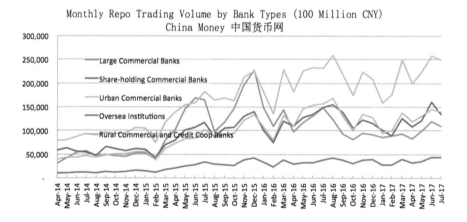

The reason for smaller banks' active tapping into interbank repo section for funding is their lack of both network to reach broad deposit base and the credit line to obtain sufficient institutional funding. In a repo transaction where credit risk is eliminated via interest rate collateral, there is no observable credit spread between large and relatively smaller banks. The increase and precipitous drop of repo rate in the first half of 2015 coincided with emerging and subsequent bursting of the equity bubble that led to increased and later subdued need for funding.

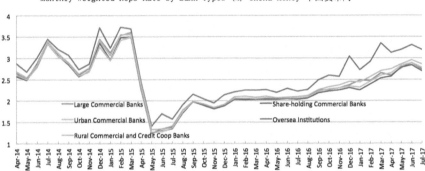

Loan deposit is a traditional funding market where larger institutions including large commercial banks and share-holding commercial banks handle short term funding request via interbank market. The end of 2015 peak was related to the fed fund rate increase and since then central bank and large institutions are much better prepared to handle volatility caused by global funding condition change. This improvement could be seen from a much smoother 2016 year end loan deposit yield condition amid the fed fund rate increase.

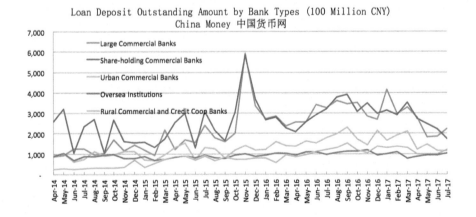

Between large commercial banks and share-holding commercial banks, share-holding commercial banks have higher loan deposit trading volumes. The peak volume in 2015 year end during fed fund rate increase and 2016 mid year

peak volume during Brexit indicated share-holding commercial banks active usage
of loan deposit market for short term funding and therefore their risk exposure to
money market volatility, while reduced usage since 2016 year-end deleveraging
suggested share-holding commercial banks' reliance on interbank loan deposit
market for off-balance sheet financing.

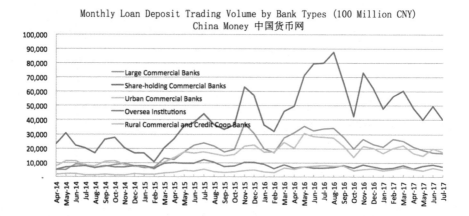

In terms of loan deposit cost, rural commercial banks had an observable spread
reflecting rural financial institutions' room for corporate governance improvement,
which resulted in a rating spread when compared against their more mature peers.

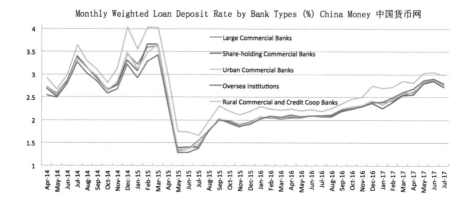

Outright repo is a much smaller segment and also more expensive source of fund
versus Repo and Loan deposit. It is a place for urban and rural commercial banks to
access fund that otherwise would not be available. Peak occurred in the end of 2015
and 2016, during which fed fund rate increase was in play that created short term
funding shortage.

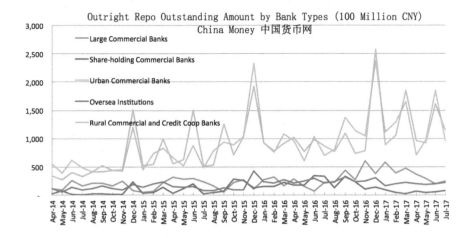

Urban and rural commercial banks relatively active outright repo trading volume corresponded to their relatively large outstanding positions, indicating both types to be consistent users of this market as funding source versus occasional surplus fund provider.

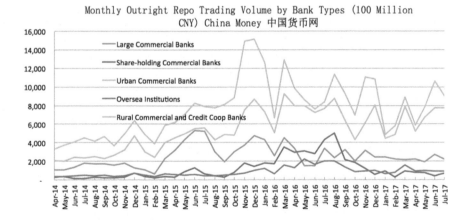

There is no observable spread among different bank types, compared against loan deposit where rural commercial banks showing a clear credit spread, indicating outright repo as an effective method in mitigating credit exposure versus uncollateralized loan deposit transaction.

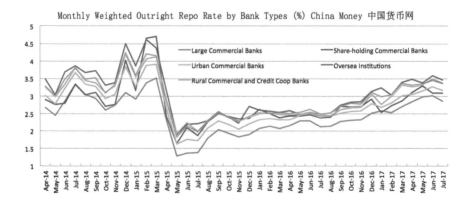

5.1.2 Banks 3-Tiered Banking Systems in Details

The active usage of money market itself illustrated the substantial changes that Chinese banking system had gone through over the last several decades. After splitting from public services, they entered commercial area burdened with large amount of non-performing loan from the previous era of planned economy. In the following economic reform, non-performing loan was unloaded, modern management structure was set up and some of the largest one became listed companies.

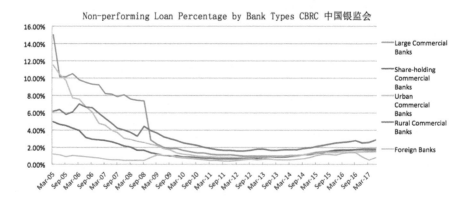

During the economic reform period, banks have gradually learnt to compete domestically and internationally to provide financial services to individuals, corporations, and many other entities. With the country's economic growth, their balance sheet size also grew substantially.

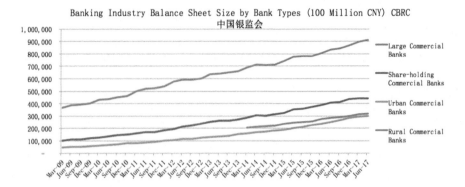

Bank is the most significant type financial institution in Chinese capital market. With their total asset size above 230 trillion CNY by the 2016 year-end, they are responsible for the lion share of both foreign exchange market making and fixed income trading/investment in China.

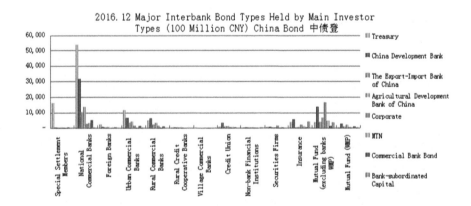

Based upon shareholder ownership, banks are mainly divided into three tiers: state-owned commercial banks, share-holding commercial banks and urban commercial banks. In terms of asset sizes, ICBC led the pack, followed by CCB, ABC and BOC. State-owned commercial banks are generally much larger than share-holding commercial banks and share-holding commercial banks are much larger than urban commercial banks. But as the market evolves, some of the smaller banks are growing faster thus blurring the line in terms of size.

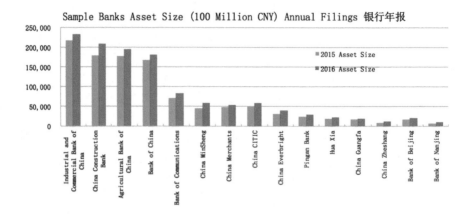

Though not exact and many exceptions do exist, the size of a bank's balance sheet is still a good indicator of its number of retail outlet, marketing reaching strength and capability to lower cost of fund via attracting deposit. Among the sampled banks, largest banks including ICBC, CCB, ABC and BOC had the lowest cost of fund, less than 2% for the year 2016. Funding cost for most of share-holding bank, with the exception of China Merchants, would be 0.5% higher. The lower cost of fund is typically caused by relative higher portion of funds coming from cash deposit, while the higher cost of fund is usually caused by higher portion of funds coming from term deposit, interbank borrowing and wealth management products.

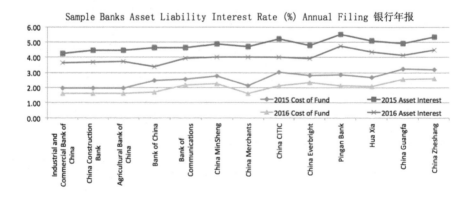

Under equal condition, the lower cost of funding would translate into higher interest rate spread. Alternatively, to generate the same level of interest rate spread, a bank with higher cost of funding might pursue riskier assets.

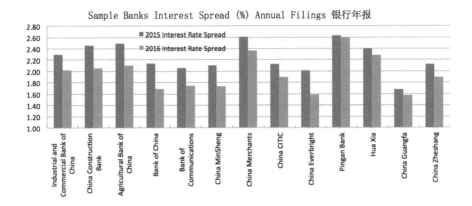

Sample Banks Interest Spread (%) Annual Filings 银行年报

Over the recent years, while all financial institutions participated in Chinese economic growth with their asset sizes increased substantially, share-holding commercial banks and urban commercial banks grew even relatively faster than their large commercial bank peers. Large national banks share of the total banking balance sheet dropped from 52.6% in 2009 to 37.4% by mid 2017. Share-holding commercial banks and urban commercial banks increased their share from 14.2 and 6.5% in 2009, to 18.1 and 12.2% by mid 2017, respectively.

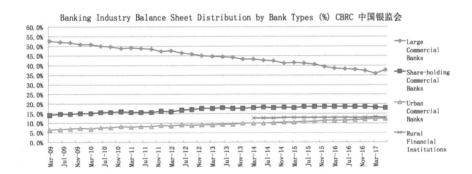

Banking Industry Balance Sheet Distribution by Bank Types (%) CBRC 中国银监会

5.1.2.1   State-Owned Commercial Banks

Of the 3-tiered banking system the first tier is the state-owned commercial banks. There are 5 of them in total. Usually people refer the largest 4 as the Big Four. They are Industrial and Commercial Bank of China (ICBC), China Construction Bank (CCB), Agricultural Bank of China (ABC) and Bank of China (BOC). These 4 banks all have fairly large balance sheets. For the year 2016, they reported balance sheet asset value at 23.26 trillion CNY for ICBC, 20.96 trillion CNY for CCB, 19.57 trillion CNY for ABC and 18.15 trillion CNY for BOC. Bank of

Communications is the smallest national bank in this category by comparison, with its balance sheet size at 8.4 trillion CNY.

These five banks play significant roles in the financial sector. Their combined asset values represented 38.90% of the Chinese banking industry's total by the end of 2016. They are also large players in the fixed income investment universe, with combined bond portfolio stood at 18.2 trillion CNY at the end of 2016, about 41.64% of the total Chinese bond market.

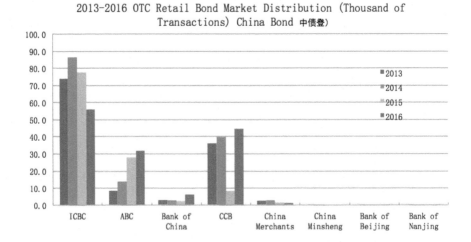

Based upon 2016 OTC retail bond market analysis, ICBC, ABC, BOC and CCB dominate the market distribution, a clear testament to their wide retail outlet outreach and marketing strength.

The cost of funding of the large banks, due to their extensive retail network, is comparatively lower than other types of financial institutions. Based upon annual filing for the year 2016, ICBC's cost of funding was at 1.6%, CCB at 1.61%, and ABC at 1.61%. BOC has a strong focus on international business, with slightly higher cost of funding at 1.69%. BOC's cost of funding was 2.17%.

ICBC, CCB, ABC and BOC and Bank of Communications for year 2016 had reported net balance sheet interest rate spread at 2.02, 2.06, 2.1, 1.69 and 1.75%, respectively. The spread was lowest for BOC for its relatively large exposure to difficult international business versus other 4 banks. The interest rate spread was the highest for ABC due to its competitive strength to bring financial service to the rural and remote area.

The funds put into fixed income investment by these large banks are generally originated from two sources. The first source is the excess assets after lending is carried out. The secondary source is the off-balance sheet Wealth Management Product that has grown tremendously as part of the market liberalization. WMP's return is much more competitive compared with the meager return offered by deposit product, therefore its growth is higher than the amount of fund deposited at the banks.

Over the years, with the interest rate liberalization taking place, the cost of funding increased for most banks even though it has had a more modest impact on the larger banks. That increase forced many banks to shift their fixed income investment portfolio allocation to higher yield instrument.

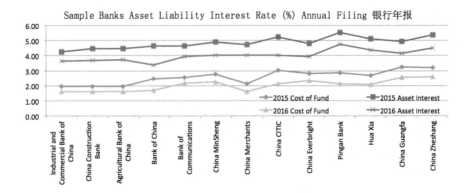

Large commercial banks implemented rigorous counterparty credit risk management practice to minimize their credit risk exposure for outright repo, where collaterals are marked-to-market. The stringent credit policy practice encouraged them to engage more in loan deposit and repo trading and reduced their market share in the outright repo segment of the MM market. They generally trade with counterparty with good credit status. Therefore, the weighted rate of Repo, Outright Repo, and Loan Deposit trades are comparable.

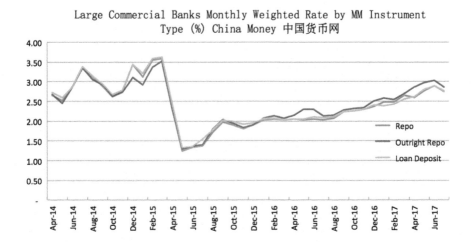

For large banks, relatively low cost funds from both deposit and MM market translated into their preference for Treasury bond, CDB bond and other interest rate bonds. Credit instrument is a small percentage of their total fixed income investment. China Bond definition for national commercial banks roughly combines both large state-owned national commercial banks and share-holding commercial banks into one group.

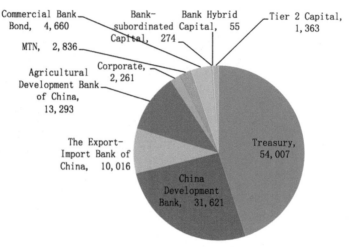

Main Bond Types Held by National Commercial Banks
2016. 12 (100 Million CNY) China Bond 中债登

Both the total amount of credit issuance and each individual credit issuance are relatively small for large banks portfolio. Hence the overall preference for interest rate product has been relatively stable in the recent years.

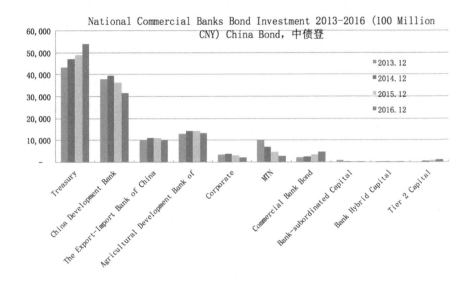

National Commercial Banks Bond Investment 2013-2016 (100 Million CNY) China Bond, 中债登

5.1.2.2   Share-Holding Commercial Banks

The next tier is 12 share-holding commercial banks. Their size of balance sheet varied from about 100 billion USD to about 800 billion USD, much smaller than the State-owned commercial banks at the end of 2015. The cost of funding was often 0.5 to 1.0% higher than that of the larger national banks. For 2016, China Minsheng Banking Group had cost of funding at 2.27% and China Everbright had cost of fund at 2.33%. To achieve comparable financial results with higher cost of funding, they tend to have higher risk preference than the state-owned commercial banks and urban commercial banks.

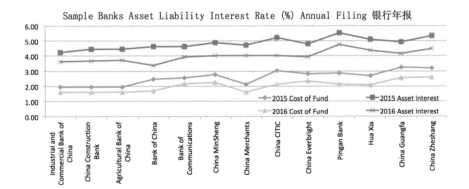

Sample Banks Asset Liability Interest Rate (%) Annual Filing 银行年报

Share-holding banks engage in loan deposit plus repo and do not use outright repo as much. There was an observable credit spread for these banks in outright repo segment. But that was rather insignificant since their engagement in outright repo segment had been rather occasional.

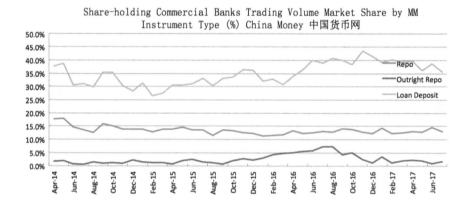

Share-holding Commercial Banks Trading Volume Market Share by MM Instrument Type (%) China Money 中国货币网

5.1.2.3   Urban Commercial Banks

The 3rd tier banks include urban and rural commercial banks. Urban commercial banks gained importance over the recent years. They usually started from a series of merger of local credit institutions within a metro area during the start of economic reform, therefore heavily involved in local economic development. As a result often they are viewed to have obtained local government support and in return also shared the some of the responsibilities to support local economy. To compensate for their lack of extensive branch coverage to attract deposit, urban commercial banks make extensive usage of interbank money market to fund their balance sheet expansion.

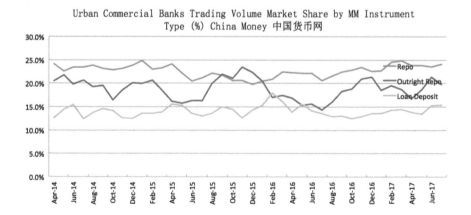

Urban Commercial Banks Trading Volume Market Share by MM Instrument Type (%) China Money 中国货币网

Due to their stronger funding need for money market resource and relatively lower rating status versus national and share-holding commercial banks, urban commercial banks utilize both repo and outright repo more often, which is different from large national banks or share-holding commercial banks that have preferred loan deposit over repos.

Actively pursuing higher yield in traditional lending, carry trade and trust segments caused urban commercial banks weighted repo rate to be about 0.5% higher than large commercial banks and share-holding commercial banks. For the same reasons, their use of outright repo was voluminous and credit spread clearly observable.

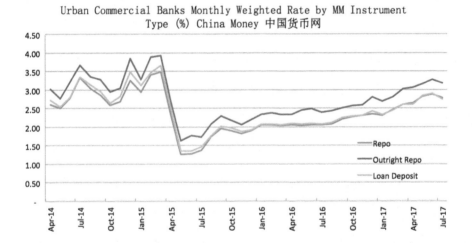

Urban Commercial Banks Monthly Weighted Rate by MM Instrument Type (%) China Money 中国货币网

Analyzing urban commercial banks investment behavior requires some basic understanding of class structure of various Chinese cities. Chinese city regions are classified into 4 tiers. First tier cities usually refer to Beijing, Shanghai, Shenzhen and Guangzhou. The second tier cities usually refer to provincial capitals or certain cities that have achieved successful economic development, such as Hangzhou, Tianjin and Nanjing. The third tier cities are those with government administrative level above county but lower than provincial capital. The forth tier cities are those at the county level. Based upon their different geographical location and sizes, an urban commercial bank might choose a specific type of operating model best suited for their own business condition. We could roughly classify all urban commercial banks into three types.

The 1st tier urban commercial banks are largest urban commercial banks that usually headquartered in a first tier city. An example of such is Bank of Beijing. Over the years these 1st tier urban banks grew in a competitive business environment where large state-owned commercial banks and share-holding commercial banks are both omnipresent and active. Tough regulatory environment caused by the presence of larger financial institutions and 1st tier urban banks competitive advantage related to local development projects made these urban banks choose to compete in local credit loan and be less willing to venture into risky bond investment that requires large technology and expertise investment. In the case of Bank of Beijing, for the year of 2015, had about 19.364 billion CNY of investment, with overall low taste of risk.

The 2nd type may be located in economically developed second tier city, such as Zheshang Bank or Bank of Nanjing. They have sophisticated business models and can be more actively utilizing interbank and corporate term deposit to fund their balance sheet growth. Interbank funds and corporate term deposits are generally more expensive and volatile, therefore better investment strategy, risk management and asset liability management processes have to be in place for these banks.

The 3rd type of bank includes those located in areas that need further development. These urban commercial banks still have relatively heavy reliance on cash deposit especially from the retail customers to fund their balance sheet growth.

Deposit is the main source of urban commercial banks funding and its size is a good measure of a bank's competitiveness. The following figure illustrates the size and composition of 5 sampled urban commercial banks' 2015 and 2016 reported deposit.

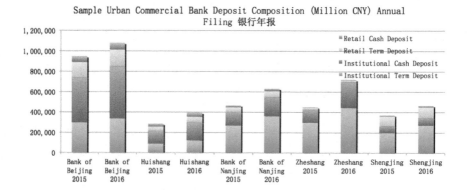

Sample Urban Commercial Bank Deposit Composition (Million CNY) Annual Filing 银行年报

The mixture of a bank's deposit type is also important for a bank's financial competitiveness. Cash deposit pays much lower interest for both retail customer and institutional clients, often at less than 1%, while the term deposit's return is often at more than 3%. While banks generally prefer cash deposit to term deposit, higher percentage of deposit coming from cash may reflect the general strength of local economic environment and contribute to a bank's growth prospect.

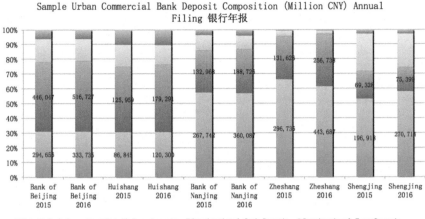

Sample Urban Commercial Bank Deposit Composition (Million CNY) Annual Filing 银行年报

The source of a bank's income is another important measure for bank competitiveness. As Chinese banking industry as a whole gaining on business competence, banks are trying to diversify their income away from traditional interest income so as to increase return on equities and simultaneously lessen their dependency on capital on growth, which has become increasingly expensive as financial interest rate liberalization takes hold. From this perspective, banks' interest income to total income ratio is also a good indicator to assess the level of financial progress in both the local bank and local economy. In the sample population, Bank of Beijing maintained low interest income to total income ratio. Zheshang made large improvement from 2015 to 2016 partly due to local export industry recovery in Zhejiang province.

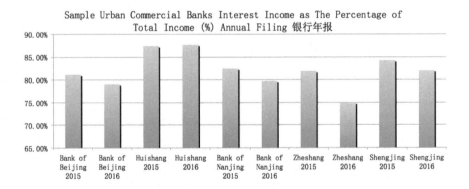

Sample Urban Commercial Banks Interest Income as The Percentage of Total Income (%) Annual Filing 银行年报

The type of loan administered is also important for assessing a bank's local business condition and growth potential. The rapid industrialization of Chinese economy has made it difficult for the regulatory framework to keep up with the pace of change. To guard against business irregularities and strengthen their risk management practice, many banks have designed their own approaches to reduce risk exposure in their respective business environment. One way to analyze an urban commercial banks' stringency of their risk management practice is to compare the loan percentage administered by the pledge type. Collateralized loan is the most stringent form of loan, while credit loan is the least. Bank of Beijing's relative low percentage of collateralized loan and highest percentage of credit loan may point to the overall better business environment in Beijing.

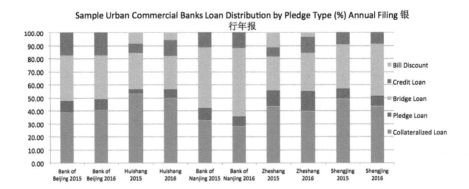

Though a bank's distinction from each other has been blurred in the process of market liberalization, urban commercial banks have been generally risk-averse in their fixed income portfolio more similar to national banks versus share-holding commercial banks. Policy bank bonds offer higher yield than treasury while still retain good liquidity, and can be readily used as collateral for interbank money market repo operation. Policy bank bond therefore became the most favored asset class in their bond portfolio.

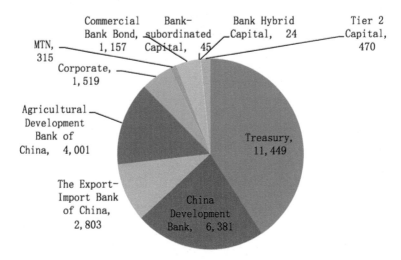

Main Bond Types Held by Urban Commercial Banks 2016.12 (100 Million CNY) China Bond 中债登

The preference for interest rate product has been consistent and striking for urban commercial banks. Given the pressure to increase return has forced them to venture more into the volatile money market for funding, to administer high yield loan with various credit-enhancing techniques and to generate more fee income versus interest income, bond portfolio is still viewed more as a excess liquidity asset pool versus a yield-enhancing asset class.

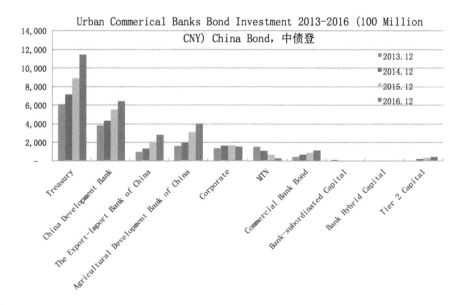

5.1.2.4 Rural Commercial Banks

Part of the 3rd tier banks, rural commercial banks are the result of merger of regional rural credit institutions. Similar to urban commercial banks, they lack extensive retail network but have access to local projects. To fund their balance sheet expansion, rural commercial banks have become very active in money market especially the repo segment.

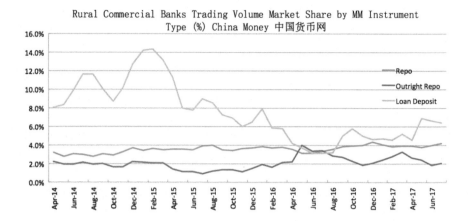

Having made strides since their inception, rural commercial banks still have some room for improvement. The credit risk spread is observable for both outright repo and loan deposit against repo transactions, which is not the case for urban commercial bank type that has only outright repo showing a clear segment spread. They also have clear loan deposit and outright repo credit spread against other bank types.

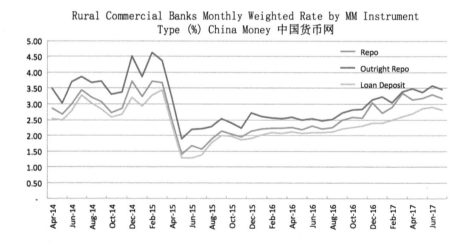

Rural Commercial Banks fixed income portfolio composition is quite different from either urban commercial banks or national commercial banks. The largest difference is the higher allocation to CDB bonds and lower allocation to Treasury bond.

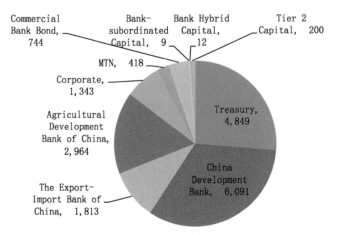

Main Bond Types Held by Rural Commercial
Banks 2016.12 (100 Million CNY) China Bond
中债登

As the combined result of gaining on fixed income market expertise and under
the pressure to deliver return, the increased allocation to CDB bond actually sped
up in 2016 for rural banks.

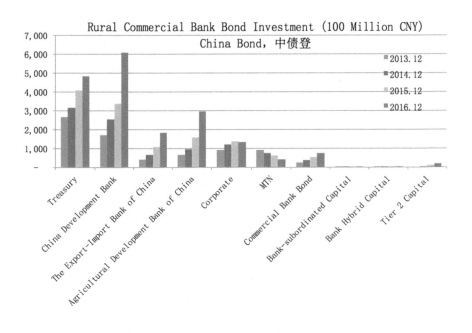

5.1.3   Mutual Funds, Tax Policy and Carry Advantage

The mutual fund industry in China stood at just over 10 trillion CNY at the end of 2016. Most of the funds are open-end funds. The general perception of mutual fund as a temporary solution during low equity return or high equity market volatility is fundamental to bow mutual fund industry trades and invests in China.

For the 10 trillion plus CNY investment by the end of 2016, 50.25% went to money market fund, 8.28% to equity fund, and 23.57% to hybrid fund. Fixed income instrument, which includes bond fund and money market fund, took 66.95% of the fund industry total. Money market fund took a much larger share of the total fixed income segment. 16.7% of the fund market, or about 1.42 trillion CNY, went to bond mutual fund.

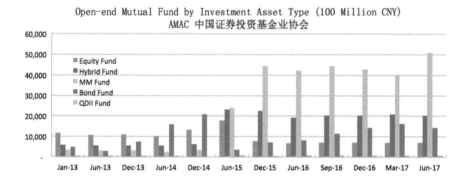

By regulatory definition, at least 80% of the assets under management by a bond fund must be bond assets. Similarly, for an equity fund, at least 80% of the assets under management must be equity-related assets. For a fund of fund, 80% of assets must go to various types of fund. Money market fund must invest in money market instruments. The rest is classified as hybrid fund.

There are three types of bond fund, based upon product type mix in the fund: pure bond fund, which invests mostly in credit bonds; type 1 bond fund, which also invests in newly-issued stocks and convertible bonds; type 2 bond fund, which also invests in newly-issued stocks, convertible bonds and stocks on the secondary market. For type 1 and type 2 bond fund, the weight of the stock-related investment should be between 0 and 20%. Therefore type 1 and type 2 bond funds are not hybrid funds even though they have equity-related components.

Bond funds face competition from bank-issued WMP products. WMP products have the following advantages: (1) WMP is not restricted to access high yield assets including trust or credit assets; (2) Its liquidity management is made easier by funds pool and preset redemption dates; (3) Default risk is substantially lower due to implicit guarantee with banks' large balance sheet. Some recent reforms have made WMP less competitive, but it remains a strong competitor for bond fund. On the other hand, most of the bond funds are open-end funds with active management. This has made fund liquidity management difficult, as the investment inflows are mostly unrelated to retirement investment plan and can have huge short term fluctuation.

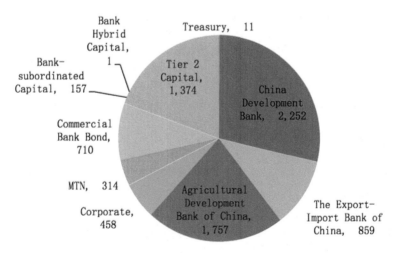

Main Bond Types Held by WMP 2016. 12 (100 Million CNY) China Bond 中债登

Better positioned to deal with redemption and volatility risk versus bond funds, WMP bond investment pattern has been fairly stable. WMP maintains little Treasury bond position for liquidity management and has large allocation to illiquid bank-related bonds to enhance yield. Its exposure to ADBC and EIBC is also relatively large to gain on small ADBC and EIBC liquidity premium versus CDB bonds.

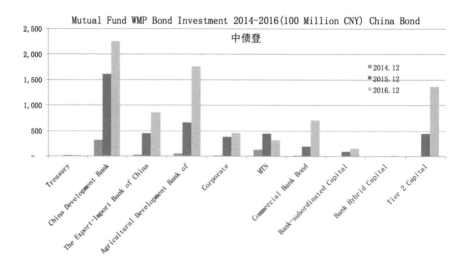

The other main challenge bond fund faces comes from money market fund. MM fund is a simple financial product, in terms of product composition and service complexity. Overtaking bond fund and hybrid bund in just over a couple of years, from 2013 to 2015, the faster growth of MM fund was a result of both the interest rate market liberalization and the internet technology's capability in market penetration.

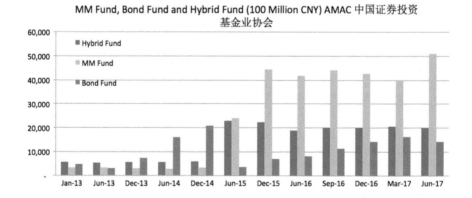

The root cause for bond fund's problem is that bond market is heavily populated by state-owned issuers thus bonds are often perceived to be of low credit risk. From the perspective of an active investor, lack of credit premium and presence of bank account investment flow together make bond yield spread against money market fund unattractive to compensating for its simultaneous lack of liquidity. Hence, more retail investments went into money market fund than into the bond fund. A prime example was the money market fund YueBao. This particular money market fund took full advantage of the internet technology to access large client base of Alibaba, a lot of which had small amount of idle cash deposit that previously earned little return. Money was aggregated into money market fund that mostly invested in interbank borrowing with much higher interest income. This is a model business case of using internet technology to access large amount of small investors from defragmented market, the so called "fragmented long tail" client resource. Money market fund became a serious competitor for banks' deposit resource and there was a heated debate in 2014 and regulatory change regarding third party payment companies.

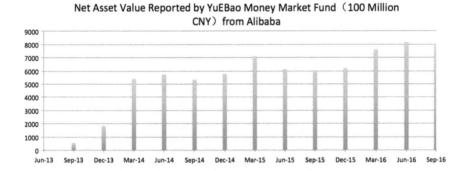

The third party payment player is not a direct participant in the investment world, but the importance of its future role cannot be discounted. A large third party payment system arranges goods delivery, and upon subsequent clients satisfactory acceptance confirmation, releases payment. This type of system in China was crucial in reducing small merchandize sales irregularity and cutting down complicated sales network overhead. In the process of helping their clients, they had gained more knowledge of their clients' need and their clients' spending behavior than banks, in certain areas could provide more tailored financial services to clients. Therefore third party system was simultaneously both a good partner and a potent challenger to banks.

To compete against money market funds, WMP and other financial products, Bond funds have tried in many ways to increase product yield and attractiveness. Gaining access to equity market is one of them. For the actively managed bond funds, a substantial amount belongs to type 1 and type 2 bond fund to gain higher return and better liquidity offered by the equity market.

Specialization is another way to enhance fund return. The fund industry has entered a new phase where niche specialization is advantageous, and the dominance of the top 10 players regarding market share has come down from a much higher level to about 50%. The top 20 pure bond funds had recently achieved return between 15 and 29%, a substantial value amid low yield market condition.

Repo combined with leverage is also applied to enhance fund return. Bond fund is allowed to conduct repo transactions. Leverage ratio is limited to 1.4. This ratio is relaxed to 2 for principal-guaranteed fund and close fund. There is no leverage ratio restriction for leverage fund.

Bond mutual fund's yield strategies typically involve credit strategy, term strategy and leverage. With leverage ratio limited by regulation, credit strategy limited by credit worsening macro environment, and traditionally low term spread, all these have added difficulties for bond fund to compete against money market fund, wealth management product, and other financial investment products.

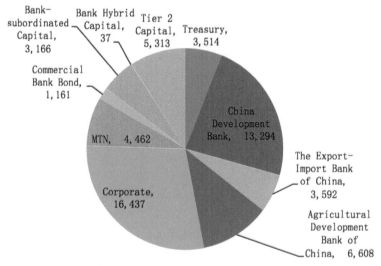

Main Bond Types Held by Mutual Funds
Excluding Bank WMP 2016.12 (100 Million
CNY) China Bond 中债登

Bond fund allocation into different bond segments reflects a balancing act between managing liquidity and maximizing yield. Mutual funds pay tax on their profit, while banks are usually profitable and have to pay tax on interest earned. This has made bond fund more attracted to policy bank bonds with higher before tax coupon versus Treasury. Still, bond funds have relatively higher Treasury allocation versus WMP to prevent possible liquidity run and volatility risk hike. So was the reason for bond fund higher CDB exposure versus EIBC and ADBC bonds to gain on liquidity and forego the small liquidity spread offered by EIBC and ADBC bonds. Exposure to corporate bonds with credit premium and repo leverage advantage is very large to increase yield return.

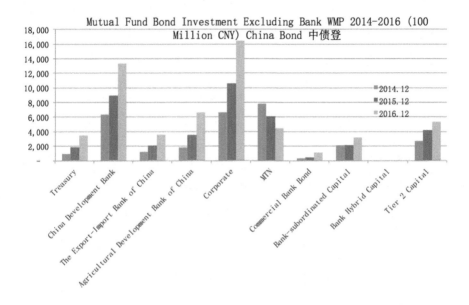

5.1.4 Insurers and Long Investment Horizon

There are three types of insurance service provided in China. The first type is social security that is administered by government. The second is corporate annuity provided by corporates for their employees as supplementary benefits. The third is insurance-related services provided by private insurance companies.

In 2015 the government issued new rules to allow social security to invest in wider ranger of asset classes to tackle negative real return and deal with the fact that China is gradually becoming an aging industrial society. Specific investment guidelines included: the amount of liquid instrument, including deposit with maturity less than 1 year, central bank bill, treasury less than 1 year, repo, money market retirement annuity product and money market fund, should be no less than 5% of the net asset value of any fund; bond and other fixed income instruments including convertible should be no more than 135% of NAV of any fund; equity-related products should be no more than 30% of NAV; large national project should be no more than 20% of NAV; equity index future, bond future, defined as derivatives, are only allowed for hedging purposes, with book value not exceeding hedged assets book value.

New guidelines were also issued in 2015 for pension fund companies including: liquid asset should be no less than 5% of the total assets value; basis infrastructure, real estate and other similar financial assets should not exceed 75% of portfolio value; any single project investment should not exceed 50% of portfolio value;

liquidity management plan is mandatorily required; the solvency adequacy ratio of an insurance company is the size of its capital relative to all risks it has taken and the insurance companies that have solvency ratio less than 150% can not invest in equities, credit assets or trusts.

After the reform in 2015, some pension firms started to engage in equity market via universal insurance product to wrestle control from management of companies that deemed being undervalued. The objective was to increase investment return via management and corporate restructuring. The actions by pension firms proved to be controversial leading to further regulatory guidelines issued in 2016 to rein in universal insurance product to prevent over-borrowing in the pension industry.

5.1.4.1   Social Security

Based upon the data published by Ministry of Human Resources and Social Security, social security expenses increased faster than domestic product growth to provide better coverage for the society. Social security in China provides coverage on retirement, medical insurance, work-related injury, unemployment and birth insurances. The allocated coverage is largest for retirement insurance and medical insurance.

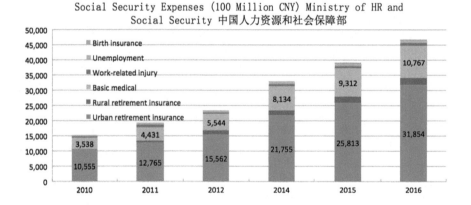

One major change over the recent years regarding social security expenditure was the increased coverage for rural retirement. This was aimed at reducing living standard inequality between urban and rural areas so as to foster labor mobility between industrial and agricultural population.

In terms of investment community participation, resources collected to for pay for future social security benefits need to be invested to preserve their value. Historically social security investment was tightly regulated and its real return was usually in negative territory. To increase investment return and provide better coverage, guidelines were issued in 2015.08 to broaden the range of financial products allowed for social security investment. The investable products included bank deposit, interest rate bond, investment grade credit bond, convertibles and equities of listed companies, among many others.

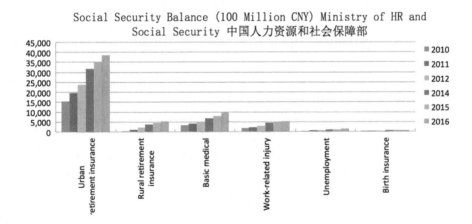

It is worth breaking down social security balance by segments since different outstanding social security segments could have theoretically different investment time horizon and different investment risk profile. Among these segments, retirement insurance including urban and rural took about 72% of the social security balance in 2016. While the relatively faster increase of rural retirement over urban retirement balance reflected the effort to increase future coverage to the rural area, the weight of retirement insurance as a whole had been generally stable. Social security fund is very different from other types of investors for its strict due diligence requirement, long investment time horizon and conservative investment behavior. As social security fund's gradual expansion into capital markets in terms of amount and range of investment progresses, the fund impact on the investment community will be felt more clearly in the future.

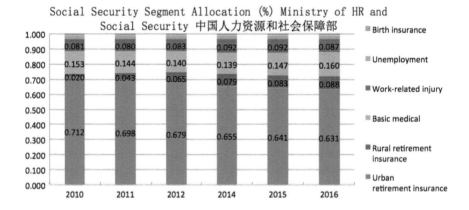

5.1.4.2 Corporate Annuity

Annuity Insurance provides coverage for both individuals and groups. Corporate annuity for employees is provided in addition to the mandatory social security coverage. There are 4 roles involved in annuity management, trustee that acts as the legal entity representing the interest of the annuity investor; account manager that manages the cashflow of investment accounts; custodian that are commercial banks offering accounts; investment manager responsible for investment management. The most lucrative among these roles is the investment manager. There is a license requirement for being an investment manager. At the end of year 2015, only 7 licenses were given to investment manager participants.

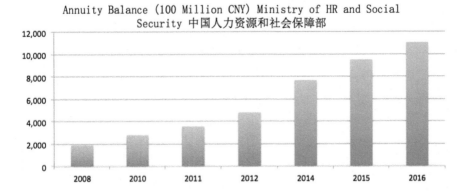

Annuity Balance (100 Million CNY) Ministry of HR and Social Security 中国人力资源和社会保障部

5.1.4.3 Commercial Pensions

Commercial pensions provide coverage to both individuals and groups. Commercial pension funds can be both open-end fund and close-end fund. For individual commercial pension plan, there will be 10% cut from the management fee as risky capital charge, until it is 1% of the total asset value under management for individual commercial pension management. This was designed specifically to cover losses resulted from violation against management contract and others.

Insurance business provides coverage on both property and personal insurance. Property insurance tends to be of shorter maturity, typically within 1 year. Personal insurance tends to be of much longer maturity. Personal insurance includes life insurance, health insurance and personal accident insurance. It has long been the case for the industry that more fees are generated from personal insurance and more fees within the personal insurance is generated from life insurance.

Areas within life insurances, ranked from low to high in terms of investment risk, include traditional life insurance, dividend insurance, universal insurance and investment-linked insurance. Currently most of the market share of life insurance is taken by dividend insurance, from which a dividend will be paid and any profit or risk beyond that are shared by both the insurer and the insured based upon preset proportion.

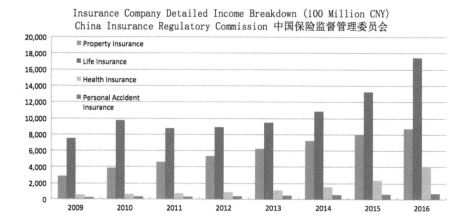

Insurance Company Detailed Income Breakdown (100 Million CNY)
China Insurance Regulatory Commission 中国保险监督管理委员会

Since most insurance income is generated from personal insurance, the largest portion of investment assets for the industry belongs to the personal insurance business line, with property insurance taking a distant second spot. The domination of life insurance within personal insurance, combined with the domination of personal insurance assets within the industry, has decided the asset allocation for insurance industry investment is long maturity in nature.

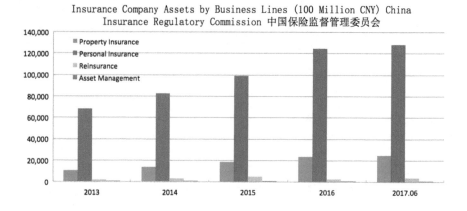

Insurance Company Assets by Business Lines (100 Million CNY) China Insurance Regulatory Commission 中国保险监督管理委员会

An important regulatory change was the removal of upper limit on insurance premium that was put in place to protect insurance industry. Stipulated in 2015, the premium upper limit could be decided by each company, but no more than each company's most recent five years' average investment return. This change eliminated the protection for insurance industry against interest rate liberalization in the financial industry, but also had the effect of making the industry to be more competitive in their product offering. Partly because of that, the fee income rose substantially in 2016.

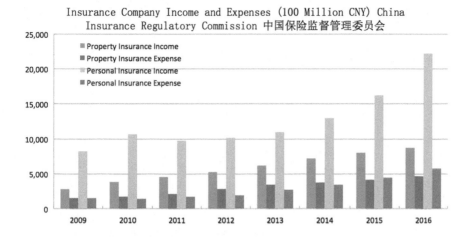

Insurance Company Income and Expenses (100 Million CNY) China Insurance Regulatory Commission 中国保险监督管理委员会

Since 2014, both incomes and expenses have risen with the fast growth of the insurance industry. The Personal insurance saw a much larger increase, a result of the market liberalization of the insurance sector and the new found competitiveness of the life insurance investment product. Historically property insurance has always been much smaller part of income stream to insurance companies compared with personal insurance, its income also grew, but to a much less extent.

Insurance companies' asset management business can be divided into two main business areas. The first is investment business, which includes basic infrastructure/real estate fixed income or equity investment plans; asset-backed investment plan; PE; value-enhancing platform. Basic infrastructure/real estate investment tends to be long maturity investment, between 5 and 10 years that matches the long duration requirement of insurance investment.

The second business line is the more traditional asset management business, which includes insurance asset management, corporate annuity, third party insurance asset management and investment-linked insurance. Insurance asset management holds the advantages of large size of insurance issuance, relatively less regulatory restriction and longer maturity. These advantages made insurance asset management more compatible with the term of insurance capital, which is long-term and large-scale diversified assets lead to lower funding cost and relatively higher return. Therefore insurance asset management has enjoyed fast growth in recent years.

The reduction of bank deposit rate in 1999 caused large pressure on life insurance product, which was considered a competing product. To lessen this pressure, upper limit of life insurance was fixed to 2.5% to prevent insurance companies from competing with each other by offering higher insurance return. As market liberalization progressed this fixed ceiling eventually made the insurance industry products less competitive. In 2013 the upper limit of life insurance was raised to 3.5%. In 2015, the upper limit was further raised to a company's 5-year average investment yield. At the same time, the type of allowable investments is becoming increasingly more complex. Proportionally there is less invested in bank deposit and investment grade bonds, which are simpler instruments that offer less return but also retain less risk. More investments are allocated to the more volatile equity products and other financial products.

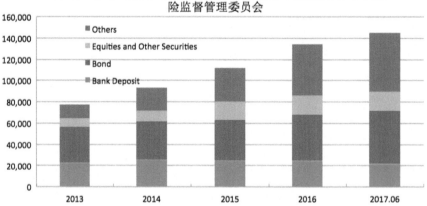

An area that recently attracted much interest from the insurance industry was the government-sponsored infrastructure projects. These projects tend to be of long maturity. For their long maturity, they offered high yield above 6% in 2015 compared against average return from quality long bond investments that offered yield in the range from 3 to 4%. These government-sponsored large projects also have relatively low credit risk.

The outstanding bond positions by insurance industry in 2016.12 showed the industry's particular favor for treasury and CDB policy bank bond for liquidity and long duration, and high-grade corporate bonds for higher yield. Regarding bank-subordinated capital bond, banks and insurance companies often practice reciprocal holding of subordinated capital instrument to increase their capital base and this was not encouraged.

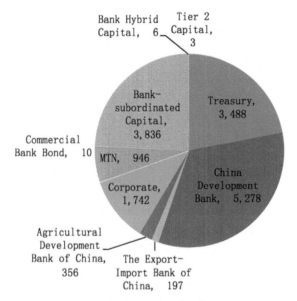

Main Bond Types Held by Insurance 2016.12
(100 Million CNY) China Bond 中债登

Within insurance companies' decreasing bond inventory, Non-CDB policy bonds are still consistently avoided mainly for maturity reason. Compared with ADBC and EIBC policy bank bonds, CDB has more bonds with maturity beyond 5 years, and even more so in maturity beyond 10 years. Regarding credit instruments, we have to keep in mind that only a portion of corporates and MTN are eligible for investment due to ratings.

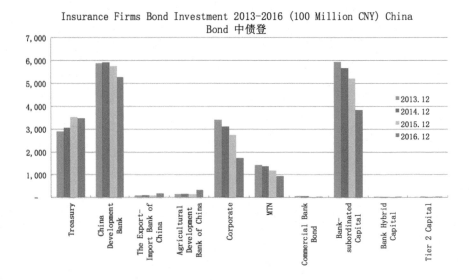

Insurance Firms Bond Investment 2013-2016 (100 Million CNY) China Bond 中债登

5.1.5 Foreign Financial Institutions

Overseas In stitutions can be foreign-owned or joint-owned financial institutions. They can also be classified into banks or non-banks. Most activities conducted by overseas financial institutions in China's money market and bond market are actually executed by foreign-owned banks. In its published data China Money does not distinguish between foreign-owned versus joint-owned, or between banks versus non-banks. Overseas institutions combined accounted for a large percentage of repo and outright repo activities in money market compared with their bond market presence. This disproportionally higher money market participation is more in line with their heavier involvement in international commerce trade that is short term financing in nature and with less willingness to commit to long-term capital under the current condition. Their footprint was smaller on loan deposit due to domestic bank technical difficulties in conducting oversea due diligence on foreign banks to get credit line approval.

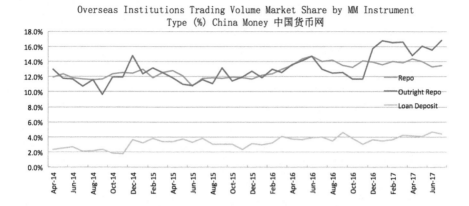

The clearest evidence for credit limit difficulty was in the money market repo spread, which in theory should not have existed with the elimination of counterparty risk within a repo transaction. The higher cost of MM rate during a repo transaction for foreign institutions is almost a reversal of situation, as Chinese financial institutions in Hong Kong (China) generally have to pay a higher so-called China Premium in money market financing. Spread aside, overseas financial institutions funding cost historical pattern largely followed their domestic peers in China's money market, illustrated a generally homogeneous money market capital management style for domestic and overseas financial institutions.

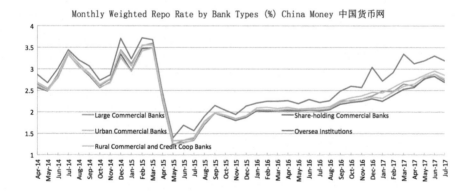

Credit limit is even a bigger issue in a loan deposit transaction given the presence of counterparty credit risk and the limited credit access generated a clear spread between repo instruments and loan deposit trades that did not exist for large domestic peers.

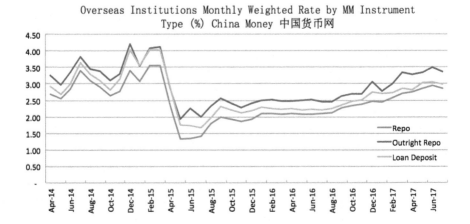

Most trading activities by overseas financial institutions in China's interbank bond market are also generated by foreign-owned banks. Smaller than many domestic peers, their bond trading volumes could be more influenced by international market view, which makes them somewhat different from domestic peers. For example, within the second half of 2016 after Brexit, domestic banks quickly resumed business as usual in bond market while foreign institutions remained muted until the beginning of 2017.

There are many reasons contributing to the lack of presence of foreign banks in China's bond market. Difference in regulatory framework, capital account restriction, quick-paced market growth and difficulty in reconciling the quantitative approaches across markets all played their respective roles.

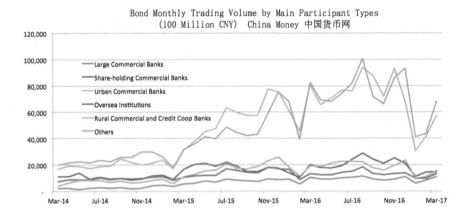

Most of what the foreign banks have purchased on the bond market were Treasury bonds for liquidity reason with less tax complication. It was also an efficient way to take bond yield arbitrage between domestic and international markets with minimum complexity.

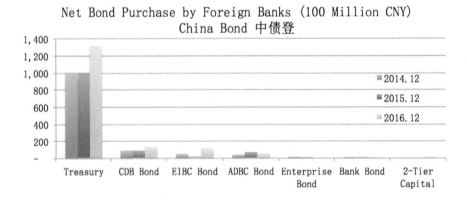

Foreign banks limited involvement in interbank bond market was evident in their bond portfolio. Investment in credit sector requires liquidity capital support and detailed issuer analysis. Therefore most of the foreign banks bond investment was in interest rate sector including Treasury and policy bank bonds.

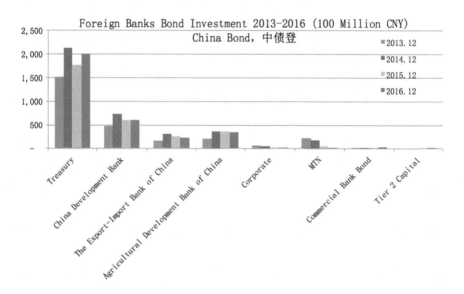

While foreign banks have encountered problems in money market credit limit access that can be traced back to the lack of experience by domestic peers in international market, and problems in local credit issuer analysis that can be traced back to the lack of experience by foreign banks in domestic market, a perspective can be given based upon comparison on foreign banks different participation rate in various market segment. In mid 2017, foreign banks accounted for about 13.5% of the repo market share and 8.3% of bond trading market share, but only about 0.99% of total bond holding. This suggested the willingness to engage and expand in short term profit-taking trading activities on behalf of foreign banks without committing deeply in building local franchise. Low interest spread and stringent capital requirement after the financial crisis and difference in complicated regulatory framework between domestic and international markets have all limited the ambition of global financial institutions.

The so-called overseas institutions designated by China Bond executing bond transactions on interbank bond market could be a non-bank garden variety including overseas legal entity branches of domestic financial institutions. With very limited bond market participation, they were engaging in heavy cross-border capital arbitrage until the capital charge loophole was closed. Cross-border yield arbitrage without tax complication makes Treasury their favorite instruments.

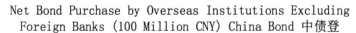

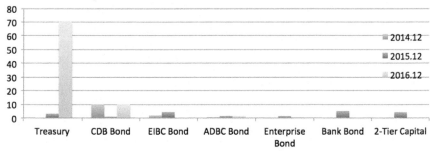

These overseas financial institutions are much different from foreign banks. Much larger credit exposure could be seen within their bond portfolio, which demonstrated their knowledge of domestic market and readiness to invest in local credit instruments. Their sharp increase in Treasury holding in 2016 could be seen as a combined result of preference for liquid interest rate bond used in cross border yield arbitrage and low tax spread between Treasury and policy banks bonds in domestic market.

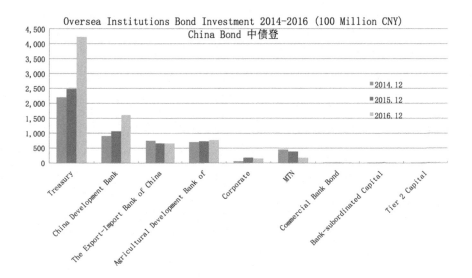

5.1.6 Private Equities, a Growing Presence

With a scale much smaller than bank lending, private equities grew by competing in the same space with securities firms' asset management division, mutual fund sub-affiliates and trust with more flexibility. The sector was not as regulated until 2013 when rules specifically targeting PE area were issued. Recent trend was to bring more order and transparency, including regulations issued in 2016 on various leverage ratio limits. Specifically, from the perspective of types of funding source, equities and hybrids-financed leverage ratio should not exceed 100%, fixed income-financed leverage ratio should not exceed 300%, other structured products should not exceed 200%. From the perspective of allocated investment, invested structured assets versus net assets should be under 140%, invested non-structured (1 to many) versus net assets should be under 200%. In addition, any structured product investment needs to be validated via a pass-through test.

Private equities invest mostly in equities. As China market is very different from US market, the applicable strategies are also quite different. Most common strategies include (1) traditional equity trading strategies, which include value investing, growth investing, trend investment, equity-backed tranche, industry, alpha and hedging; (2) bond-related strategies, which include bond future-related strategies, convertibles, leveraged repo carry and high yield; (3) event-driven strategies, which include M&A, new issuance, private placement and special event; (4) macro strategies, which include commodities trading and macro hedging; (5) relative value strategies, which include cross market arbitrage, cross product arbitrage and ETF arbitrage; (6) portfolio strategies, which mainly include FOF and MOM.

As market evolves and demands more accountability, the so-called Sunshine PE funds that usually specialize in secondary market are gaining wider acceptance. These PE funds are often designed and operated by asset management companies. In practice the asset management teams would reach out to banks and solicit funds via bank-affiliated trusts. Periodical reporting of net asset value brings much desired transparency to the table.

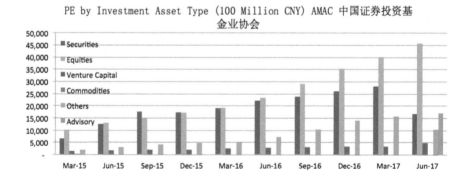

PE by Investment Asset Type (100 Million CNY) AMAC 中国证券投资基金业协会

An important platform for PE participants to operate upon is Interotc under the supervision of CSRC. It is a place where various participants, including banks, securities firms, insurance firms, mutual funds and private equities can issue products, solicit quotes and arrange buy/sell transactions that are not meant for the general public. The products covered by the platform include private placement bonds, equities, OTC derivatives and consumer financing products. Most of the transactions were simple Certificate of Receipt under private placement bonds, an instrument comparable to WMP but issued mostly by securities firms. Nevertheless, Interotc is a useful platform that brings various players together with more efficiency and better regulatory compliance.

5.1.7 Trust

Based upon data published by Chinese Trustee Association, the trust industry by the end of 2016 managed 20.21 trillion CNY. An off-balance sheet financing vehicle, with high yield and low default probability during the years of economic boom, this sector experienced tremendous growth starting from 2009, due to the fiscal stimulus package put into place by the government after the 2008 global financial crisis. WMP as an off balance sheet funding source, was connected to high yield non-standard fixed income product based upon various development platform. The combination of high yield and low capital requirement was very attractive to financial institutions especially banks. During that period, a trust could mainly serve three financing purposes: (1) Raising capital for state-owned companies; (2) Raising capital for government-sponsored development platform or local government; (3) Raising capital for local government and injecting funds into development platform.

The industry's overall growth slowed between 2013 and 2015. Significant events include: in 2013, more rigorous regulatory environment was in place regarding banks' off balance sheet financing via WMP to trust; in 2014 redemption risk exposure in trust became evident, especially in the real estate sector; in 2015, the volatile equity market exposed the leverage risk inherent in the "umbrella structure" in trust investing in securities, and regulatory instruction was issued to amend the situation.

During the same period, a generally more streamlined regulatory environment and easing monetary condition had made financing through other venues, including municipal and corporate bonds more viable choices. In order to reduce the debt burden of local government, large quantity of local government bonds was issued to replace high yield outstanding loan, amount to 3.2 trillion CNY in 2015 alone. This loan-to-bond swap had reduced the need for high yield financing vehicle such as trust. Also the rules are more stringent for trust industry to deal with many of the irregularities observed during the earlier expanding period. The most overriding catalyst for change was it was getting harder to justify trust's industry position as a high cost financing vehicle, as the Chinese economy entered a period of more modest growth.

Since 2016, trust industry growth recovered to certain extent. Ample liquidity led to a recovery in the real estate sector projects first in the 1st tier cities then spreading to 2nd and 3rd tier cities, supported by continuous easing monetary policy and global export recovery. Stock market crash in 2015 reduced equity investment allocation further amplified the effect of liquidity on bank-related trust.

[Origination] From the perspective of origination, trusts can be originated as a single fund trust, an assembled fund trust, or as an asset management trust. Single fund trust has only one trust settlor. Usually set up by a bank as an off-balance sheet vehicle with underlying loan assets, single fund trust is structured to meet single institution's investment need using a single institution's fund. Banks, through single fund trust, either obtain funds via Wealth Management Product and invest in trust; or make a safer investment in high priority tranche, where risk is limited via stop loss and other measures, and let the trust to obtain its own fund to invest in riskier equity tranche.

Assembled fund trust involves multiple trust settlors. A trust of this type may select one or a number of investment projects into its portfolio. Projects are further assembled into investment products based upon maturity and other risk factors. Interested investors will then invest into these products based upon their risk appetite and yield requirement. Assembled fund trusts are usually proprietary investment business operated by trusts, therefore are actively managed by trusts, and tend to entail greater complexity and offer higher yield. Much of the funds come from individual investor. Within the trust industry this area may have the greatest potential for growth.

Asset management trust typically serves as a legal entity of a corporation to manage its own assets.

At the end of 2016, analyzing data published by Chinese Trust Association, based upon the origination of any trust, 13.65% went to asset management trusts set up by the receiving side this financing transaction. 62.28% went to assembled fund trust, which is set up based upon the assembly of individual investors fund. The majority, 50.07% went to single fund trust.

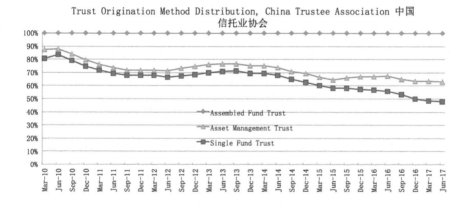

[Investing method] From the perspective of investment method, the fact that trust often serves as an off-balance sheet financing vehicle for banks and banks are prohibited from direct involvement on equities together decided that largest percentage of trust investment is executed via loan issuance. As Chinese economic growth shifted from high gear to more moderate growth rate accompanied by market liberalization process, assets investment methods by trusts also shifted accordingly, from mostly high interest loan to a more diversified liquid outlays, including trading, AFS (Available for Sale) and HTM (Held to Maturity) assets, many of which could involve credit bonds, ABS and others high yield instruments. Specifically regarding bond assets, trust is limited in two ways when carry out bond transaction in interbank bond market. First, it can not directly conduct a repo transaction, which is the most efficient approach to obtain short term funds; 2nd, due to regulatory restriction, later obtained accounts type B can only conduct transaction with market dealers.

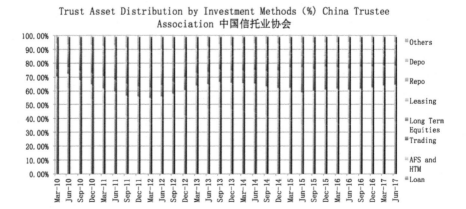

[Investment distribution by market segment] Based upon the market segment distribution of trust investment, trust can be classified into the following areas: basic industries, real estate, equities, mutual fund, bonds, financial institutions, commercial corps and others. Over the years, the percentage of bonds, commercial corps and financial institutions increased, while the reduction came most from basic industries. At the end of 2016, 11.02% of trust investment went to bond segment.

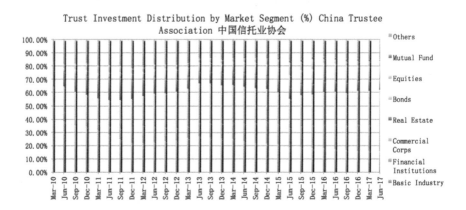

The rationale behind the grouping of these 7 categories quite accurately reflects the basic regulatory and economic policy implementation structure for trust investment assets. We can categorize the above listed 7 types of trusts into two sub-categories: securities subcategory, which includes bonds, equities and mutual funds; non-securities subcategory, which includes real estate, basic industries, financial institutions and commercial corps.

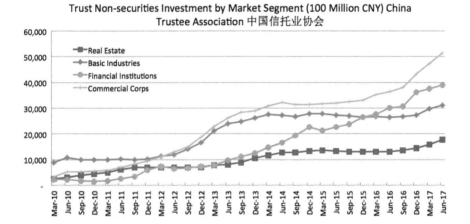

Within the non-securities category, the basic industries trust is often referring to a trust entity with investment destined to areas providing public utility function. Public utilities cover basic infrastructure, transportation, mining, energy and others. Often in collaboration with government initiatives, these trusts were important in the delivery of infrastructure projects around the country. More recently they have benefited from various stimulus packages after the global financial crisis. During basic industries trust setup there is often collateral based upon government receivable from managing the public project. Received payment on debt by local government is the return to the trust investment. Though still important, they have become less so partly for two reasons. First, there are less high yield local development initiatives since the economic growth moderated. Second, the bond for loan swap initiative that is aimed at lowering the debt burden of local government reduced the need to pursue expensive trust funds investment. In addition, while total amount of local debt is generally considered manageable, concern over debt-to-GDP ratio for various levels of local government surfaces periodically and this slows the growth of basic industry trust. With that in mind, looking ahead, further urbanization could provide more room for moderate growth in this area.

Real estate trust had its booming years. Trust Investment in this segment rose substantially up to 2013. The real estate sector risk caused by large inventory, leverage in the industry (measured by trust assets versus trust equities), aggressive regulatory arbitrage via WMP and interbank money market repo operation have caused serious concerns among economists and regulators. Various regulatory policies followed led to the slower growth of trust since that time. Still, the current state of real estate trust segment presents both risk and opportunities. Urbanization is still proceeding forward, with 1st tier cities and some of the 2nd tier cities exhibiting strong economic vitality and housing inventories in some areas in short supply. Asset geographical distribution, affordable housing project progress, local tax reform, property tax legislation and anti-speculation measures should all be taken into consideration when a real estate trust investment is to be evaluated.

While basic industry trust and real estate trust growth slowed down, commercial corps trusts and financial institution trusts have gained. Commercial corps trusts often provide liquidity lending support. Financial institution trusts act as conduit for banks hence consistently showed a strong presence. It is worth noting that all four trust subtypes within the non-securities category had enjoyed fast growth since mid 2016 after local government debt level was getting attention and deleveraging effort was in motion. Banks being the core of Chinese financial industry, amassed large liquidity from monetary easing policies and with retained channels to high yield investment, use trusts to connect the liquidity and investment opportunity at the expense of entrusted loan, the other major form of shadow banking.

In the securities sub-category of trust investment, bonds were consistently favored. Equities had a spike in 2015 during an ill-fated boom but otherwise were less attractive to trust asset allocation for their high volatilities and many other concerns. Mutual fund had strong exposure to equities and money market and weak exposure to bond market. The relatively small financing role played by equities market and lower yield produced by money market compared against high yield bond market with leverage, resulted in a lukewarm reception from investors to mutual fund products.

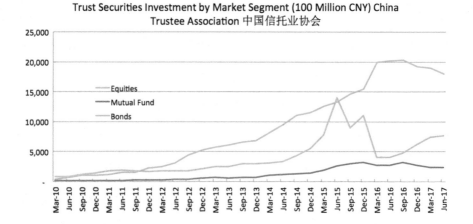

[Trust by collaboration style] Trusts are boutique financial entities that often have domain expertise in certain industries but otherwise generally lack broad capital market experience and customer penetration. Therefore they are often formed in collaboration with various other entities, including government-sponsored platform, private equities and banks. Here government provides public project as assets for investment, private equities provide investment area expertise, and banks provide broad investor base, investment assets diversification, risk mitigation and source of stable funds.

Due to banks' strong influence in China's financial area, banking-related trust is the most common form for trust collaboration. Government-related is also an import segment. PE-related type may play a more important role in the future. Trust and PE collaboration can mutually benefit each other in many ways, including PE follows the lead of trust to invest; PE assist trust in providing certain capital market expertise while trust can raise fund for PE.

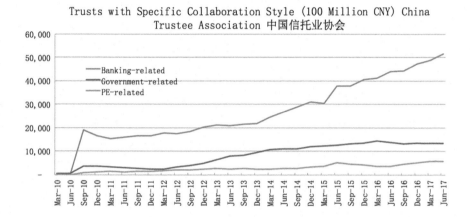

Trusts with Specific Collaboration Style (100 Million CNY) China Trustee Association 中国信托业协会

[Trust investment by industry] It is also interesting to analyze the types of industries that trust had provided funding for. Financial had always been the strongest one, a reflection of banking influence in China's capital markets.

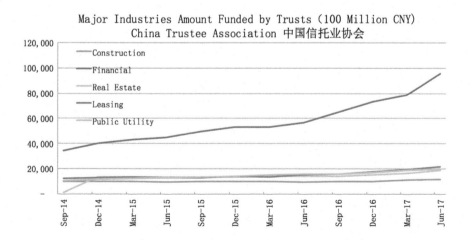

Major Industries Amount Funded by Trusts (100 Million CNY) China Trustee Association 中国信托业协会

Among the non-financial industries, construction, real estate, leasing and public utilities, public utilities and leasing trust investment enjoyed the strongest growth. Leasing will make more efficient usage of existing capital base, while improvement on living standard will require continuous investment support. The need for both construction and real estate trust investment had mostly stabilized until 2016. This largely reflected the stage of economic development in China, where wide spread construction and real estate development had seen their best years even though urbanization will still proceed forward for many years ahead. With liquidity support, deleveraging on local government and banking access to projects, trusts investment in non-financial industries resumed growth from mid 2016.

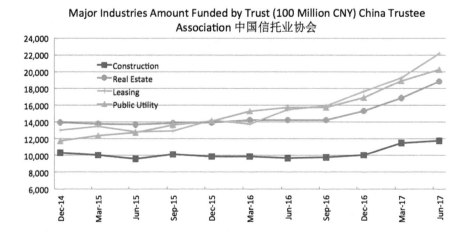

5.1.8   Securities Firms

Securities firms have much higher percentage of their bond portfolio in Corporates and MTN, followed by liquid interest instrument when compared with most banks, including large, urban and rural commercial banks. Securities firms' bond inventories are relatively small, and mostly for trading purposes. Unlike banks or insurance business, where constant cash inflow offers stability during volatile funding periods, securities firms face ever-present redemption pressure and yield pressure therefore compromise must be constantly made to achieve optimal balance between yield and liquidity.

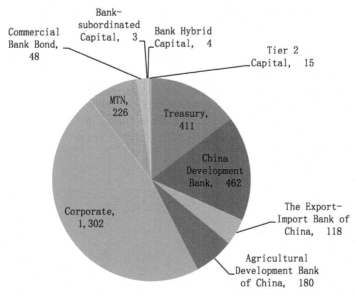

Main Bond Types Held by Securities Firms 2016.12 (100 Million CNY) China Bond 中债登

The most frequently used bond strategy by securities firms is to apply leverage via repo on exchange-traded corporate bonds. Over the recent years with ample liquidity on exchange repo market, securities firms had continuously increased their corporate bond inventory. Interest rate bond, including treasury and CDB policy bonds were mostly used for liquidity support with yield objective being secondary, hence very little EIBC and ADB bonds were held.

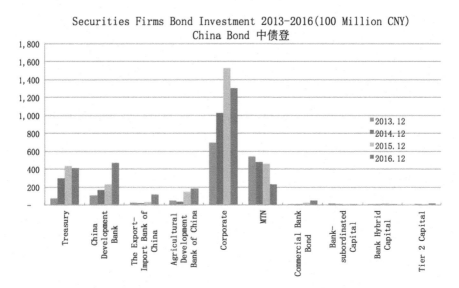

Securities Firms Bond Investment 2013–2016(100 Million CNY) China Bond 中债登

Securities firms have ventured into asset management sector via various asset management plans. Collective investment scheme is set up for a collection of investors for investment and profit sharing by pooling resources together. Targeted asset management plan is typically started from a particular client request and also as a collaboration effort between a securities firm and a bank, focusing mainly on standard products. Specific asset management plan is typically started by a securities firm to focus on a particular project. Direct investment plan is to provide direct investment in a particular company. The large allocation to targeted asset management plan shows banks playing prominent role in securities firms' asset management business.

5.2   FX Trading Players

In the interbank market, banks, non-banking financial institutions and foreign financial institutions (mostly banks), after receiving approval from SAFE, can trade foreign exchange. There are hundreds of these institutions, covering most of the large commercial bank, share-holding commercial banks, urban commercial banks, some foreign banks, and some rural cooperative banks and corporate treasury.

This interbank FX market is a wholesale market where some dealers make market after they submit their applications to appropriate regulatory agencies and receive respective approvals. Dealer and members use CFETS to trade with each other. Market makers drive the market via two-way quote. Interbank market members execute transaction with market makers, using either bilateral trade mode or anonymous trade mode.

The retail market is operated by designated banks to reach individual and corporate customers via internet, phone and mobile banking service. Trading services include limit order, RFQ, stream market making with one click trading. Banks typically net their internal positions first. The netted risks are offloaded to other interbank members and international markets. Large banks offer FX trading services around the clock. Central bank is an active member and intervenes when market is under stress.

Chapter 6
China, International Trade and Global Supply Chain

Global supply chain has fundamentally changed international trade structure. China's rapid ascendance in the last couple of decades in global economic order can be largely attributed to its successful integration into the global manufacturing supply chain. Many of today's essential goods are produced by international supply chains that integrate material processing, production technology, participating labor and delivery network across different geographical locations. The current state and future direction of supply chains are relevant for analyzing global and Chinese economic condition and therefore important for applying suitable trading and investment strategies regarding China.

6.1 Major International Supply Chains

Computer and communication technology supply chain is the most important global supply chain at work. Fast changing, with high risk and high margin, this supply chain is largely organized around design technology providers in the US, production technology and equipment provider in Japan, Korea, Singapore, Taiwan (China), and manufacturing process provider in China, Korea.

Automotive and parts supply chain remains important for its sheer size in terms of both values created and the amount of labor employed. While US and China provide two largest auto markets, Germany and Japan are the strongest international supply chain players in this area of technology complexity.

Electric equipment and appliance supply chain requires competitive capabilities on cost control and operations management. Advanced economies have largely exited this area for its low margin and relatively high environment cost. Important for providing employment for less skilled labor from populous countries, the chain is heavily concentrated in China, Mexico other emerging market countries.

Textile supply chain is more sensitive to labor cost input and is more mobile than the electric and appliance supply chain. It moved from Japan and other Eastern Asia

© Springer Nature Singapore Pte Ltd. 2018
X. Zhang, *Capital Markets Trading and Investment Strategies in China*,
https://doi.org/10.1007/978-981-10-8497-3_6

countries/regions to China, and now in the process of moving to other emerging countries as wage and other costs in China grew.

Aerospace products remain to be the pinnacle of modern manufacturing technology. This supply is dominated mostly by US and to less extent the European Union.

For the past 30 years these major global supply chains moved manufacturing process, good and wealth around the globe, changing fortune of many countries. While they lifted many from poverty in emerging countries, it also brought with it structural dislocation in both advanced economies and developing countries for its uneven cost benefit distribution. To decipher the current state and future direction of macro economic condition of various countries including China, it is important to analyze supply chain's impact using relevant countries' trade and other statistics, based upon which policy makers are also trying to address their constituents concern and finding possible remedy to influence the future direction of economy.

6.2   Electronics and Electric Supply Chains

At the top of electronics and electric supply chain, the US has the largest and also one of the most innovative economies often takes the leading position in international supply chains. Large companies including Apple, IBM, Oracle, Microsoft, Boeing and Intel dominate the global technology landscape. Its export strength in aerospace is a prime example of technology system integration at the highest level.

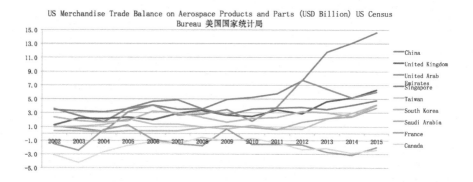

Even though US economy remains technologically competitive, the effect of global supply chain is under heavy scrutiny in the US, especially regarding large trade deficit. Many associated the manufacturing employment loss to the enduring merchandise (goods) trade deficit. One of the alternative possible explanations suggests the export of US dollars as the reserve currency by definition would inevitably lead to US trade deficit. Any possible policy solution to the US merchandise trade deficit would have large international economic ramification and significant impact on investment outlook.

The US international trade pattern has two important characteristics. First the size of US international trade is moderate by international comparison relative to the size of its GDP. That is one of the reasons US market is able to withstand large event shock during time of international turbulence, as was the case during the Asian Financial Crisis in the 1990s. Second the size of US trade deficit includes large goods merchandise deficit and sizable service surplus. Based upon data published by US Bureau of Economic Analysis, US trade on goods in 2015 was 761.5 billion in deficit, and trade on service was 263.9 in surplus. That made US total trade number at −497.6 billion in red for 2015.

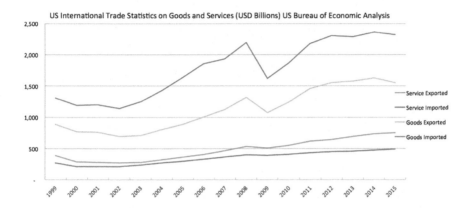

The US total goods and services deficit-to-GDP ratio is relatively modest when large US GDP is taken into account. This ratio came down significantly after 2008 financial crisis, as US trade on goods took hit during the crisis, and service export sector continued its growth, especially within the Other Personal Travel segment. The relatively modest deficit to GDP ratio suggests the issue at the heart of US trade deficit, the discussion upon which could influence the future direction of US international trade relationship including Sino-US trade relationship, is more centered upon certain economic dislocation caused by global supply chain versus the size of trade deficit.

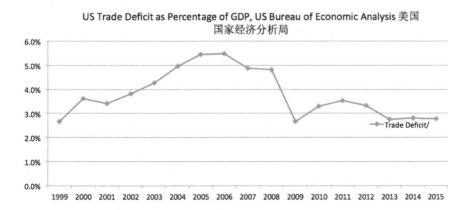

One of the economic dislocations, the US manufacturing job had endured two large losses since 1996. One caused by the burst of dot-com bubble and the other caused by the 2008 financial crisis. While education and health services employment grew, the population severely impacted by manufacturing job loss was a different population group from those in education/health care services and policy remedy was called for to help improve their economic situation.

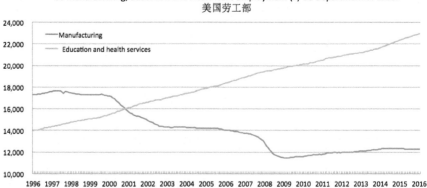

The deficit in the manufacturing areas, which includes computer and communications equipment, apparels, automotive and parts and some other manufacture sectors, was often suggested as the root cause for the loss of manufacturing jobs, while others have also argued that the loss could also be partially caused by technological improvement, US production moving to higher environmental standard or export of US dollar as the reserve currency.

From the traded merchandise type perspective, the largest source of US trade deficit was concentrated within a few goods segments including Computer and Electronic Products, Oil and Gas, Transportation Equipment, Apparel, Electrical Equipment, among many other traded merchandise categories.

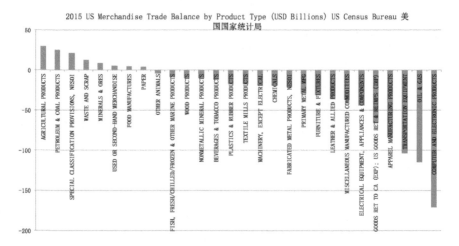

From the traded merchandise geographical origin perspective, the majority of US merchandise trade deficit was encountered during its trading with a few large trading partners that are all manufacturing powerhouses. Besides China, Germany, South Korea and Vietnam also increased their respective surplus over the recent years, with Germany and South Korea for their technological strength and Vietnam for being the alternative low cost manufacturing hub to China. US deficit to Japan was stable. US merchandise deficit to the rest of the world excluding countries mentioned above actually shrank.

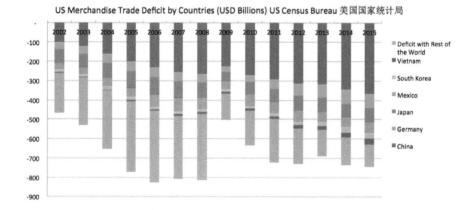

US Merchandise Trade Deficit by Countries (USD Billions) US Census Bureau 美国国家统计局

The continuous US trade deficit with China had attracted attention from US policy makers. US trade deficit with China was concentrated in the following areas: foremost was Computer and Electronic Products category, with Electrical Equipment and Appliances category being the distant second, followed by apparel, leathers and others. Services category has been a continuous source of surplus for US.

2015 US Trade Balance with China on Goods by Product Type and Services (USD Billions) US Census Bureau and US Bureau of Economic Analysis 美国国家统计局和美国国家经济分析局

As large as it is, China's share of the source for US computer and electronic products import has peaked in recent years. Rising labor, real estate and other costs, and the general maturing nature of the existing US market, limited market segment growth potential. At the same time, Countries including Mexico and Vietnam have gained their manufacturing prowess.

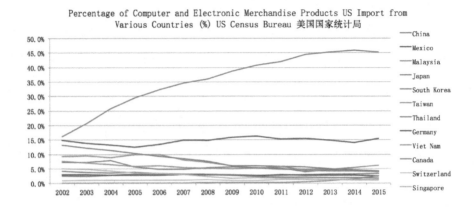

A detailed look at US deficit with China within Computer and Electronics category showed that most of the deficit was in computer equipment and communication equipment. In this area China is part of an expansive supply chain took off from the beginning of this century powered with core technologies provided by global giant including Microsoft, IBM, Google, Intel, NVIDIA and Samsung.

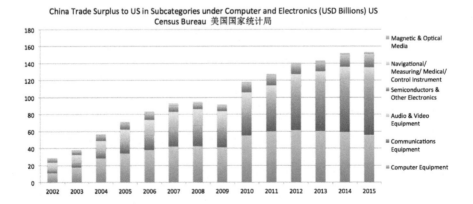

An example is the semiconductor area that is strategic for some of the global giants to be able to rapidly deploy application of new technology with economically affordable cost for consumers around the world amid volatile demand. Positioned within 4 segments, including equipment, materials, semiconductors and electronic end equipment, the top 20 companies in this semiconductor industry chain are from

US, Japan, Korea, Taiwan (China), with the top 7 based upon 2013 revenue being Intel (US), Samsung (Korea), TSMC (Taiwan, China), Qualcomm (US), Micron (US), SK Hynix (Korea), Toshiba (Japan). Here US provides technology design and specification, US, Japan, Korea, Singapore and other places provide high-end technology equipment and components, and China provides mid to low level components and labor. As goods flow within the manufacturing chain, about 217.7, 230 and 242 billions USD worth of integrated circuit are imported into China respectively for 2014, 2015 and 2016 based upon data published by China Customs. Besides being the manufacturing hub that supplies sufficient amount of mobile labor essential for volatile consumer demand, China also provides a substantial market for testing new technologies. While computer-related growth plateaued, with artificial intelligence expected to play a bigger role in daily life, this supply chain could morph into another important area with potentially explosive growth. The segment investment risk involves fast technology turnover that could render past large investment useless and for the size of investment loss, substantial macro impact for involved countries and companies. Another possible investment risk comes from the large structural imbalance this supply chain brings to the international and respective domestic economies, which if not properly addressed, could lead to severe policy reaction. There could also be large investment reward associated with these risks as Chinese technology companies gaining their competitive edge based upon a large consumer base.

The technology flow pattern could be approximated by Mach and Elec trade flow statistics reported by World Bank. Data suggested China was the final destination for international machinery and electrical equipment trade, with other countries/regions being either the supplier or conduits for these traded equipment.

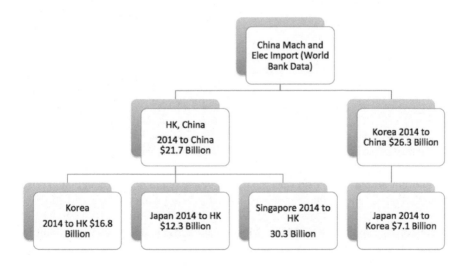

One player gaining significant technological edge was Korea, Rep. Over the resent years it has built up considerable amount of surplus with US, China and HK China, while being able to reduce its deficit with Japan.

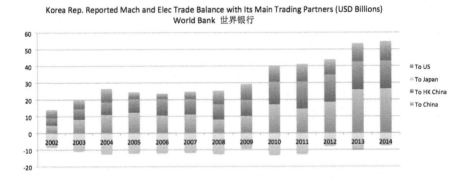

Relative to Computer and Electronics Equipment category that is often high value-added and produced with fully distributed global supply chain, US deficit in Electrical equipment, appliance and components category is much smaller. Out of this category, Electric Lighting Equipment and Household Appliances are overall low margin manufacturing business where Mexico is also a strong market player taking advantage of its geographical proximity to large US market and the size of its labor market.

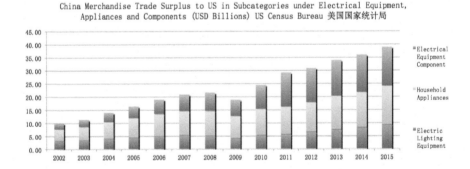

The household appliance and electric lighting equipment production is concentrated in China, while Mexico is also showing competitiveness in this low margin business that is sensitive to labor and transportation cost. Continuously manufacturing migration to China, Mexico and some eastern European countries could be expected, assuming no major change of existing business environment.

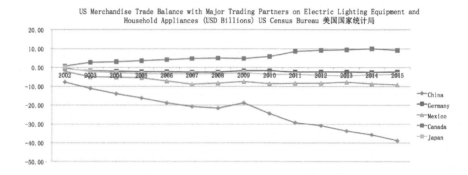

There is embedded efficiency in producing household appliances in China and Mexico, for the production quantity required to satisfy existing domestic demand is already large. In this low margin business segment, besides labor cost, the efficiency provided by scale of production is also important. While the investment reward in this area could be modest compared with high tech area, as large household appliance makers improve on their production skills and have business prospect supported by solid domestic and international demand, the downside risk is limited.

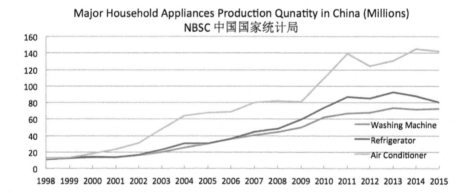

Within the much smaller area of Electrical Equipment, where Germany, Japan and US are all very competitive market players, China is slowly expanding its footprint with technological improvement.

Supported by solid demand and improvement on production capability, invest-ment risk and reward in Electrical Equipment and Component area is comparable to those in household appliance area.

6.3   Automotive Supply Chain

Compared with other important supply chains including Computer Electronics and Household Appliance, automotive supply chain puts particular emphasis on just-in-time production management to cut inventory cost and hence requires pre-cisely integrated production delivery process. Germany, Japan and US lead global automotive manufacturing supply chain. One of the large change over the past two decades was the German auto manufacturers' successful integration of mid European industries from Poland, Czech, Slovakia and Hungary into their manu-facturing supply chain, with very broader economic ramification. The integration had both expanded market in Europe for German auto products and lowered the manufacturing cost of German industries. Therefore the core strength of Euro, which is heavily dependent upon German economic vitality, is on a much solid foundation. The increased investment from Germany to Poland illustrated the supply chain integration.

The investment from Germany to Poland had increased substantially since Poland joined the European Union in 2004. Investment from Germany to Spain kept up with investment from Spain to Germany, while investment from Germany to Italy did not keep up with investment flow from Italy to Germany.

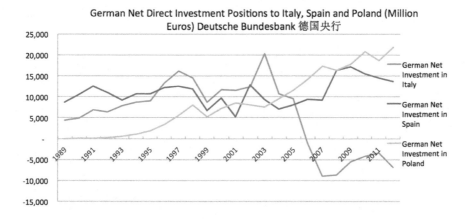

As a result, the net investment from Germany to Poland increased. In comparison, German net investment to Italy had decreased substantially. This change of direction for net investment flow within Europe is fundamental to the current mid Europe economic strength and southern European economic difficulty.

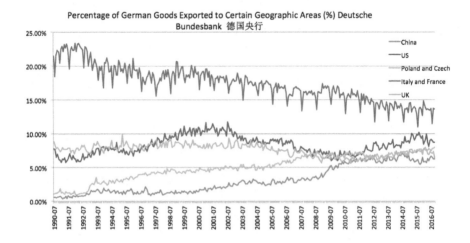

Czech, Hungary, Poland and Slovakia together have a combined population of more than 60 million, and a combined GDP roughly about a quarter of German GDP. The German net investment and subsequent supply chain integration in Mid Europe region has lowered German auto manufacturing cost by tapping into a less expensive and well educated labor force. As German technology investment improved the manufacturing skill level and efficiency within these four countries, these countries have also gained importance as US automotive product providers.

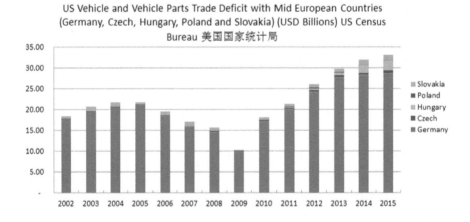

The European auto supply chain's impact was global. Currently two largest automotive markets in the world are the US and China market. In 2015, 4.0 million vehicles under different German brands were sold in China, and German surplus in Vehicle and Auto Parts with US reached $28.7 Billion. German auto and parts supply chain, including related electronics and chemicals business, had a stabilizing effect on German and mid European economies during large economic shocks in

Western Europe, including Brexit, referendum and elections in Italy and France. The amount of real economic impact would be larger when German-affiliated auto production and export from Mexico were taken into calculation.

For China's capital market, the main effects of German auto supply chain strength were the followings: (A) a stable European economy translated into a stable external market for various European-bound export industries; 2nd the strength of Euro economy was often underestimated, which translated into incorrect estimate for pace of European economic recovery and ECB interest rate policy. These are important factors for export industry analysis and domestic monetary liquidity forecast.

The other strong automotive supply chain leader is Japan. Japan has been a strong technology supplier on the global stage for both electronics and automotive industry. Based upon trade data from Japan Ministry of Finance, the largest source of country's trade surplus with a single trading partner is the US.

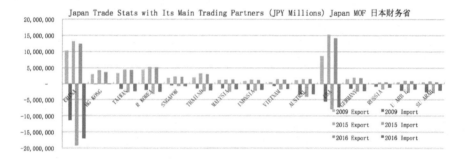

Within US Japan bilateral trade, the largest source of Japan trade surplus with US was the automotive sector. This shows both the competitiveness of and the country's heavy dependency upon automotive industry.

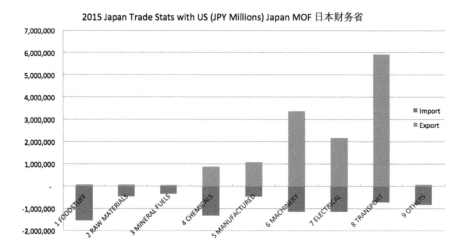

For US auto market, one of the relatively recent developments was the increase in auto manufacturing activities in Mexico and accelerated growth of US auto deficit with Mexico. Many of the production activities were resulted from auto-related investment from global automakers. The rapidly gained competitiveness of Mexico manufacturing base and this large auto deficit are becoming concerns for US policy makers for auto industry's importance in US economy.

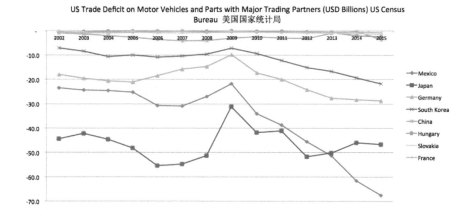

For China auto market, the competitiveness of global automotive supply chain especially those led by automakers from Germany and Japan is evident as well. Passenger vehicle market is often sub-categorized into three sections including car, SUV and MPV. In the year of 2016, foreign brands took 80.7% of the car section and 41.8% of the SUV section in China, based upon number of vehicles sold data published by China Auto-stats. When the value of vehicles sold is accounted for, since foreign brands usually occupy the higher end on the value chain, the relative strength of global auto supply chains in China is even larger.

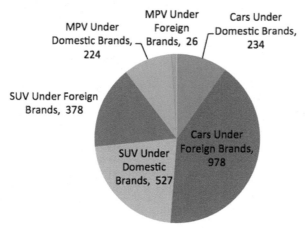

Type of Vehicles Sold in China in 2016 (10K) Auto-Stats 中国汽车工业协会

The ratio of cars sold under domestic brands versus total number of cars sold in China had shown a declining trend, from 29.11% in 2011, 22.42% in 2014, to 19.3% in 2016, as customers demanded better cars and foreign manufactures were responding by moving into compact and subcompact car segment. The falling ratio suggested the technology gap between existing supply chain leaders and market followers was actually widening at least for now.

Number of Cars Sold in China Under Domestic and Foreign Brands (10K) Auto-Stats 中国汽车工业协会

Unlike the US automotive market, the amount of direct automotive imports into China and export from China remained modest. Vehicles sold in China under German and Japanese brands are mostly manufactured in China, hence bilateral automotive trading data with China does not directly exhibit the competitiveness of German or Japanese automotive industry in China's market.

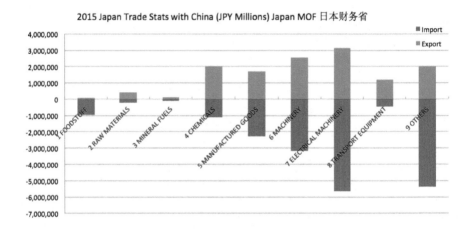

From 2009 to 2015, compared against large increase of phone import from China, motor vehicle parts import from China to Japan only increased slightly again illustrated China playing the role of final market but not an intermediary export base for international auto supply chain.

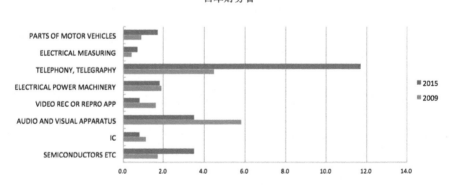

The Japanese economic recovery after 2008 financial crisis was relying heavily on success of Japan auto industry, with 3.79 million vehicles sold in China under Japanese brands in 2016, and Japanese surplus in Vehicle and Auto Parts with US reaching 46.6 billion in 2015 by report US Census data.

In summary, the current operating models in China by international automotive supply chain from Germany, Japan, US and Korea Rep are to focus on manufacturing or making final assembling of vehicles in China for auto sales in China. These leaders have so far not incorporated China as an exporting base into their global manufacturing supply chain the same way Mexico was set up to be. The understanding of this business model helps us to conduct analysis on China capital market investment from several perspectives. The first is regarding automotive industry's importance for US, Germany and Japan, China is more of a final consumer versus a global supplier, hence the current global auto trade conflict risk for China domestic auto industry is limited. The second point is since German, Japanese, American and Korean automotive supply chain leaders all have extensively integrated local supplier into their production network and therefore have established large domestic economic presence, their sales data can be useful for both analyzing the state of Chinese domestic auto consumption level, future trend and domestic auto makers' growth prospect. The third is automotive industry including international suppliers forms a large part of China consumer market, producing more than 23 million vehicles in 2016. The statistics of the international auto suppliers in China provides a context for both analyzing and assessing domestic economic health regarding GDP, commodity price, inflation and other macro matters.

6.4 Chemicals and Pharmaceutical Manufacturing

Another global supply chain that is often considered having significant entry barrier is the chemical industry. Based upon World Bank data, US and Germany are the main leaders in the area of global chemical business. Belgium, Netherlands and Japan are also established players in the segment. Though emerging countries including China made strides in areas including basic chemicals, the entry barrier remains high for newcomers for a couple of likely reasons. First chemical manufacturing process itself is technology and capital intensive. Second the volatile commodity price and long investment cycle requires large amount of knowledge and resources for careful planning to weather capital investment risk. Third the patent law implementation regarding chemical and manufacturing process protection can also complicate an investment decision.

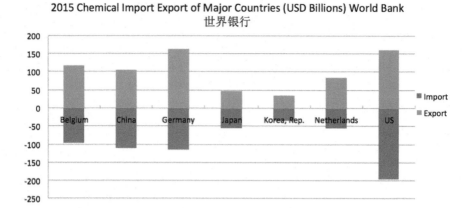

2015 Chemical Import Export of Major Countries (USD Billions) World Bank
世界银行

While US has a very large chemical industry and market, over the years it has also built up trade deficit in this segment with some countries including Ireland, Germany, Switzerland, Israel and India. Germany and Switzerland have been traditionally strong players in pharmaceutical manufacturing business. Ireland enlarged its market presence partly because of its favorable corporate tax policy. On the export side, US chemicals also had slowdown in export to emerging economies in various chemical subcategories.

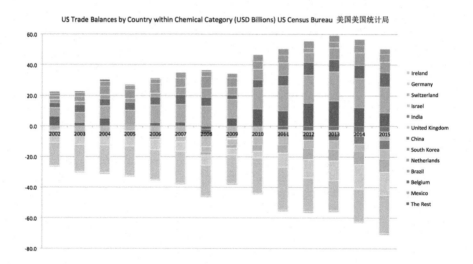

US Trade Balances by Country within Chemical Category (USD Billions) US Census Bureau 美国美国统计局

From the perspective of chemical product type, US trade deficit in chemical area is mostly concentrated in pharmaceutical subcategory. Surplus in Resin, synthetic rubber and fiber reflects US strength in industrial chemical production involving technology complexity.

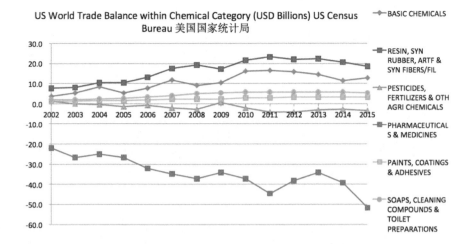

Within the important pharmaceutical and basic chemical area, US export was stagnant while import has increased.

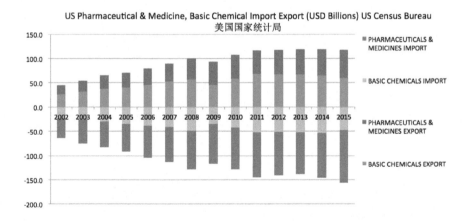

Specifically regarding international pharmaceutical business, Ireland has a favorite corporate tax policy put in place. Germany, Switzerland and UK have been traditional strong players in the pharmaceutical industry. India acts as an efficient low cost production site. All five countries that had surplus with the US have certain entrenched competitive advantage in the high margin segment.

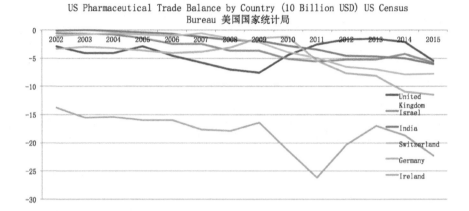

German competitiveness in chemical manufacturing area is illustrated by its large and increasing surplus with the US, most of which is concentrated in pharmaceutical and basic chemical areas.

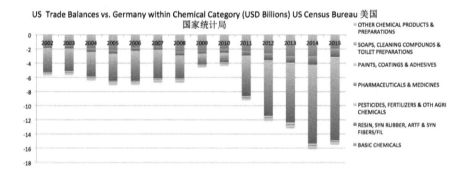

German pharmaceutical surplus to US is roughly 30% of German global pharmaceutical surplus, suggesting the large surplus to US is possibly due to the very large US market demand for high quality medical and pharmaceutical products.

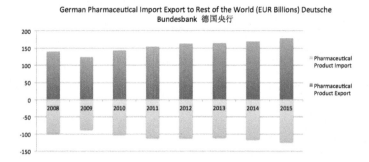

German Pharmaceutical Import Export to Rest of the World (EUR Billions) Deutsche Bundesbank 德国央行

UK, long after ceding its top position in international trade to the US and giving up imperial preferential system in order to join the European Economic Community in 1973, has nevertheless managed to remain competitive in the very high-end segment of the manufacturing business, exemplified by aircraft engines and pharmaceutical production. It is an important player in global chemical industry and runs a sizable surplus with US on pharmaceuticals.

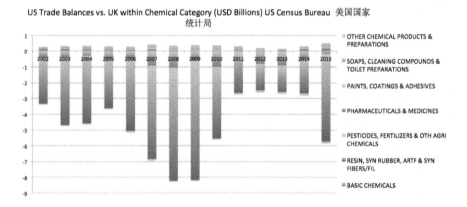

US Trade Balances vs. UK within Chemical Category (USD Billions) US Census Bureau 美国国家统计局

When analyzing UK chemical industry more broadly based upon data published HM Revenue and Customs, within the chemical category, UK ran a sizable surplus in pharmaceutical area, and a smaller surplus in organic chemicals area.

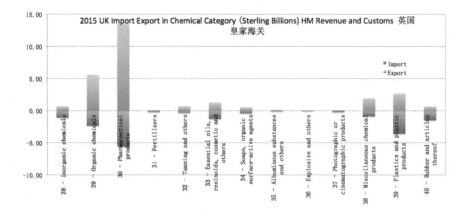

UK's largest trade surplus by country in 2015 was with US, a large part of it was related to pharmaceutical products within the chemical category. Its largest deficit was with Germany and China.

Japan ran a pharmaceutical deficit with US while keeping a sizable deficit in the area of basic chemicals. This bilateral chemical trade pattern is quite different when compared with other industrialized countries regarding their respective trade relations to US in chemical business.

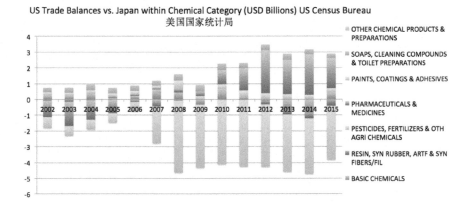

US trading with China in chemical segment illustrated a traditional bilateral trade pattern between an existing player and a newcomer. US ran a surplus in Resin Synthetic Rubber area, and a deficit in less sophisticated basic chemicals area.

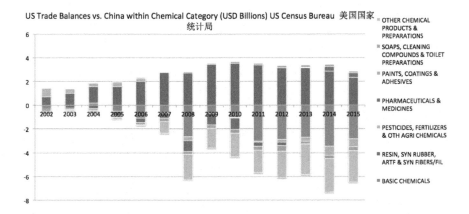

The relatively low growth of US chemical import from China except basic chemicals again demonstrates the difficulty in overcoming technology difficulty by emerging countries. Similar to its competitiveness in the global appliance industry, China does have built-in advantages in basic chemical area, where the large amount of capital can be mustered, the technology barrier is relatively low and the demand for quantity is large in its domestic market. Even in this area, some difficulties exist and international corporations including BASF and others operated quite amount of production facilities in China.

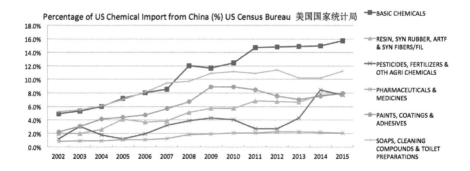

Another difficult area hence with potential growth opportunity is environmentally safer US pesticide and pesticide production technology export to China due to increased environmental awareness.

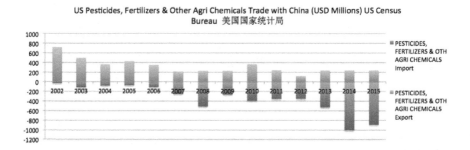

Pharmaceuticals and Medicines area does not play a big role in US and China trading relationship and there are several possible reasons for that. One of the reasons was major difference in the patent protection. It is also difficult in making pharmaceutical products in China to meet western pharmaceutical standard.

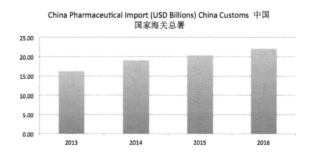

We also need to recognize that the healthcare industry in China is mostly a public-funded industry. Though the medical budgetary expenditure saw steady increase over the recent years, but as the economic growth moderates, the increase from the government spending on the medicine will inevitably also moderate.

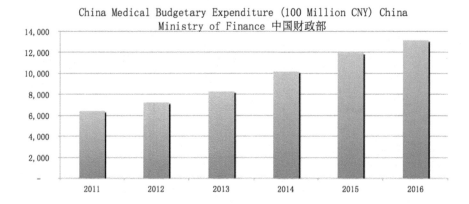

China Medical Budgetary Expenditure (100 Million CNY) China Ministry of Finance 中国财政部

Regarding capital markets investment analysis for the chemical industry in China, its industry capability is still mostly on the beginning side of the learning curve hence it will less likely be subject to international trade conflict risk. Chemical export will continue to be mostly within low-end chemical area including pesticide, basic chemical and others. Growth on high-end chemical products and pharmaceutical products will be challenging. Opportunity for foreign capital and technology investment does exist. Growth prospect specifically within the pharmaceutical area will be moderate given the overall economic growth has moderated.

6.5   Apparel Sector

Apparel industry growth has peaked over the recent years. Rising labor cost and the value of CNY had eroded China's competitive edge on textile production cost over other developing countries including Vietnam, Bangladesh and Mexico. While still important when domestic demand growth is taken into consideration, the overall growth potential in terms of export by China apparel sector is limited. This translates into an industry assessment with overall limited investment opportunity. Single credit opportunity can still be identified by focusing on niche player with successful reorientation from international demand to domestic demand with improved cost control measures.

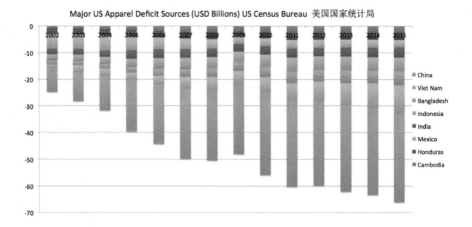

6.6   Agricultural Sector

International agricultural sector interacts with China mainly in the areas of grain import, soy import and seed technology-related import. Grains are the most important part of the agricultural sector for China. The country had traditional processed more wheat among major crops imported. More recent imports favored wheat and corn while domestic rice supply is abundant. For a large populous nation, food safety is a paramount national security issue hence being mostly self-sufficient on major crops will limit the import growth regarding grains segment.

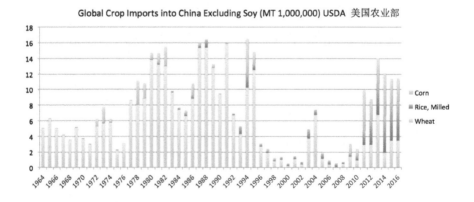

Meat import took off over the recent years as demand for protein diet enjoyed solid growth. The amount of both major crops and meat import themselves is not large enough to sway inflation index calculation.

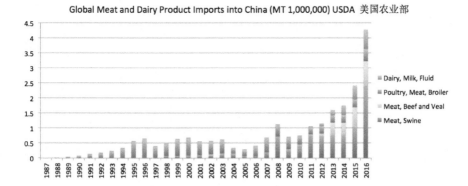

Global Meat and Dairy Product Imports into China (MT 1,000,000) USDA 美国农业部

One of the agricultural areas with large quantity of import is soy. China imports very large amount of soy, mostly because availability of arable land and the yield advantage of foreign soy growers make foreign soy production much more competitive.

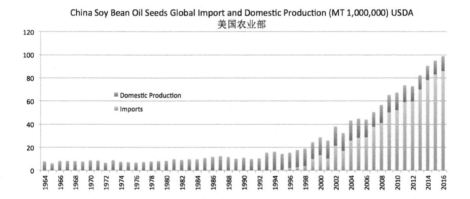

China Soy Bean Oil Seeds Global Import and Domestic Production (MT 1,000,000) USDA 美国农业部

Brazil had replaced US to be the largest soybean provider to China. These two combined provided about 70 million tons of soy to China. The soybean imported is used for direct food consumption, cooking oil and soy meal production. Soy mean is a major source of animal feed.

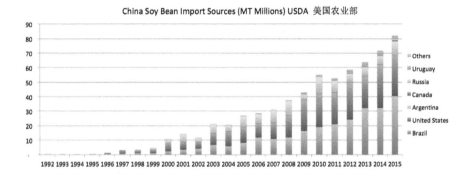

China Soy Bean Import Sources (MT Millions) USDA 美国农业部

One of the critical technologies in modern agricultural sector is the capability to genetically modify produce DNA to enhance yield and make them more adaptable in various natural environment, more pest-resistant and drought resistant, etc. Controversial in many corners of the world, its wide usage is a commercial reality and demand for GM seeds remains high. China imports significant amount of seeds from foreign countries and US dominates in this technology area. For China's emphasis on food self-sufficiency, the relevance of seeds import for investment analysis is pertained to assessing whether seed technology plays significant role in a specific agricultural area and whether it gives or takes away competitive advantage of any industry leaders especially regarding merger acquisition opportunities.

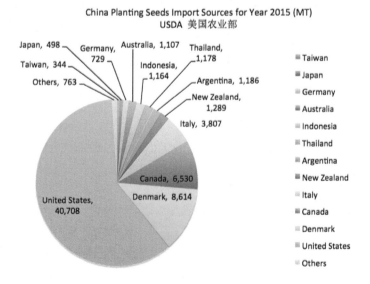

China Planting Seeds Import Sources for Year 2015 (MT)
USDA 美国农业部

The amount of sugar and sweeteners import is large, with large amount of import coming from Brazil. The international market is competitive and the amount imported is not large enough to impact inflation and interest rate analysis in China.

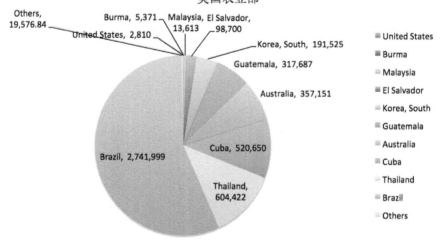

China Sugars & Sweeteners Import Sources for Year 2015 (MT) USDA
美国农业部

In summary, agricultural sector dependence on foreign production and technology is expected to grow because of continuously improved living standard, but
at a very gradual pace for food security concern. Soy import will persist for
international cost efficient and concern for domestic GM-related soy production.
Investment analysis needs to be particularly focused upon regulatory change's
impact on land usage, price control and trend.

Chapter 7
Portfolio Objectives and Trading and Investment Strategies

7.1 Onshore CNY Liquidity Portfolio Management Objectives

Long-term, short-term, global and domestic economic changes result financial and other resources to be reallocated among different countries, among different economic sectors and among different financial market segments. In an event of reallocation, liquidity of different economic sectors and market segments could sustain certain upsets. Central banks, PBOC included, often apply long-term and short-term monetary rates as anchorage points, recalibrate the target rate of those anchorage points, and utilize various market operations and others measures to manage and smooth out anchor points large swings to achieve financial and liquidity stability. Still, in time of large adjustments with possibly concurrent economic shocks, short term money market liquidity can change dramatically, causing violent swing on short money market rates. During the second US QE, there was a big decrease of US long bond yield and subsequent rise when its effect wore off, CNY 7 D repo rate had large swings and PBOC eventually managed to return China 10Y long bond yield back to stable territory. Similar events occurred during the mid of 2013, when the US economy was more assured of its recovery. That raised the prospect of Fed fund rate increase and USD appreciation, which in turn drove up yield curves globally causing a severe draining on CNY money market liquidity and a large increase of CNY repo rate. To manage liquidity portfolio in such a rapid changing environment was not a trivial task. That task had since 2015 became relatively easier and liquidity in CNY money market became more stable, as many of the interest rate management reforms by PBOC are put into place.

© Springer Nature Singapore Pte Ltd. 2018
X. Zhang, *Capital Markets Trading and Investment Strategies in China*,
https://doi.org/10.1007/978-981-10-8497-3_7

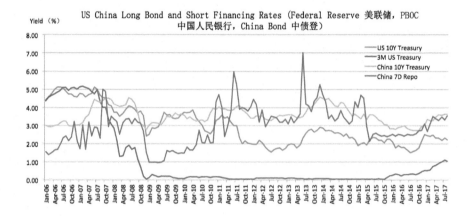

Liquidity portfolio management often includes asset liability management, reserve management, fund level forecasting, trading management for maturity, price, counterparty, direction, position and support for central open market operations.

7.1.1 Asset Liability Management (ALM)

Financial institutions management their expected and unexpected liability changes with liquid assets. Some of these liquid assets are money market short-term assets. Others are long-term liquid interest rate assets such as treasury bonds and bond futures.

For banks some of the unexpected ALM changes are caused by retail clients withdrawal from cash account and matured term deposit to invest in competing wealth management product or large amount of IPO during stock boom time. Some of the unexpected changes come from institutions to meet fiscal deposit requirement. Changes can also be caused by PBOC market operations and regulatory policy updates. An announcement on reserve level requirement change would either take away or release large amount of liquidity.

Banks have to maintain enough funds in money market portfolio to handle short-term liabilities, and at the same time, maximize the portfolio' return. Often higher return is associated with less liquidity, for instruments with lower rating, longer maturity, and larger transaction amount. In essence asset liability management is a compromise between liquidity and yield.

7.1.2 Reserve Management

Reserve requirement is mandatory for all banks. Banks are assessed based upon their capability in reserve management. The reserve level needs to stay above the mandatory reserve requirement, but at the same time the level is managed to be close to the mandatory requirement level so the capital usage efficiency is maximized. This is often the case for large banks with large deposit base and surplus funds to lend to those in need in money market. Compared with large commercial banks, some of the aggressive share-holding commercial banks do not have as large retail deposit base and they usually borrow via money market and WMP. Money market liquidity tends to dry up quickly when funding need is severe and this translates into very high short-term borrowing cost. Competition for funds can also push up WMP rates quickly. On the other hand, borrowing long term can be costly. For those banks, reserve management means a balancing act between safely meeting reserve requirement and minimizing funding cost.

7.1.3 Diversification on Maturity and Counterparty

An institution pays and receives different amount of cashflows on different dates. Cash assets to be used for payments later need to be timely invested to maximize return. Payments made earlier than received cashflows need to be financed with cheapest funding rate possibly using receivable as collateral. Accurately forecasting and managing incoming and outgoing cashflows with maturity and counterparty diversification facilitate asset liability matching and funding process. Concentration positions on specific maturity dates and counterparties in any direction could pose potential funding risk when liquidity is tight.

An example is some share-holding banks often relied upon large banks and rural commercial banks for interbank surplus fund to cover liquidity needs. As interest rate market liberalization progressed, large state banks started to have less retail surplus fund, while rural commercial banks often preferred to invest in high yield trust assets. This leaves s some share-holding commercial banks exposed to liquidity stress risk. A diversified funding schedule can help to reduce funding cost spike risk in time of stress. Another example is mutual funds. Mutual funds are vulnerable to redemption thus timing investment maturity to redemption forecasting helps to ensure portfolio duration and yield plan will not be interrupted by funds redemption.

7.1.4 Support for Central Open Market Operations

PBOC manages its open market operations via a list of selected financial institutions. Those institutions will then release funds to a wider ranger of participants in the money market. PBOC monitors activities in the market, making sure cornering market does not occur during liquidity crunch. Lessons from Solomon Brothers Treasury hoarding and Enron concentrated energy future contract position taught us draining market liquidity for profit can bring regulatory consequences.

7.2 Offshore FX Liquidity Portfolio Management Strategy Objectives

For offshore liquidity portfolio manager, cashflow forecasting and matching on maturity ladders and amounts also have to be performed on a currency-by-currency basis. Some of the currencies are more liquid than the others. The most liquid USD is often chosen as the base currency for offshore liquidity portfolio.

7.2.1 Funding Cost, Return Rate and Liquidity

The base rate, in most cases the USD base rate, is the baseline funding cost for other currency sectors. Funding from USD is swapped into other currencies to fund non-USD liabilities. Non-USD funding rate is calculated as USD base rate + USD to Non-USD funding swap spread. The swap spread, which is the relative non-USD cost of funding, is dependent upon the monetary supply and demand of the non-USD currency in offshore market. Offshore liquidity portfolio managers compare and adjust their funding positions constantly, based upon which currency liability provides lowest funding cost and which currency asset provides highest return while maintain appropriate level of liquidity for each currency. The main funding currencies typically include a home currency plus main global funding currencies, including USD, EUR and JPY.

Main Currency Funding Rate （Federal Reserve 美联储，China Money 中国货币网， Bank of Japan 日本央行，ECB 欧洲央行）

7.2.2   SAFE Limit, Cross Border Flow and CNH Liquidity Condition

CNH is not a global reserve currency and its offshore liquidity is dependent upon the amount of activities that Chinese financial institutions can engage in. Every year SAFE will publish short-term foreign debt limit for different types institutions. For example, the limit for 2014 was 13.9 billion USD for central-managed domestic banks, 16.5 billion USD for central-managed foreign banks, and 12.9 billion USD for other domestic financial institutions and foreign financial institutions. These numbers set the upper limit of foreign borrowing the institutions combined can take, hence the amount of activities they can engage.

CNH is a managed float currency and its offshore liquidity is also dependent upon the amount of cross-border capital flow. PBOC can increase or decrease offshore CNH liquidity using various measures, including oversea asset capital requirement, amount of flow allowed into China via the CNH clearing banks and others.

7.3   Trading Accounts FX MTM and Strategies

7.3.1   FX Strategies

【Trading Mechanisms】 The FX business model can be generalized into two categories: passive price taker or active market maker. An institution can act as a price taker or price giver based upon capabilities and circumstances. Transactions can be carried out in bilateral RFQ mode, where a price taker makes contact to a price giver to find out an agreeable price. Transaction can also be carried in anonymous mode, which includes click-to-trade with streaming quotes, anonymous RFQ and limit order. A quote is two-sided to prevent price taker trying to take advantage the information. Click-to-trade and limit order tend to be fast and reliable, but may not cover less liquid currency pairs. RFQ tends to cover more currency pairs, and offers better price on transactions with large amount, but this mechanism is slow and error-prone.

Global FX trading evolves heavily around electronic trading platform, which have made strides over the years. The most prominent platforms include Reuters and EBS, both of which are multi-dealer platforms, and some single-dealer platforms offered by Deutsche Bank, UBS and others. Similar to other commoditized products, FX Spot, FX Forward and FX Swap transactions all went though substantial electronification globally and in China. However, when compared with equity markets where supply and demand flow with price and quantities are posted to concerned parties, FX flow information is still not transparent. Therefore financial institutions in general take one of two roles in FX market based upon information available to them, those who control the information of order flow and unload the net aggregated risk to the market, and those who control the information of market sentiment from different sources of order flow and try to make market.

Trading Electronification of Various Asset Classes (%) BIS 2015

With better-developed electronic trading platforms and a broad base of fast moving institutional clients including Principal Trading Firm, the market making effort in global FX market is still dominated by small number of global leaders. Domestic commercial banks are mostly taking the order flow management role. The well accepted business model for them is to make market to domestic corporations and business personnel based upon bid ask quotes in the international market, offset positions internally, and unload netted risk to market makers in global market, via RFQ, streaming one lick and limit order. This has certain advantage for two reasons. First large banks in China have substantial retail and corporate clients and demand for FX products, and secondly there is substantial risk capital and technology investment requirement for market making in global FX area. Thus it is more feasible at the current stage for large Chinese banks to take the order flow approach in international FX market.

This above framework could change substantially during a high volatility period. PBOC publishes strict guideline for the amount of FX risk banks can take on, and it may step into prevent the exchange rate market from substantial deviation from what it considers to be a fair valuation of the CNY exchange rate. This could possibly be the case in the end of 2015, when anticipating US rate increase and Chinese economic slowdown these was a large capital outflow from China, PBOC stepped into prevent CNY from fast depreciation which might brought disruption to domestic capital markets and instability to international trade pattern.

In domestic FX trading, the spot transactions are mostly carried out against CNY, with the USD-CNY being the most important pair. Pairs without USD, the so-called cross currency pairs, are often split against USD, which is the industry convention. Efforts were made to make it more convenient for some merchandise importer and exporter, for example, for business located in Japan and China involved in China Japan trade to carry out foreign exchange transaction in direct JPY-CNY pair to reduce transaction cost, but overall USD-CNY is still by far the largest traded currency pair. Forward transactions also follow industry convention, where it is structured as a package composed of a spot and a swap trade.

The spread in the interbank FX market can be very thin, but it gets a lot higher in the retail market, a reflection of both the risk to offset the position in the wholesale market, and the cost for building and maintaining a retail network. The retail spread on mainland could be twice the spread level in Hong Kong (China), which has active FX retail activities with more concentrated geographical distribution.

【Currency View Formation—Macro condition and relative strength of currencies】 Views on macro conditions and currency movement directions have to be formed before a position is to be taken via trading mechanism. FX trading involves the relative strength comparison of two currencies thus requires assessment of macro conditions, which was discussed earlier, and also market sentiment of both currencies.

With or without timely central bank rate responses, strong macro condition changes tend to lead to strengthening currencies. Some of the macro economic assessments are more stable and some of them are more volatile. Market is more active when European market and US market open. Market makers digest large macro economic news and the expected IRP triangulation kicks in. During Asian hours, the trading focus of domestic banks is more on CNY-related events. Since CNY is a managed float currency, the market tends to be stable but enters into volatile trading period when significant changes on China's economic outlook and monetary policy start to occur.

Specifically for USD-CNY currency pair, traders have to form views on macro conditions of both US and China. Components for US macro economic conditions include new home construction, CPI, hourly wage, employment level and PMI, among many others. Components for China macro economic conditions include GDP, retail sales, export, outstanding foreign exchange, fixed investment growth, M2, electricity generation, steel production, among many others. A trader must also be mindful of US monetary conditions including the current level of fed fund and swap rate, Federal Reserve's view on the state of US and global economy, the future target level of fed fund rate and details within published fed meetings notes. Monetary assessment of China includes the current level of M2, Aggregates Social Financing, the interest rate on repo, loan, WMP, PBOC's view on interest rate, recent open market operations, and other monetary actions such as MLF and PSL.

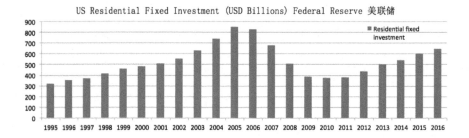

The analytical complexities on the US macro condition lie in deciphering the meaning and interaction of large quantities of economic data, on the US monetary condition lie in the instant changing nature of global liquidity and its interaction with US economic condition, monetary condition and subsequent US monetary policy. For example, published residential fixed investment and annualized new housing construction back to historical average level did suggest the overall recovery of US economy, which increased Fed's confidence in US domestic economy. Fed could raise fed fund rate to long-term neutral level based upon domestic monetary concern to reduce potential asset bias caused by cheap money. That would move global liquidity back to the US, amplifying the rising of dollar from US economic recovery.

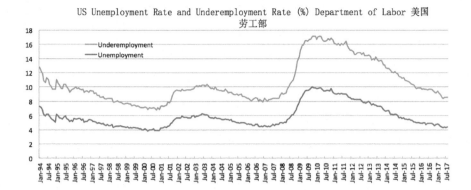

But one was to derive a simple conclusion based upon the main unemployment numbers could lead to economists or traders missing another large component that could have a profound impact on future direction of US economic and monetary policy. Data from US Department of Labor reported the employment level of Caucasian Male was down from 46 million before the financial crisis to 43 million, indicating a large segment of society had not fully recovered after the 2008 crisis. So from domestic economic perspective, raising interest rate would lead to a strong dollar that could put US manufacture on competitive disadvantage further hurting a segment that was impacted by the 2008 crisis. This is a good example that macro economic condition improvement, while it can change the value of a country's currency, it is not necessarily perfectly correlated to an interest rate policy change.

General unemployment rate in other advanced economies including Japan and European countries have also come down since the 2008 financial crisis. As was the case in US, the progress on employment recovery is not evenly distributed. EU Stat published data showed the employment recovery progressed more in the wider European Union versus the Euro area. The mandate is still there for more structural reform and monetary easing implementation.

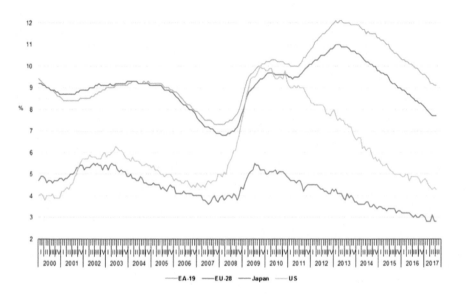

More specifically, European Union's level of unemployment recovered mostly back to its historical average level, while in the Euro area the number of unemployment grew from historical average of around 13 million to the peak level of more than 19 million in 2013, to below 15 million in 2017.

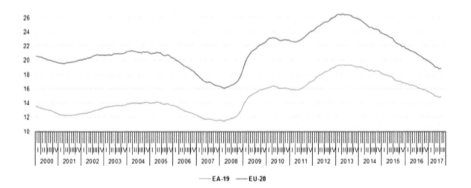

Japan also recovered mostly from the havoc of global financial crisis. An export power house, its levels of export to its two largest customers, China and US, are mostly back to their pre-bubble period levels.

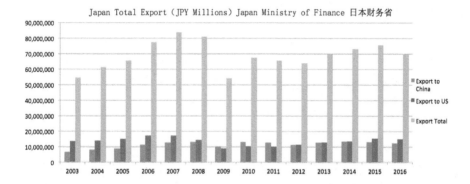

From global monetary perspective, due to dollar's reserve currency status, the US recovery and the prospect of rising US dollar funding rate would also raise the global level of funding cost, which could have certain negative consequences on global economy, and therefore certain repercussion for US export and growth. EU and Japan recoveries are more complicated working progress. Both have recovered mostly from financial crisis, but aging and other structural issues make predicting their future economic growth, funding cost level, hence EUR-CNY and CNY-JPY levels more difficult at this time.

Compared with mature industrialized nations, the analysis on the China is complex from different perspectives. First, the fact that different sectors of Chinese economy are moving at different speed towards modernization with different degrees of privatization has decided that the framework used to analyze Chinese economy would be different from the framework used to analyze industrialized countries. Second, different financial sectors including money market, loan, bonds and equities market all have different levels of funding rate transmission sensitivities and efficiency and each financial sector has different interaction mechanism with various Chinese economic sectors. The compartmentalized working mechanism has huge monetary policy implications. Equity markets do not respond to interest rate policy with a clear correlation. Loan is generally held to maturity so it is much less sensitive than the bond market to an interest rate cut or reserve ratio cut. The situation is very different from US where a rate cut would often lower the yield on bonds and also give a boost to equity market. In 2015, stock market segment boomed in China without firming of economic foundation after a series of rate and reserve ratio cuts. For that reason liquidity poured into stock market did not signal the credit market condition improvement. Rather it drained fund from bond market and elevated the level of interest rate on the fixed income market, increasing cost on borrowers. The rising stock price in this case was not a lead indicator for broad Chinese economic bottoming out and monetary policy forecast should be a continuously easing liquidity environment, which would have an impact on CNY strength expectation.

In a nutshell, strong US and EU economies in cyclical recovery with uneven structural benefit distribution, plus stable but slow Japan economic performance, lead to rather loose monetary environment lacking fast tightening rate policy updates, with gradually strengthening USD and EUR. So macro economic performance can but may not produce a central bank rate policy response and nevertheless can move exchange rate due to expectation therefore its accurate grasping is fundamental. On one hand, we may assume strong US dollar drives up CNY valuation since CNY is heavily pegged to USD. But on the other hand, recovering US economy could also draw capital from global markets hence draining domestic CNY liquidity. Without a corresponding rising CNY yield to mitigate the capital outflow, CNY exchange rate could fall. Strong European macro condition could have the same effect on CNY exchange rate, but to less extent versus USD.

【Currency View Formation—Global trade balance, interaction of rate policies】 The level of FX is also dependent upon relative trade positions, relative interest rate forecast based upon Fed and PBOC interest rate policy, China currency reserve level and the attitude of PBOC on the level of CNY. From trade perspective, China trade data from 2014 to 2016 showed weak export with stable surplus. There was debate on the validity of the export data, some of which could be fraudulent disguise for capital export to get around capital control regulation. China's export competitors had substantial devaluation since 2008 and this was partly the cause for China's weakened export since stronger currency often leads to weaker export. Weak export data tends to lower exchange rate expectation as a country may devalue in the hope of boosting its export. Besides relative export strength, relative interest rate policy implementation also changes the currency value expectation. US, EU and China monetary policy changes cause different interest rate parity expectation. Strong US rate increase expectation since 2015 changed what had long been a China capital account inflow into a capital outflow draining China's FX reserve. The speed of draining on the reserve caused by capital outflow, the speed of trade slowdown and the volatility of currency without intervention will decide the extent of CNY intervention management. There seemed to be a consensus among regulators and policy makers from major countries that a steep devaluation or volatile CNY exchange rate could have a destabilizing effect on global trade, therefore the amount of resources and level of commitment for stable CNY exchange rate are both very high.

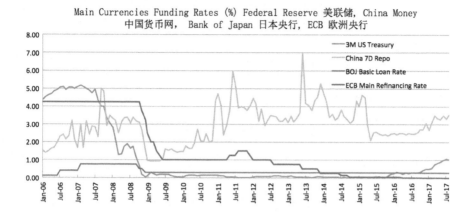

The Euro's share in global foreign exchange reserve is not as large as the US dollar's share. Therefore the impact on global and China domestic liquidity by ECB's interest rate policy is large but relatively smaller in comparison to Fed rate policy. On the export side, Europe is a large destination for China export industry. Since much of the China export is priced in US dollar and European export market is relatively fragmented versus US market, much of the CNY relative valuation study is focused on USD CNY interaction.

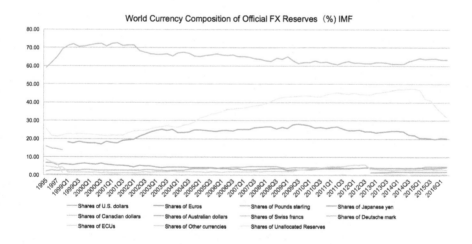

For JPY's relatively small share in global currency reserve and perennial low interest rate, BOJ's interest rate policy impact on CNY exchange rate is rather limited. JPY is nevertheless important due to the country's export performance. Lower JPY value adds competitive currency devaluation pressure on Korea Won and TWD. When JPY, KRW and TWD devalue together, the pressure on USD-CNY peg will be greatly felt. In fact, since 2006, China's currency in terms of

USD had appreciated against some of the manufactured goods exporter country currencies including JPY, KRW, EUR and TWD, and this had an adverse impact on China's export, especially after the labor cost and real estate cost made China's export industry much more expensive in the recent years. Besides direct competition in manufactured goods export, Japan also attracts large amount of tourists and tourist spending from China that can drain China's currency reserve when JPY value is low.

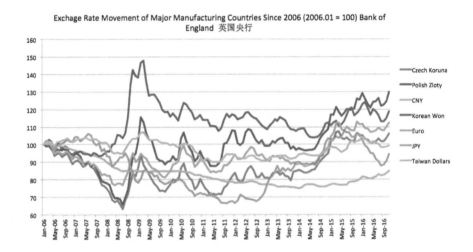

Exchange Rate Movement of Major Manufacturing Countries Since 2006 (2006.01 = 100) Bank of England 英国央行

In summary, strong export performance from China strengthens CNY expectation. Strong export performance from the US and EU suggest strong economic growth for these two large markets that are vital for China export industry and so CNY expectation could be stable. US and to less extent, EU rate policy affect global liquidity. USD and Euro rate increase could drain global liquidity and add devaluation pressure on CNY if PBOC does not take corresponding action. JPY exchange rate policy could add pressure on other export-driven economies' currency. JPY, KRW and TWD devaluation together could weaken CNY expectation.

【Currency View Formation—Various events】 Traders also need to pay attention to large international economic, financial and political events and estimate their impact on exchange rates. Examples of important political events with economic complication including Brexit in the mid of 2016, US presidential election in the end of 2016 and constitutional amendment vote in Italy in the end of 2016, all of which could change the preexisting understanding of political and economic condition in US and the Euro zone and therefore move respective exchange rates.

British voted on UK exit from European Union on Jun. 24th, 2016. After the Brexit vote was confirmed, Sterling exchange rate came down. EUR and US Dollar index went up. This was somewhat different from a more 'typical' European risk event, during which the value of USD and Gold would rise and the value of Euro would decrease.

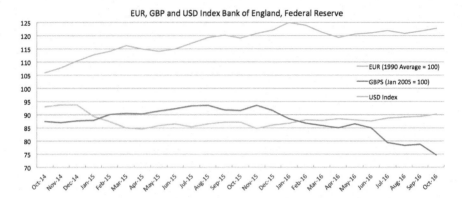

Under normal risk circumstances, USD and gold would go opposite directions as gold is priced in USD. During Brexit, liquidity change caused by the global capital movement in London looking for safe heaven drove both Gold and USD index higher in July of 2016. The up movement of USD index drove down CNY exchange rate during that month.

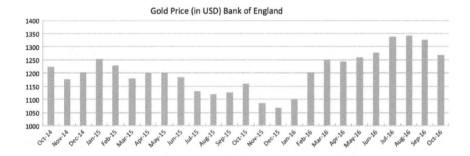

An example of US Fed policy event and its impact on exchange rate was the end of 2015 Fed meeting on rate increase. The end of 2015 saw strong US economic growth leading to Fed interest rate policy change. That rate event translated into the rise of US dollar index and the drop of gold price. This fit the more probable pattern of US dollar and gold going opposite direction. The rise of USD was mirrored by the fall of CNY exchange rate. US policy event led to US monetary policy expectation, USD currency value increase and CNY currency value decrease.

Besides Europe and US, another location with important international financial events is Japan, especially regarding its decision announcements on interest rate, various easing measure and tax reform, since Japan is a significant source of global liquidity. In terms of economic events, traders need to pay attention to the level of import and export published by Ministry of Finance of Japan that would indicate a certain state of Japanese economy, which is heavily dependent upon its auto export industry. Large change on its auto data changes Japan economic outlook and its close economic link with China lead analysts in China to update their domestic economic analysis result.

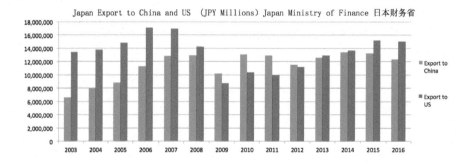

【Design Strategies and Implementation】 Based upon macro, interest rate and event analysis, executable views are formed and be summarized into directions, durations and extent of pricing targets of currency movement: directions include bull, bear and volatility; extents include quiet, shallow and steep; durations include long and short; pricing targets include spot price, forward spread and volatility.

With these executable views, traders or institutions will start to build up their positions. If there is a confident forecast for a long bull market, positions are accumulated when price moves lower. Stop-loss trigger needs to be set at a rather safe distance to prevent it from being easily triggered.

Building up positions in the case of spot means accumulation of a particular currency, and in the case of volatility means accumulations of FX option position.

Building up positions in forward requires the selection of one or a number of traded tenors. Liquid tenors typically involves 1-month to 3-month positions. Beyond 3-month money market instruments liquidity decreases for most currencies, making it difficult for efficient IRP trading. Forward Traders seldom have naked forward position. Usually a simultaneous spot and FX swap are done to create a synthetic forward position. If the view is EUR-USD or USD-CNY spread going higher, long positions in the contract currency will be accumulated, in the EUR-USD case, 1M or 3M EUR will be accumulated, in the case of USD-CNY, 1M or 3M USD will be accumulated. The spot leg will be a short of the contract currency. As MTM profit/loss is accumulated, a trader can choose to either settle at maturity with P&L or close the position with offsetting trade. The P&L threshold for clearing position is dependent upon trader's view, whether the current movement is for or against trader's position and closing transaction cost.

7.3.2 Trade-Financed CNY CNH Interest Rate Arbitrage

These are popular transactions for clients engaged in international trade to either take profit from interest rate differential, usually between USD and CNY, or expected forward exchange rate move.

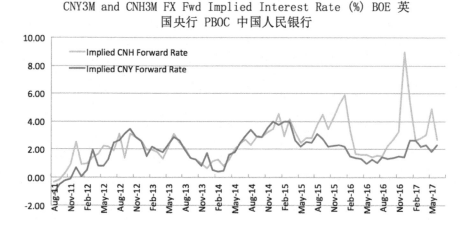

CNY3M and CNH3M FX Fwd Implied Interest Rate (%) BOE 英国央行 PBOC 中国人民银行

The execution of this strategy has a couple of variations. The first is when a client starts with an existing FX deposit. Based upon client's request, the bank will execute forward sell FX trade. The forward settlement date matches the maturity of FX deposit. Upon settlement date, FX deposit will be cashed out and delivered as part of the maturing FX trade to receive CNY.

(A1) If a client invests in 3M USD Deposit and carries out a 3M forward USD sell:

	USD position	CNY position	Action
Day 0	1,000,000		Sell USD 3M Forward at 6.6
3M	1,002,500 (1% annual)		Sell USD at 6.6
3M	0	6,616,500	

(A2) A client carries out a spot USD sell and invests in 3M CNY deposit:

	USD position	CNY position	Action
Day 0	1,000,000		Sell USD 3M Spot at 6.4
Day 0	0	6,400,000	
3M		6,448,000 (3% annual)	

The difference is $6,616,500 - 6,448,000 = 168,500$. In this case, the clients' tradeoff between A1 and A2 is to lose the interest rate differential between USD and CNY, but gain on the upside of USD appreciation.

(A3) A client can also use the deposit to finance an import export trade using USD deposit as collateral, and receive approved CNY loan.

When USD appreciation against CNY is expected, a client may carry out A1. If trade financing in USD is needed, A3 can be used in combination with A1. A1 and A3 combination is important in facilitating small merchandise export business with proper risk mitigation. When CNY exchange rate is stable, A2 can be used.

(B1) A client starts with a cash deposit of 6,400,000 in CNY and invests in a 3M CNY deposit, while taking on a trade-financing USD loan.

	USD position	CNY position	Action
Day 0		6,400,000	Buy USD 3M Forward at 6.4
Day 0	1,000,000		Arrange a USD loan at 1%
3M		6,448,000	3M 3% CNY deposit matures
3M	1,007,500		Settle USD Fwd receive USD at 6.4
3M	-1,002,500		Pay back USD loan
3M	5,000		Balance

(B2) Replace the USD forward buy trade in (B1) with an USD buy window trade

(B3) Replace the USD forward buy trade in (B1) with an USD buy FX option trade

In all three B cases, the underlying expectation is that the exchange rate of USD-CNY is stable and the client is trying to gain on the USD CNY interest rate differential.

It is important to remember that fraudulent activities present serious risks in trade-related financing, an important business area in China with a large export sector. Trading returns based upon view on interest rate differential or the direction of currency appreciation, in either A or B, are all made possible by using deposit as collateral to control potential fraudulent risk.

7.3.3 Cross-rate Split Strategies

Cross currency pairs refer to those currency pairs that do not involve USD, for example, EUR-JPY. Traders will quote EUR-JPY in Euro Zone. Outside Euro Zone, EUR-JPY may be split into EUR-USD and USD-JPY. For example, a spot trade to buy EUR sell JPY will be split into buy EUR sell USD and buy USD sell JPY.

Assume at this time EUR/USD spot is at 1.08, USD/JPY spot is at 104, and a cross pair spot of EUR/JPY is 112.32. On the market, a EUR/USD bid ask quote can be 1.0798/1.0802, a USD/JPY bid ask quote can be 103.98/104.02, and that may translate into an EUR/JPY bid ask quote at 112.28/112.32.

The cross-rate split gets more complicated when a client requests quote for forward. For example, if a client wants to execute a 3M buy EUR sell JPY forward trade.

	EUR	JPY
Cross forward	+	−

A dealer will execute two spot trades, buy EUR sell USD, and buy USD sell JPY.

	EUR	USD	USD	JPY
Spot	+	−	+	−

And simultaneously execute two FX swap trades, in first swap sell EUR buy USD on spot leg and buy EUR sell USD on 3M forward leg, in second swap sell USD buy JPY on spot leg and buy USD sell JPY on 3M forward leg.

	EUR	USD	USD	JPY
FX swap spot leg	−	+	−	+
FX swap forward leg	+	−	+	−

The rationales behind this common and seemingly complicated strategy are that USD quotes are usually more liquid than cross pair quotes and swap is more liquid than forward. Forward trade being replicated as a combination of more liquid FX spot and FX swap is that FX forward traders trade on interest rate risk, and interest rate parity is locked in when an FX swap is executed.

If we assume USD-JPY spot at 104, we further assume USD 1 year rate at 0%, JPY 1 year rate at 2%, based upon interest rate parity, 1 year from spot date, 1 USD is still 1 USD, 104 JPY becomes 106.08 JPY, thus 1 year USD/JPY will be quoted at 106.08. The difference at 2.08 reflects the arbitrage-free 1 year quote.

In an FX Swap trade, on spot leg, buy USD sell JPY, on forward leg, sell USD buy JPY, is equivalent to borrow USD for 1 year and lend JPY for 1 year. If 1-year USD/JPY forward rate difference from spot USD/JPY rate is not equivalent to 2.08, there will be arbitrage profit to be made. When a forward trader buy spot USD sell forward USD, or sell spot USD buy forward USD, the interest rate difference of 2% between USD and JPY is locked in. Therefore if a forward trader is asked to give a forward quote to client, a trader will give a forward spread quote, which is the result of a profit margin spread on top of arbitrage-free market forward spread, in the above case, 2.08%. Trader will simultaneously execute a package of spot and FX swap. The FX Swap, equivalent to a combination of loan and deposit, is used to lock in the interest rate differential with a profit margin, and the spot trade and the spot leg of the FX swap will net out each other, so the end result of the package is to create a forward equivalent position.

7.4   Trading Accounts Bond Strategies

【Global Context】 Varying substantially from country to country, trading strategy in fixed income markets is one of the most difficult for designing and execution. Globally the most liquid fixed income market is the US market, followed by the Euro market. The maturity of the US market is reflected in its arbitrage efficiency between different product types, between different issuers within the product type and between different tenor points within the term structure. Different qualitative and quantitative measure can be applied and supported by solid liquidity across a wide spectrum of products, including for interest rate products, treasury bond, treasury bond future, for credit products, high-grade credit bond, high yield, CDS, CDX, interest rate swap and currency swap, for volatility products, cap floor and swaption. With sufficient amount of liquidity at asset class level, product level, issuer level and term structure level, not only it is possible to execute a variety of trading strategies to arbitrage from different analytical perspectives, it is also possible to execute a variety of portfolio strategies, with asset allocation based upon sector exposure including credit quality and industry.

One of the common misperception in global investment community is that for global fixed income markets, at least when liquid products are considered, rules applicable in the US market and Euro global market, can be uniformly applied in other sovereign markets. In practice US market is about the only fixed income market at this time that is dominated by non-banking institutional investors, therefore the frequency of trading and demand for transparency that support the market liquidity can not be easily replicated in other markets, including Japan, Germany and China. In those markets, the majority of fixed income activities are executed by banks and banks are heavily regulated entities and therefore do not exhibit the same active behavior as the non-banking institutions. As a result, fixed income trading and investment in non-US market could be quite different from the US market.

For instruments that are considered relatively safe in China's market, including treasury, policy bank bond, and short commercial paper, there is good liquidity, bid ask spread is generally thin and certain trading strategies can be supported. Credit product liquidity is much lower in comparison and further detailed legal framework is required to facilitate the quantification of default risk and recovery measurement for credit products from different issuers and different issuance.

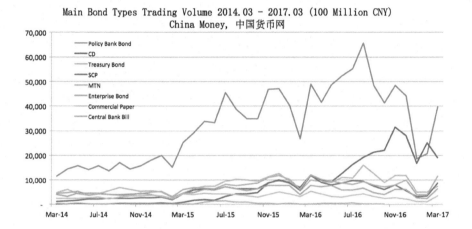

Main Bond Types Trading Volume 2014.03 – 2017.03 (100 Million CNY)
China Money, 中国货币网

7.4.1   Trading Mechanism

Traders give stream quotes on liquid treasury, policy bank bonds and short-term credit instruments, or respond to RFQ on less liquid instruments, first by forming a rate view based upon a list of factors. Those factors usually include macro economic condition, monetary liquidity condition, instrument supply and demand forecast, important economic announcements and other market events. Once a view is formed, a trader may adjust spread on a specific instrument based upon its market-making portfolio liquidity and duration.

The spread a trader will charge on a specific instrument increases with the instrument duration, to compensate for their liquidity risk. Longer duration instruments tend to be less liquid for their larger duration risk that introduces volatility into portfolio valuation. To manage portfolio duration risk and other risks, institutions put into place rigorous risk control measures for traders' books, including maximum loss, DV01 and counterparty limit.

Buy-side quote and sell-side quote may not be symmetrical and there are two important reasons for that. The first is during strong bull or bear market, the quotes are often only effective on only one side since traders do not want to take a falling knife in a unidirectional market. The second reason is the regulatory requirement limiting the extent of naked short positions and this makes it difficult for traders to hedge their position risk in a volatile market condition. Therefore during a bear market, the quoted yield on the buy side can be very high. These two issues can be alleviated to certain extent once the CDS and bond future segments become more mature.

Liquidity spread will also differ among different trading venues including CFETS and exchanges. The vast majority of bond trading is conducted in CFETS and this brings concentrated liquidity. Trading on exchange brings liquidity of certain corporate instruments as it employs centralized risk management measure in repo transactions.

Spread also differs based upon trading methods and clients. The spread on electronic market making towards institutional clients, via one-click stream quotes or RFQ methods, tends to be modest, though RFQ quotes could be slightly higher for its dealing with less liquid instruments. The spreads on electronic market making towards retail customers tend to be much higher than the spreads towards institutional clients.

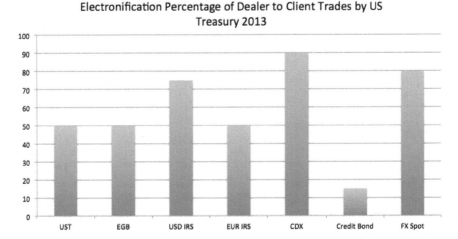

A major difference between the domestic bond market and global bond market is that electronic market making via high frequency methods in bond market among institutions is hard to execute, due to the fact it is difficult to offload interest risk position using bond future, a market itself hampered by naked short regulation designed to prevent large amount of speculation. It is also difficult to offload credit risk, caused by the relatively recent CDS introduction and improvement needed regarding bankruptcy legal framework and loss recovery procedure. All these make identifying and locking in arbitrage profit with proper hedging trade difficult to execute in high frequency market, and the bond market itself is still relatively dominated by buy-to-hold banking accounts. Still, progress was made in China fixed income electronification outside HF trading. Started from the bilateral trading mode, the fixed income trading went through RFQ and single dealer platform/multi dealer platform developmental stage, comparable to FX electronic platform, with its focus on different products being rolled out in different market venues.

7.4.2 Rate View from Global Perspective

Here we define the asset classes in terms of interest rate product, credit product, equities and commodities. We form the view based upon the international macro and monetary condition, domestic macro economic condition, monetary policy, budgetary policy and instrument supply demand.

【Global macro impact on domestic macro condition】 Global markets have significant influences on China's domestic market yield due to macro economic interaction. EU and US are two largest trading partners with China. When US and European economies grow, their imports from China tend to grow and this will have a pulling effect on Chinese economy. Vice versa, global economies also benefit from Chinese economic growth. An example is the damage done to global iron ore exporters from Australia and Brazil in a China steel production slowdown. Therefore macro conditions of large economies including EU, US, Japan, ASEAN and other economic areas need to be studied prior to forming a rate view on China's capital markets.

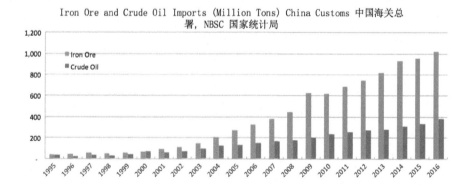

Iron Ore and Crude Oil Imports (Million Tons) China Customs 中国海关总署, NBSC 国家统计局

Europe has one of the world's largest economies. Based upon European Commission's report published in April of 2016, China was its second largest trading partner. With coordinated monetary easing and many other structural measures, Europe gradually recovered from the 2008 economic crisis. Eurostat reported Eurozone GDP growth rate at 1.2% for 2014, 2.0% for 2015, compared with −0.9% for 2012 and −0.3% for 2013; it also reported GDP growth rate for the whole European Union economic growth at 1.6% for 2014, 2.2% for 2015, compared with −0.5% for 2012 and 0.2% for 2013. By the end of 2016, while the recovery progress was to certain extent still unevenly distributed, the general unemployment rate in EU-28 area was again close to its historical average. US and EU economic recoveries together provided a generally improving external macro context for China domestic economy.

【Global Rate level on domestic rate level】 The funding cost impact of US dollar as the global reserve currency during a time of a global economic slowdown and subsequent recovery can not be underestimated, especially for many parts of the world with relatively large international trade exposure and cross border monetary flow. US rate reduction provided easing liquidity globally during global slowdown but its rate increase was difficult for many countries including China and southern European countries that still proceeded with various structural reform. For policy makers in Europe and China, it is preferable for their benchmark 10-year European AAA-rated government yield curve and Chinese government curve to be maintained at stimulative level to provide more financial help during their reform process, and that preference would be part of the Fed interest rate decision consideration.

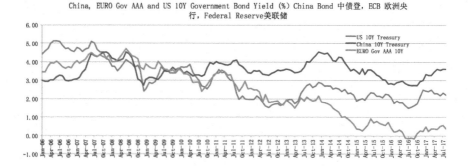

China, EURO Gov AAA and US 10Y Government Bond Yield (%) China Bond 中债登, ECB 欧洲央行, Federal Reserve美联储

To address severe GDP contraction in 2008, US started its first round of quantitative easing program. Around the same time, with a severe export decline, China embarked on a 4-trillion CNY stimulus package that some estimated equivalent to 20 trillion when multiplier effect was taken into consideration. The treasury yields in both China and US came down substantially. Starting from the end of 2010, stable yield spread between two countries treasury curves began to form and took its shape at the end of 2011. After many years of trade liberalization, with its export at 2.28 trillion USD (14.14 trillion CNY) and import at 1.68 trillion USD (10.45 trillion CNY) in year 2015, the large amount of exchange flow in trade account inevitably led to China's capital market deep linkage to the external capital market. Quantitatively the capital markets linkage is expressed in the form of relatively stable yield spread between the liquid China and US 10 year treasury instrument. The spread was often between 100 and 150 bps, reflecting risk capital charge and perceived currency risk by international capital markets when investment strategy towards China was being formulated. Between the end of 2011 and 2013 the spread went through a cycle of first coming down and rising up, mostly a reaction to of US yield increase prospect.

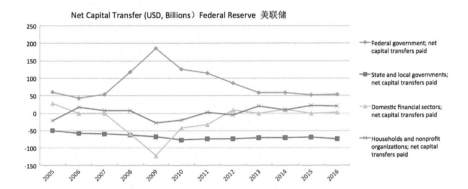

By the end of 2013, US economic recovery was firming up. The process of deleveraging of individuals and corporates, accomplished by leveraging transfer to the federal government, was mostly finished. This could be observed by looking at the level of net capital transfer from federal government to corporate and individual back to its normal level. But there was concern at the time that the US economic recovery still needed to be firmed up further with additional monetary support. In addition to that, there was a general realization of global structural economic reform difficulty. Both international condition and domestic concern caused the US treasury yield to come down, with hopes that the benefit of more recovery could be better distributed among different sectors and demographics in US and that more improvement of global economic condition would be helpful. Still the improving US macro condition will be the most important deciding factors for US treasury yield change. The detailed movement of the 10-year US treasury yield and US GDP growth rate illustrated linkage between the GDP growth and 10Y yield, which is a target of Fed's monetary management. Therefore US GDP growth and resulting Fed yield management had close links to China domestic yield movement, China domestic economy and its general investment condition.

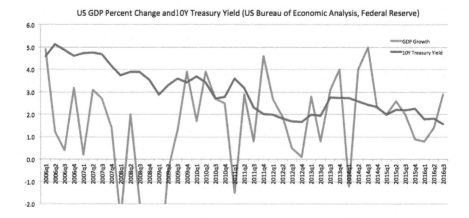

【Level of USD-CNY and domestic yield】 While US Treasury yield provides current indication on US macro condition, US dollar index prices the relative attractiveness of dollar-denominated assets therefore the relative health of US economy over its major trading partners. Since 2014 the Fed managed to keep treasury yield staying at relatively low level, nevertheless the continuous US economic recovery improved the future prospect of dollar-denominated assets and led to increased relative attractiveness of those assets. The US dollar index rose sharped since then, until it stabilized at the end of 2015. Until the end of 2016 Fed did not raise Fed fund rate again not only for domestic US economic concern, but also for the effect of raising rate of reserve currency on global liquidity for emerging market economies that struggled with overcapacity and rebalancing of their economies, including China. Those structural factors together created a pause for the rise of USD index.

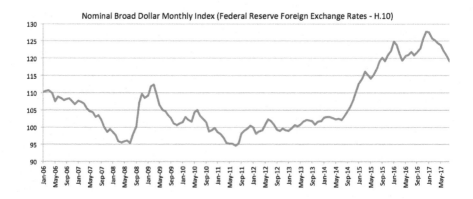

The rise of US dollar index coincided with fall of value of CNY. The rise of US dollar index could also explain from time to time the pressure on CNY, since the value of CNY is linked to a basket of currencies, the largest share of which belongs to US dollar. Slower rise of CNY versus USD could drain the domestic market liquidity through global capital flow. On the other hand, the rise of CNY with USD could hurt the export industry of China. Interest rate is an important tool in managing the rise or fall of an exchange rate. Thus in keeping domestic CNY yield within certain range of international yield to achieve stable CNY exchange rate, the extent of CNY management needed has a direct impact on domestic China yield movement and investment environment.

An important note is that the linkages among US macro condition, US treasury and Chinese treasury yield can be more quantitatively observable, the linkages among US macro condition and US dollar index and CNY exchange are less so. A possible explanation is that interest rate is the instrument both Fed and PBOC utilize as direct response to macro condition changes and the international trade flow and capital arbitrage keep the two treasury yield spread with certain levels, hence two treasury yields and the spread between are very sensitive to major macro economic indicator changes from both countries. On the other hand, both Fed and PBOC apply interest rate instrument for counter-cyclical management purposes, hence the signal transmission from macro change to currency assets could be muted by those policy implementation. Also CNY is a managed-float currency priced against a basket currencies back up by large currency reserve and its stability is part of economic management agenda as important as the yield level itself. These two reasons make USD index plus CNY exchange rate less indicative than two treasury yields and spread on indicating China domestic yield management and investment condition.

【Level of Gold and domestic yield】 Gold is priced in US dollar and that makes it a natural alternative investment asset to US dollar especially during any inflationary period. Gold price complements the dollar index to provide additional information on global capital flow and domestic inflation that can influence China's capital markets investment return. Under normal circumstances, gold is stronger when dollar is weaker. Vice versa, when dollar is strong gold becomes less desirable. The decrease of the price of gold, which corresponded to the rise of US Dollar since 2013, also coincided with the timing of US recovery. On occasions, when there is large amount of capital looking for safe haven during a volatile period, both gold price and US dollar index could rise. This was the case during the Brexit, when the price of both gold and US dollar index were up, which would be interpreted as a bull indicator for Chinese fixed income market due to probable capital inflow from London, versus a normal rise of US dollar index with gold price decrease, could be interpreted as a bear signal due to capital outflow.

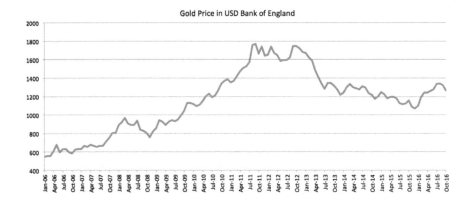

【Level of Euro and domestic CNY】 Next to USD, Euro is also an important global economic input for forming a China rate view. Euro area is not only a large trading partner for China, it is also both a large global capital provider and an important capital investment destination. The area's quickened growth did not translated into Euro relative currency strength against USD until 2017, with its slide started in 2014 and stayed at relative low level against US dollar through 2015–2016. In times of economic difficulties, weakening Euro could be followed by large capital outflow leaving Euro zone leading to the rise of US dollar index and capital inflow into China, creating a circumstance of rising US dollar index without a weakening CNY. On the other hand, strong Euro could cause capital flow out of China therefore draining domestic liquidity.

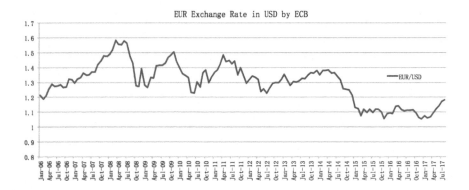

7.4.3   Rate View from Domestic Perspective

【Macro economic contributors】 Some of the domestic input factors applicable to form a rate view include GDP growth-related macro factors, budgetary expenditure and deficit, monetary cycle statistics, various industries statistics and others. Three main macro-contributing factors to GDP growth include trade export, real estate and public expenditure. On export, WTO statistics suggested China export contribution for about 22% to China's GDP growth in 2015 and about 20% in 2016. On real estate, NBSC's statistics on consumption sales and investment suggested real estate contribution for about 23% to China's economy for 1st half of 2016. On government spending, Department of Treasury published the 2015 national budgetary expenditure at 17.59 trillion CNY, relative to NBSC's GDP figure at 68.55 trillion CNY. Therefore the government expenditure contributed to 25.66% of China's economy. Combined assessment on export industry, real estate industry and government expenditure will form a large picture of current state of China's macro economy.

When a country enters slower GDP growth period, counter-cyclical budgetary policies are often implemented to support economic growth and recovery. Budgetary deficit tends to enlarge with more monetary stimulation injected into the system to prevent deflation. The driving factors in the monetary system are deflation and lower rates that will have the bull effect on yield curve and credit spread. When a country enters a faster GDP growth period, its budgetary deficit tends to shrink with less monetary stimulation injected to prevent inflation. The driving factors in the monetary system are inflation and higher rates that will have the bear effect on yield curve and credit spread.

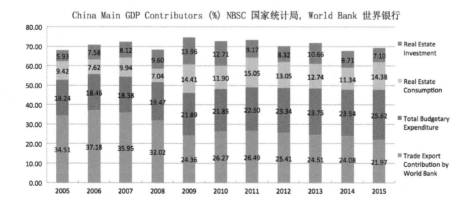

At the end of 2016, the overall economic condition in China was a mixed picture. Internationally, major economies led by US moved into relative recovery while global trade was still mired in stagnation for a variety of reasons. China export industry was in stable territory without clear growth prospect. Other industries that were mainly serving domestic consumptions, especially steel and coal sectors were still proceeding with structural reforms. Government budgetary expenditure and private real estate investment consumption expanded to fill in the gap left by the falling export. The state of macro economy dictated the need for continuous easing monetary condition.

【CNY effect】 Similar to other large economies with strong export industries but without reserve currency, the level of Chinese treasury yield curve is decided by both domestic macro economic concern and international capital flow, especially the flows that are priced in US dollar. A large complication to the above assessment is when the spread between US and China treasury yield narrows, in the case of a Fed rate increase without a corresponding China yield increase, there is a possibility of capital outflow that could start a serious drain on country's FX reserve. If the drainage becomes too large and PBOC becomes less willing or able to defend the CNY at a particular level, CNY could weaken further until either China export picks up to such an extent that can support the domestic yield back to a corresponding level, or the country will have to increase the yield so spread is back to the level that can stabilize the exchange rate. The compromise between supporting a level of export at a time of weak global trade market or China increases its treasury yield to accommodate rising US yield during structural reform would be difficult to make.

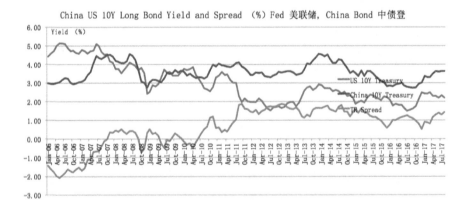

China US 10Y Long Bond Yield and Spread (%) Fed 美联储, China Bond 中债登

A weakening CNY could reduce return for international portfolio managers with exposure to Chinese assets but at the same time their portfolio valuation is denominated in USD. On the other hand, a weakening CNY will have positive consequence for domestic portfolio manager since it will stimulate country's export, assuming no international trade breakdown against the surge. A stable CNY will make international investment in China an easier decision with more predictable result, but domestic interest rate increase to keep up with US yield increase will be hard for domestic economy to digest, as the domestic economy is facing with overcapacity especially in the real estate sector in 3rd and 4th tier cities, which could not be solved with current market mechanism. Hence, a stable CNY could render domestic investment a difficult process, since the negative financial condition will likely persist as long as US is in a strong dollar and rate increase period.

PBOC calibrates and releases certain amount of liquidity. The monetary supply and monetary demand reach equilibrium level to produce a domestic interest price, which determines the value of CNY together with the US interest rate and other factors. In this process, central bank has to weigh considerations from different aspects during their policy formulation. Still the most important factor driving their policy decision is the domestic economic concern and this suggests the relative stimulative monetary policy is the probable course in the foreseeable future until the overcapacity issue in China is resolved.

【Liquidity and deposit reserve ratio】 The total amount of liquidity in Chinese economy is measured in terms of aggregated social financing. Aggregated social financing is the amount of funding provided from the perspective of funding user. One tool PBOC uses to manage the amount of aggregated social financing by setting the target ratio for deposit reserve. The financial institutions include banks and non-banking financial institutions provide funding to the economy of China. Close to 80% of the funding to these financial institutions was deposit, again underscores the prominent roles played by deposit-taking banks. At the end of 2015, banking balance sheet stood at 200 trillion CNY. A 0.5% reserve ratio cut would be a 1 trillion CNY released into market, and with multiplier factor. Hence the importance of deposit reserve ratio.

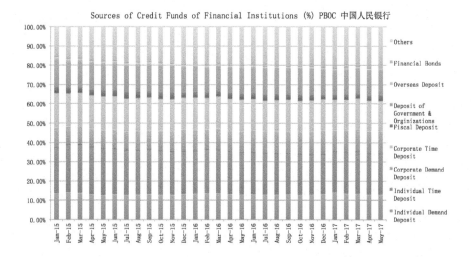

Among the changes of funding sources, the continuous decrease of individual's time deposit from 24 to 21% over the short 2-year period between 2015 and 2016 was noteworthy, as retail customers shifted their investments from low yield time deposit to other asset classes with higher return.

Up to 2008 China's export industry accumulated large amount surplus of foreign exchange amid a period of rapid global trade expansion. Exporters sold the trade surplus in foreign exchange to PBOC and received CNY in return for domestic usage. To prevent the large amount of CNY from overwhelming the monetary circulation that could be highly inflationary, deposit ratio at banks was increased rapidly. The export growth was interrupted in 2008 by the financial crisis and that stopped the increase of deposit reserve ratio. Since 2010 net export mostly recovered. This combined with the large stimulation package resulted more liquidity in the monetary system and deposit reserve rate resumed climbing until it reached its peak in 2011. After the financial crisis, China tried to shift its economy more towards internal consumption and its commercial trading with the rest of the world gradually became more balanced. China's interest rate liberalization also resumed after the crisis. As reform progressed, consensus was reached, that as a quantity management instrument deposit reserve ratio is not as fine-tuned as a price management instrument. For those and many other reasons, the ratio was kept stable until 2015, when both the slower domestic growth prospect and capital outflow have demanded more liquidity support into the financial system to stimulate domestic growth and reserve ratio had been cut multiple times since that time.

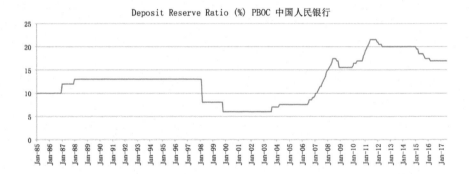

Deposit Reserve Ratio (%) PBOC 中国人民银行

【Liquidity and market operations】 Besides deposit reserve ratio, PBOC can also apply various types of market operations to change the amount of liquidity. Both deposit reserve ratio and market operations are PBOC policy implementation tools that are directly targeted at commercial banks. Through these tools PBOC could manages the amount and price of credit flows to support funding activities of all non-banking entities and individuals effectively since banks are the most important part of the larger financial intermediary network that supports the real economic activities in China. Market operations including SLO, SLF, MLF and PSL together have provided more than 6 trillion CNY financing outstanding since the mid of 2014. PBOC releases short-term liquidity via SLO and SLF, and lowers the mid to long-term borrowing cost of specific sectors to stimulate economy via MLF and PSL.

A detailed look into those market operations showed SLO and SLF were designed to smoothen short-term monetary condition therefore they have influence on short-term rate view and strategies. MLF and PSL are designed to provide long-term credit support that would influence long-term rate view and strategies. An interesting observation could be made in the May of 2015. Starting from that month PSL was increased that would offset the drop of MLF later on. And a large increase of MLF in the beginning of 2016 provided support against temporary capital outflow and other events during that period.

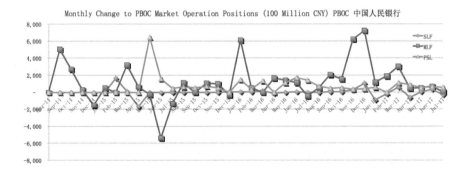

Money market operations, deposit reserve ratio, capital reserve requirement, fiscal deposit and economic activities such as property loan volume combined, decide the supply and demand of liquidity required. The results are the equilibrium short-term interest rates, which are epitomized by short-term repo rate, and equilibrium long-term interest rates, which are epitomized by 1-3Y medium term loan rate, and 10-year treasury rate. Their levels provide measurement of monetary condition at a given time, and also act as the benchmark yields of various rate asset classes. Different asset classes, such as fixed rate and floating rate loan, agency bond and credit bond, trust, wealth management product, will generate return based upon benchmark yield with their respective levels of spread.

【Liquidity by financing venues】 The resulted from deposit reserve ratio change, market operations and other monetary policy implementation was overall sufficient liquidity. Equity and bond financing expanded continuously. Trust loan and entrust loan financing were volatile. There was large reduction of paper financing, which was related to the difficult business environment for small to medium private enterprises in economic transition.

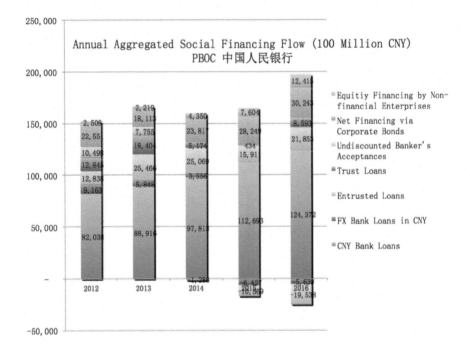

In the month-to-month PBOC data of aggregated social financing, some volatile changes could be observed. The end of 2015 large reduction of China's debt in foreign currency was related to the pressure of rising US dollar. To replenish lost liquidity due to loss of FX reserve, loan as the most applicable liquidity supply tool saw substantial increase in the beginning of 2016.

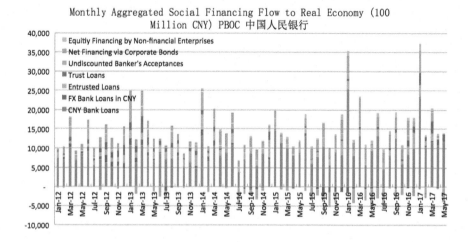

Monthly Aggregated Social Financing Flow to Real Economy (100 Million CNY) PBOC 中国人民银行

The effort by policy makers to stimulate economy could be evidenced by a correlation between the reduction of banker acceptance financing and the increase of loan financing, taking into account a latency effect.

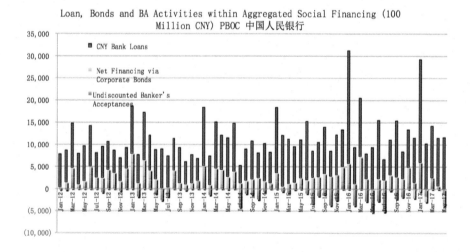

Loan, Bonds and BA Activities within Aggregated Social Financing (100 Million CNY) PBOC 中国人民银行

Due to the significance of loan, from the perspective of managing liquidity through financial intermediary, mid and long-term loan for enterprises, government and organizations, and mid and long-term loan for household consumptions, are focal points of monetary policy maker's attention. In a liquidity environment beset by specific loan deposit ratio and supplemented by short and long term market operations, banks weigh the liquidity constraint and return objectives, and may choose to either expand or reduce their loan balance sheet by changing the amount of loans they issue, or reset the size of their bond investment portfolio, while maintain certain amount of liquidity, or they could go off-balance sheet, invest in WMP, trust and other financial vehicles.

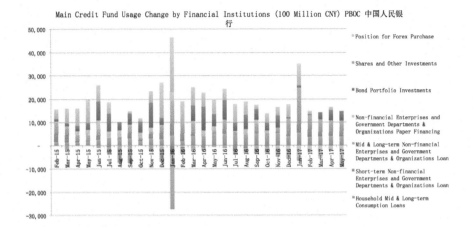

Compared against equity-based financing, bond-based financing enjoyed faster growth over the recent years, partly due to the depth of liquidity of interbank market brought by banks with large amount of funds and large customer penetration. A short hiatus was reached in 2013 when US yield curve rose sharply with anticipation for strong economic recovery and rapid pace of fed fund rate increase. Sympathetic yield increase in China's market followed, dissuading bond issuer from going to the bond market. The bond market returned to growth after the yield came down in 2014. In 2015 there was a short equity bull that reduced bond financing, but with the support of bond market reform and loan to bond initiatives, the bond market expansion continued. The US rate increase and deleveraging measure in China in 2017 again caused the bond yield increase and the falling of bond financing.

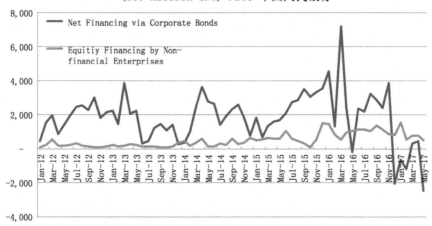

Monthly Bonds and Equities Financing Flow to Real Economy
(100 Million CNY) PBOC 中国人民银行

Policy makers assess the effectiveness of quantity management by constant monitoring the target price of financing. The price of financial resources will determine whether the general monetary environment is stimulative or tight to economic activities. Policy makers' main targets rates for the mid to long-term financial activities include medium term loan rate and long bond rate. Both fixed and floating loan issuance are often benchmarked against the PBOC reference loan rate, which is also correlated to 10Y treasury rate. Long bond rate and 1-3Y loan rate together set the overall cost level of general financing condition of Chinese economy. Central bank also has to monitor CNY exchange rate as that defines the cost for export industry.

Main Financing Cost to Chinese Economy (%) PBOC 中国人民银行, Fed Reserve 美联储, China Bond 中债登

Both the amount and prices of main financing venues paint the broad picture of macro monetary condition. From this picture, policy makers, bankers, industrialists and investment communities can assess at a specific time, whether enough amount of financial resource is provided, whether the amount of financial resource is provided at the right price. Based upon these assessment, policy makers will decide whether to further turn monetary targets for both quantity and price; commercial banks will decide whether to pursue activity expansion or contraction, whether the expansion or contraction is on-balance sheet or off-balance sheet, and what is the best mixture of their total asset portfolio; industrialists can decide whether to be bullish or bearish in terms of enlarging their footprints in business planning; finally investment communities could decide the optimal investment product mix based upon the risk return profile comparison.

Besides central bank's market operations, the size and the content of government budgetary spending also play important interactive role with other factors in a nation's monetary system. Expansive budget injects more liquidity into the system. Increase on medical spending or infrastructure will bring more growth into the respective areas. More efficient management of fiscal deposit for both collection and release could smooth out the change of outstanding amount of deposit in the monetary system.

Given the amount of liquidity and yield expectation, product supply and demand also influence short term up and down movement domestic curve movement.

【Industry analysis】   Some of the industry analysis covering real estate, export-related industries, overcapacity industries and non-capital function relocation from Beijing to XiongAn might produce analytical results in pertinence to broad economic and yield curve assessment. The analysis on the running of others more specific industries could produce more sector-specific yield curve result. Real estate segment can be further broken down along the lines of affordable versus commercial housing, for rental-only versus for buying, 1st and 2nd tier, versus 3rd and 4th tier urban demand. While the overall real estate sector for its large weight in GDP has to be sustained for stable pulling of upstream sectors including cement, glass and steel industries, more detailed analysis on real estate sector along geographical or other criteria could produce more differentiated subcategory and industry results. A regulatory restriction on 1st and 2nd tire property purchasing could shift investment demand to 3rd and 4th tier cities, support the construction and expansion of both properties and general infrastructure at county level. Cement demand is location-driven and past investment could become irrelevant depending upon whether the new demand is close to past investment. Real estate builders also have their own geographical differentiation. Detailed industry analysis thus will produce sector curve gain and loss forecast for both property builder groups and cement producers with different geographical penetration.

Some of the export industries are both domestic and globally competitive, including mobile phones, house appliance, shipping and machinery, while others mostly are more focused on domestic demand. Analysis on these industries need to take into consideration of their market share at both domestic and global level, as domestic demand and global demand may reach different economic cyclical period at different time points thus have different impact on industry yield curve and issuer yield curve based upon an industry and a company's particular market focus.

The overcapacity industries have been in fluid situation, subject to continuous industry consolidation, export market trade conflict and reform measures. Within the steel sector, there is a high demand for special alloy and other high-end material while crude supply is abundant, and iron ore price is always at play. Therefore industry's progress on technological improvement and iron ore inventory level will impact steel sector yield curve, and a producer's grasp on technology, its pension liability and holding of high-grade ore mine will impact yield analysis result for that specific steel producer. Coal is another industry facing pressure to cut overcapacity. Even though there is stabilization on the housing sector and the steel industry both with large energy demand, coal faces competition from cleaner energy sources. Yield curve on coal sector is related to both broadly positive economic growth and sub-sector competition.

From time to time certain signals from specific industries also shed lights on to the direction of interest rate. Agricultural sector market reform historically unlocked large economic growth potential, and certain pricing signal such as pork price index signals both future inflation and economic growth. Car industries can be segmented into heavy vehicles, which are dominated by domestic producers, and passenger vehicles, which had a strong joint adventure presence. Stable performance of passenger vehicle sector is a good indicator for overall consumer confidence. Copper import and iron ore import indicate strong real estate investment, an important driver for economic growth.

【Credit spread versus interest rate】 Credit spread movement generally reflected the interest yield curve change albeit at more pronounced level. The credit spread increase from the end of 2010 to the end of 2011 was partly due to the new paradigm shift for US and China Treasury spread management. From then up to mid 2013 the reduction was the result of global liquidity supply and slower growth in China. The spread increased at the end of 2013 when US recovery firmed up. After the end 2013, the credit spread came down with the interest rate yield, a realization of long and hard work ahead for Chinese economic reform. A credit spike showed up at the end of 2014, caused by strengthened repo collateral requirement on exchange markets to curb runaway borrowing from platforms.

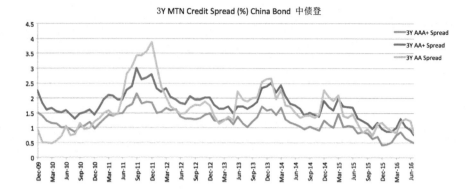

While credit spread theoretically offers more clarity than credit curve in pricing structure for credit markets, credit curve is more useful in valuation and asset allocation strategy execution in China versus US market. The reason is that the credit spread hedging methods using CDS or short interest rate bond execution have not reached maturity.

Once the direction and extent of interest rate curve and credit curve have been decided, asset class strategy, sector strategy at portfolio level, arbitrage strategy across time interval and term structure and be formulated and implemented.

【Strategy Design and Implementation】 Global macro conditions from US, EU, Japan and other economies, and domestic macro conditions especially regarding export, real estate, overcapacity industries and government spending, provide the basic foundation for China interest rate analysis. Budgetary and long-term monetary policies could provide counter-cyclical effect on interest rate movement. Short-term monetary policies and market operations from time to time reduce the volatility in liquidity market and shed light on curve movement trend. Banks are the most important channels for liquidity distribution hence their credit sourcing and usages are the focus of PBOC liquidity management and market liquidity analysis. Credit spread is largely correlated to interest rate movement. Bonds supply and demand and some regulatory measures could influence the market curve movement. Industry analysis can provide insight into both sector curve movement and broader market assessment.

Once traders and investors have formed rate views for interest rate market, credit market, sector markets and issuers, the next step is to plan their strategies for execution in their respective trading and investment domains.

7.4.3.1 Leveraged Carry Trade on the Exchange and the Interbank Market

A popular trading strategy for many trading desks, it often involves buying bonds that are eligible for repo. Repo is then executed to obtain additional financing for desks to take on more credit positions. The strategy works well when liquidity is often abundant which leads to low financing cost. The risk lies in the possible volatility of financing cost. It is also difficult to execute when the stock of credit bonds eligible for repo can be low when the strategy gets popular acceptance. In repo transactions in the interbank bond market, the less risk in a bond, the more accepted it is as a collateral.

Monthly Repo Trading Volume by Major Bond Types (100 Million CNY) China Bond 中债登

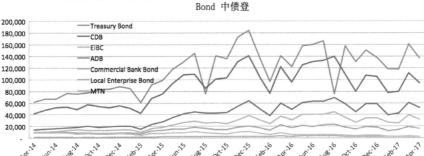

Compared to a repo transaction, in addition to being used in a leveraged carry trade, outright repo transaction can also be used for shorting since the bond ownership has changed hand. The statistics on shorting percentage versus carrying trade percentage are not available, but we might assuming less risky carrying is more prevalent. In outright repo, more local enterprise platform bonds are used than treasury until default guarantee provided by local government on those platform bonds received regulatory disapproval in the November of 2016.

Monthly Outright Repo Trading Volume by Major Bond Types (100 Million CNY) China Bond 中债登

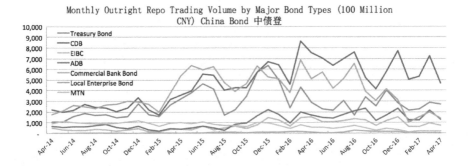

Data published by China Money covers money market instruments in addition to longer-termed instruments with a slight different bond type classification versus China Bond. One noticeable observation in outright Repo data is the large application of SCP and CD. Particularly CD became widely popular after MPA regulatory measure put into place in the December of 2016 as an on-sheet short-term financing alternative versus off-balance sheet financing WMP.

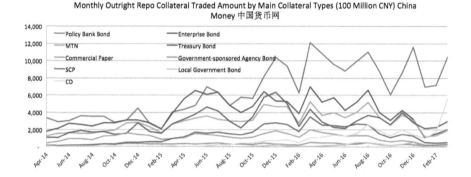

The carry strategy became popular during a time when relatively passive high yield venues such as real estate trusts became less available. Mid 2015 stock crash led to liquidity crunch and repo volume drop. Between 2016.06 and 2016.07, CBRS, CSRC and CIRC respectively issued regulatory measures to reduce financial leverage, specifically CSRC and CIRC mandated fixed income investment leverage not to exceed 300%. CBRC mandated WMP fixed income leverage not to exceed 140%. This led to a sharp decrease of repo trading for a short period. Regarding seasonality, long Spring Festival usually reduces trading in February. Also, due to tightened leverage regulatory measure including MPA, we might expect more volume volatility at the end of each quarter.

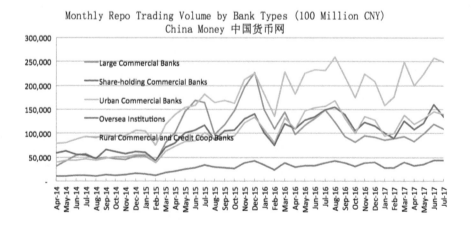

Among banks, urban commercial banks are the most active type in repo leveraging market, followed by rural commercial banks and national commercial banks, even though either urban or rural commercial banks' balance sheet is less than that of national commercial banks, based upon PBOC statistics.

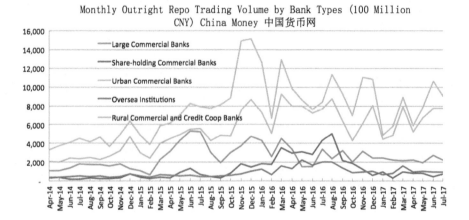

Within the outright repo segment, the two most active bank types are urban and rural commercial banks. This shows that leveraging bond trading with repo including shorting to receive high yield is one the most preferred and feasible methods for smaller players in the bond market.

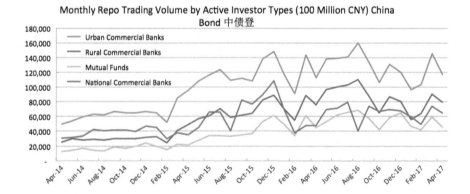

China Bond also collects repo trading data on non-banking institutional types. The most active non-banking type is the mutual funds industry, which exhibited similar trading pattern using rep leverage strategy.

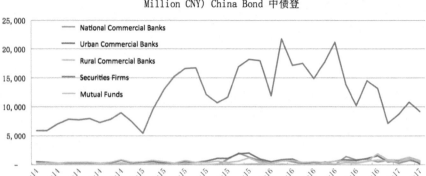

China Bond data in the outright repo segment shows the most active type in the riskier outright repo segment is the securities firm. Even though Repo has much larger trading volume versus outright repo, securities firms almost execute the same amount repo versus outright repo amount.

The outright repo trading volume versus repo volume ratio can be used as a risk appetite indicator. While the effect of 2015 stock crash was rather temporary, the deleveraging measures started in the second half of the 2016 had substantially reduced risk appetite by the more aggressive investor group in the fixed income market.

Outright Repo over Repo Monthly Trading Volume Ratio, China
Money 中国货币网

For ABS investors, the possibility of using ABS and other less liquid assets as outright repo collateral is minimal. Most of the collaterals are liquid instruments.

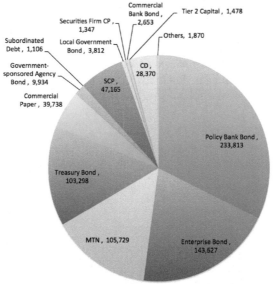

Collateral Traded in Outright Repo Transacions by Collateral Types
2014.04 - 2017.03 (100 Million CNY) China Money 中国货币网

7.4.3.2   Bull Bear Duration and Rating Strategy

The objective of this strategy is to capture the return in terms of yield times duration, or credit spread times credit spread duration, based upon macro, industry studies and issuer analysis. During a bull period, when asset price rises and default risk recedes, portfolio manager may increase their risk tolerance for both interest and credit duration. On the other hand, during a bear period, when asset price falls and default risk rises, a portfolio manager may lower their interest rate duration and credit spread duration. At this point, macro condition, budgetary condition, capital flow and monetary policy analysis all come together to form a rate bull bear assessment, upon which investor plan and execute their risk allocation.

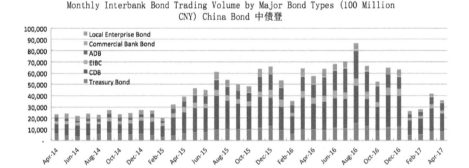

Even though portfolio managers generally do not publish their duration objectives, we may infer risk allocation change based upon bond trading volume change because trading volume decreases when bull sentiment is lower. The large volume reduction of local enterprise platform bond favored in outright repo trade, and other bond types in the interbank bond market in 2017, possibly signaled duration reduction objectives by portfolio managers amid US, China Treasury yield increase.

For comparable reasons, in addition to bond trading volume categorized by bond types, since the most active bond trading institution types in the recent years are urban commercial bank and securities firm, their trading volumes change could also approximately signal duration extension or reduction.

The base for spread calculation is interest rate instrument, including treasury, local government bond and policy bank bond. Except on the very short end, treasury distribution is overall even among different maturity tenors. This distribution pattern is useful for treasury curve as benchmark to have good liquidity across the term structure, forming the basis for fixed income market pricing.

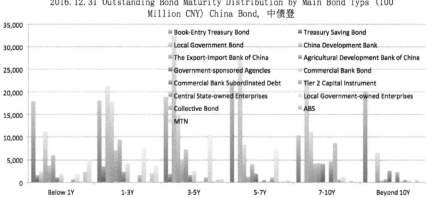

2016. 12. 31 Outstanding Bond Maturity Distribution by Main Bond Typs (100 Million CNY) China Bond, 中债登

Much of the duration adjustment is via buying the newly issued bonds that are generally more liquid. Local government issuance centers on 5–7 years. The purpose of this instrument is to support local government to lower funding cost by replacing existing loan that had much higher interest cost. As the global economy and Chinese economy entered a period of much lower economic growth, this debt swap contributed positively to the reduction of the debt burden of different levels of local government.

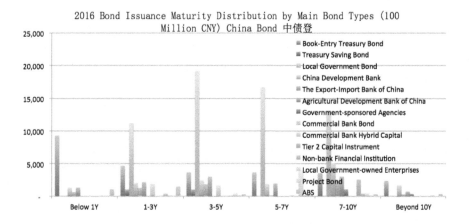

2016 Bond Issuance Maturity Distribution by Main Bond Types (100 Million CNY) China Bond 中债登

Policy bank bond issuance tends to have mid to longer maturities due to the mission they have to fulfill. For example, China Development Bank provides financing for housing targeting the low-income population and other public-related projects that support country's long-term development goal. Therefore, policy bank bond buying or selling can be used to effectively extend or shorten duration of large portfolios, while Treasury bond buying or selling can also be suitable for more subtle risk adjustment.

7.4.3.3   Term Spread Mean-Reverting Strategy

For a sector or a term bucket with its spread displaying a mean-reverting charac-
teristic, portfolio managers may apply sector or bucket allocation strategy based
upon the level of spread at a specific time, versus spread's long-term mean. When
spread is at a historical low point, as was the case for 1-3Y MTN term spread by the
end of 2015, spread duration can be shortened. When the term spread is at a
historical high point, as was the case in the middle of 2014, spread duration can be
extended to capture the term spread gain before it returns to its normal level.

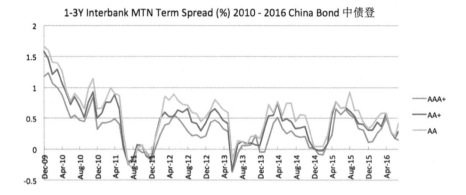

Assume there is a bond universe composed of two zero coupon MTN bonds, one
with duration at 1, the other with duration at 3. Further assume the yield has stayed
at 0% for 1Y MTN through out the investment period and transaction costs for all
bonds are zero.

One day 1, the term spread is at historical average of 0.25%.
The portfolio: 1,000,000 CNY with duration at 1 and 1,000,000 CNY with duration
at 3.
Portfolio P&L is 0.

On day 2, the term spread rises to 0.5%.
P&L: 1Y Bond = 1,000,000 * −1 * 0% = 0. 3Y Bond = 1,000,000 * −3 * 0.25% =
−7,500.
Portfolio P&L is −7,500.
Sell 1 million 1-year bond and buy 1 million 3-year bond.
The portfolio: 2,000,000 CNY with duration at 3.

On day 3, the term spread falls back to the historical average of 0.25%,
3Y Bond 2,000,000 * (−3) * (−0.25%) = 15,000
Sell 1,000,000 3Y bond, and replace it with the 1,000,000 1Y bond buy.

The portfolio: 1,000,000 CNY with duration at 1 and 1,000,000 CNY with duration at 3. Term spread comes back to where it started at 025%. So is the portfolio composition. The portfolio has made 7,500 CNY P&L, based upon mean reversion property.

7.4.3.4   Tax Spread Strategy

Compared to credit spread that can be influenced by either liquidity or credit factor or both, tax spread is mostly influenced by liquidity factor. Treasury bond coupon is tax deductible, and policy bank bond, while having sovereign status with zero risk capital weight, its coupon income is not tax deductible. The spread between policy bank bond and Treasury bond is therefore referred to as tax spread. Tax spread is mainly decided by a couple key factors. First, the interest rate curve has a significant influence on the level of tax spread. Usually the higher the interest rate curve, the higher the tax spread. Second, the tax status difference between treasury and policy bank bond has decided the type of investors for policy bank bond can be different versus treasury bond. Most domestic banks have maintained a certain level of profitability and tax is a large concern for them, but reaching taxable profitability may not the case for many mutual funds. Policy bank bond is therefore more attractive to mutual fund portfolio manager than to large bank portfolio manager. Tax spread strategy could be based upon investor liquidity condition change.

If banks' relative liquidity is larger than usual, as was the case towards the end of 2013, Treasury yield falls and tax spread expands, buying into the tax spread via purchasing policy bank bonds until the liquidity condition improves for wider investor community would produce tax spread profit for investors.

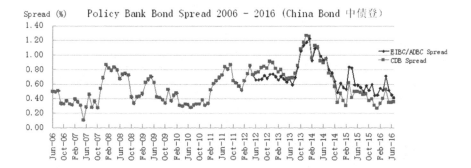

7.5 Bond Future Net Basis Strategy and Negative Implied Repo Rate

Bond Future contract trading is active but its application relatively limited. The trading volume pattern suggests that the main trading strategy is a macro interest rate strategy. Traders take bond future positions during an interest rate bull market for quick profit. Bond future is therefore a high leverage alternative to cash bond, where interest rate view strategy can be executed, without large upfront capital required to buy cash bond or shorting limitation.

One example was during the last 4 months of 2014 10Y treasury yield dropped around 60 bps and this contributed to increased buying activities in November of 2014. Another example was during the second half of 2015 10Y treasury dropped by 78 bps from 3.60 to 2.82%. The consensus was formed after stock market's volatile performance in the early half of 2015 that the interbank bond market and banking lending would be the main venues through which liquidities would be released to help the economic reform and bond future positions were created to take advantage of yield drop.

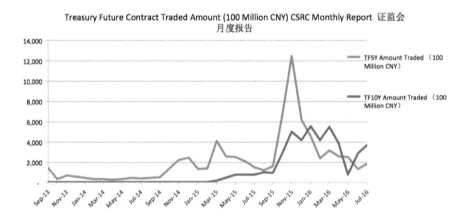

7.5.1 Net Basis Strategy

Net basis usage in bond future trade is similar to its application in the US. Net basis strategy is executed based upon the value difference identified between theoretical future value and observed future value. Long position of future contract needs to be compensated due to optionality embedded in the future contract. This is reflected in implied repo rate lower than actual repo rate, or future price lower than theoretical future price. Once net basis range is established, deviation from the normal net basis offers trading opportunities. High net basis suggests undervalued future contract and a long future trade can be executed. Low net basis suggests overvalued future contract and a short future trade can be executed.

Net basis strategy is not without limitations in real trading exercises. Net basis can be much higher from time to time because of the possibility of dated treasury issuance with low liquidity being delivered, which is disadvantageous for traders with long future position.

Net basis strategy sometimes is executed as implied repo rate strategy. A higher than expected implied repo is equivalent to a lower than expected net basis, suggesting an overvalued future price. Lower than expected implied repo is equivalent to higher than normal net basis, and long future position can be established.

7.5.2 CTD Conversion Strategy

For each bond future contract, its CTD bond is not fixed and can change over time from bond to bond due to issuance liquidity and other concern. It can also change when the interest rate yield crosses the 3% yield used in conversion factor calculation.

When yield changes from above 3% to below 3%, CTD bond switches from long duration to low duration bond, the net basis between long duration bond and future widens, and net basis between low duration bond and future narrows. A strategy of opening the long duration cash bond basis before 3% switch and close the basis trade after the switch can be executed.

Vice versa, when yield changes from below 3% to above 3%, CTD bond switches from low duration to long duration bond, the net basis between low duration bond and future widens, and net basis between long duration bond and future narrows. A strategy of opening the short duration cash bond basis before 3% switch and close the basis trade after the switch can be executed.

7.5.3 On-the-run, Existing Issuance and Tax Spread

CTD switch from old issuance to most recently issued bonds, can make a substantial difference. A theoretical CTD from old issuance with limited liquidity is harder for long future position holder to close after taking delivery. A switch to on-the-run treasury with increased liquidity will make the CTD bond more desirable, hence adding value to the future position. A strategy can be formed by creating a long future position before the switch from old issuance to on-the-run, and make profit by close the position after the switch.

7.5.4 Domestic Market's Short Sale Implication

Bond short sale helps to hedge long future position risk but in practice shorting can be difficult before further improvement on treasury harmonization. Theoretically bond short sale can be arranged by first acquiring bond via an outright repo, sell the bond, and buy it back when bond value falls to certain level and close the repo transaction. But various leverage measures limit the amount of shorting a desk can take, and tax implication has caused bond liquidity quite specific to each issuance. The difficulty in hedging via shorting has caused implied repo rate to be negative from time to time.

7.6 Investment Accounts Objectives and Strategies

7.6.1 Some Basics

7.6.1.1 Cost of Funds

Cost of funds differs substantially based upon the type of institutions and the competitive position an institution commands among its peers. Banks often have interest rate spread between 2 and 3% on their balance sheets. A very large commercial bank with cost of funding around 2% has a wider range of investment products to choose from. A low 3% tax-exempt treasury bond can be relatively attractive as 25% institutional tax rate makes it equivalent to pre-tax 4% taxable policy bank bond. Smaller banks with limited deposit base and higher percentage of funding coming from WMP and interbank borrowing would be less interested in Treasury bond investment.

Insurance companies, as market liberalization process takes hold, on one hand are able to invest in a wider range of products, on the other hand have to compete for funds in a more competitive environment. Insurance companies may have to deliver 4–5% on their products to attract investors that can otherwise invest in bank WMP, and for this reason they have to procure assets that can generate at least 6–7% to keep the 2% extra spread needed to cover company overhead including channels and service management.

Trusts often function as off-balance sheet vehicles for banks financed via WMP therefore their cost of fund can be close to prevailing WMP product rate. WMP rate can often be about 1–1.5% above treasury rate and track closely AA+ corporate bond yield. AA+ rating acts as the investment grade floor for many entities is equivalent to the role played by BBB in global rating system.

Bond funds do not have specific return target hence cost of funding theoretically does not apply. In market, bond funds have to meet investors' expectation with return higher than WMP rate, which can be considered risk-free base credit rate for investment and face possible redemption during equity bull market.

7.6.1.2 Asset Liability Management Objectives

Asset liability management is an important objective for bank proprietary investment portfolios. Unlike their US and UK peers, some commercial banks in China have large proprietary investment portfolio, created by surplus funds residing on their balance sheet. Often regarded as balance sheet yield enhancing asset that plays a secondary role in support of lending activities and liquidity management, the proprietary portfolio can have its duration continuously adjusted to match liability duration on bank balance sheet using more liquid bond assets.

7.6.2 Garden Variety of Portfolio Objectives and Investment Strategies

7.6.2.1 Return Before Tax and Return After Tax

For trading books, there is a personal income tax at 20% and corporate income tax at 25%, therefore the type of active players makes difference regarding the after tax yield of various types of instruments. For banking books, the tax rate under consideration is likely to be at 25%, and only VAT is applicable when bond is held to maturity. For mutual fund trading books, the tax rate under consideration is likely to be at 0% when fund is not making profit. When performance measure is set up, often both return-before-tax and return-after-tax are used to better reflect the portfolio performance.

The risk capital weight for Treasury bond and policy bank bond is 0%. The weight is 20% for local government bond, Railroad Corp, 25% for certificate of deposit, and 100% for corporates, loan and trust. A portfolio manager will have to evaluate and compare yield after tax and risk capital charge of different instruments before an investment decision is to be made.

December 1, 2016	Treasury bond	CDB bond	Local Govy bond	RailRoad corp	CD	AA+ corp	Loan	Trust
Yield	2.77	3.26	2.81	3.55	5.66	4. 22	4.9	7.59
VAT tax rate	0	25%	0	12.5%	25%	25%	25%	25%
Tax charge	0.00	0.82	0.00	0.44	1.42	1.06	1.23	1.90
Risk capital weight	0	0	20%	20%	25%	100%	100%	100%
Risk capital charge	0.00	0.00	0.30	0.30	0.38	1.50	1.50	1.50
Real yield	2.77	2.45	2.51	2.81	3.87	1.67	2.18	4. 19

Assume capital asset ratio at 15% and return on equity at 10%

The above comparison explains the relative attractiveness of various types of instruments. CD can be attractive for its relatively high yield, low risk and good liquidity. Treasury can be attractive for its relatively high yield when tax and risk capital cost are taken into account. One instrument attracts investors with high yield before and after tax is the trust instrument. In a nutshell, during strategy formulation, banks may prefer higher allocation to Treasury bonds, while mutual fund and securities firms may choose higher allocation to policy banks bonds.

7.6.2.2 Newly Acquired Investment Yield

Newly acquired investment yield, measures the performance of a portfolio manager by using the average yield of newly acquired positions. This measurement is pertinent in assessing how well a portfolio has done in the most recent period in terms of acquiring new assets, and will be compared against average market yield during that asset-acquiring period. For portfolio with large positions and flows, this measure becomes very critical, as the average yield of the whole portfolio can be very slow changing and thus very insensitive to reflect portfolio's most recent performance, Banks with continuous deposit cash inflow may be keen to capture present interest income and be less concerned with their strategy execution in low yield environment, knowing later high yield could elevate newly-acquired investment yield to compensate the MTM loss, while mutual funds and securities firms may try to capture precise high yield moments to enhance newly acquired investment yield so as to weather other period of lower yield.

7.6.2.3 EVA

Economic Value Added (EVA) is a well-accepted concept in global banking management and in China. Net after-tax return with cost of capital deducted, for both credit risk capital cost and operational risk capital cost, it provides a measurement of profitability after considering the risky capital charge, which is becoming more significant in the decision making process.

$$\text{EVA} = \text{Net Return} * (1 - \text{Tax Rate}) - \text{Credit Capital Cost}$$
$$- \text{Operational Capital Cost}$$

Assuming there is a 3Y credit bond with yield at 3.3% in October of 2016, the institutional tax rate is 25%, the cost of capital at 1.9%, the after tax net return is $(3.3\% - 1.9\%) * (1-25\%) = 1.05\%$. The risk weight for corporate at 100%, the capital ratio at 4% and the cost of capital at 10%. The credit capital cost is equivalent to $100\% * 4\% * 10\% = 0.4\%$. Assuming the operational capital cost is small, the computed EVA of this credit bond is 0.65%. During the same time, a 3 year Treasury bond yield is 2.4, with after tax net return $(2.4 - 1.9\%) = 0.5\%$ without credit capital cost. The credit bond generates better EVA return than the treasury bond of the same maturity, but the difference is much smaller than what the absolute yield suggests on the surface.

While BASEL III is still in its implementation stage, proposal for BASEL IV is already on the table. Various capital floor parameters are being proposed in standard model calculation, and internal model application now requires more rigorous regulatory scrutiny. One of the most important regulatory impacts of various BASIL implementations is the risky capital charge, which is aimed at strengthening banks' risk control measure and capital allocation amount, so banks would be better equipped to weather a financial storm such as the 2008 global financial crisis. This business environment makes EVA, a performance measurement parameter that takes into account both return and risky capital usage, increasingly more relevant and important.

7.6.2.4   RAROC

Risk-adjusted return on capital, RAROC, is the ratio of after tax net return over risky capital usage. Assuming we do not consider interest rate risk for banking book, based upon BASEL III framework:

RAROC = After-tax net return/(Credit risk capital usage + Ops. risk capital usage)

Using the EVA calculation example, after tax net return of the 3-year credit bond is 1.05%. Credit risk capital usage is 100% weight * 4% Capital Ratio = 4%, the RAROC is 26.25%. For the treasury bond of the same maturity, there is no risky capital charge. Therefore, from the perspective of RAROC comparison, Treasury bond is more preferable than the credit bond of the same maturity. Since EVA and RAROC mostly concern banks and Treasury bond allocation improves a bank's EVA and RAROC statistics, EVA and RAROC increase the appealing of Treasury bonds to banks that are using these two numbers for their performance measurement.

7.6.2.5   Portfolio Duration and Risk Management

Portfolio duration is one of the most important portfolio management tool. Anticipating bull period, portfolio duration will be extended to capture the expected price gain, while anticipating bear condition portfolio duration will be shortened to minimize the possible price loss and risk exposure.

Portfolio duration is used for both performance management and risk management. The optimal portfolios duration target varies for different type of institutions. A mutual bond company may avoid a long portfolio duration when term spread, often measured by 10Y–1Y Chinese Treasury, versus 10Y–2Y US Treasury, does not justify the duration risk of yield increase. If a portfolio manager takes an extra

6-year duration risk to capture additional 30 bps term spread, a 5-bps yield increase will eliminate one year of that extra term spread return. 10bps yield increase will make that 6-year duration increase a bad asset allocation decision.

For banking books of commercial banks and insurance companies, for which the newly-acquired investment yield is an important performance measurement, and mark-to-market is not as important, portfolio managers will still try to capture that small term spread in a low yield market condition. Banks and insurance companies differ in the extent of additional duration risk they can take. The term of insurance companies' liability can be very long, while banks often match the duration of their proprietary banking portfolio to their balance sheet liability duration.

7.6.2.6 Sector Duration and Risk Management

Sector duration is applied to manage return exposure to desired asset classes and segments, and control risk exposure to concerned asset classes and segments. An example would be to control the risk exposure to the industries with surplus capacity in the current economy, including real estate, steel industry and coal industry, and local government-sponsored platform bonds. In practice portfolio managers often use sector duration in combination with instrument position to produce sector 01 to control the risk exposure.

7.6.2.7 Total Portfolio Profit and Loss

Total portfolio P&L is the ultimate return performance measurement and risk control parameter for portfolios. The Mark-to-market process is carries out against price provided by China Bond in the interbank market. Portfolios that hit maximum loss threshold will be forced stop taking additional positions, reduce their exposure, and liquidate the portfolio, based upon the threshold level that is hit.

7.6.3 Insurance Companies' Long End ALM Strategies

Insurance companies often apply buy and hold strategy on long duration segment when the market is perceived to be in a bear stage. While their bond holding amount can change due to liquidity available in the market and particularly the amount of liquidity available to insurance companies, their long duration preference can be inferred from the type of bond positions they have accumulated over the time. By the end of 2016, most of their bonds are Treasury, CDB bonds and subordinated bank bonds.

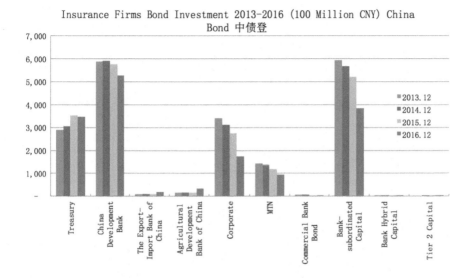

Insurance Firms Bond Investment 2013–2016 (100 Million CNY) China Bond 中债登

The reason behind the bond type preference is that large amount of CDB bonds are available between 7 and 10 years and beyond, and so are the bank-subordinated bonds. Treasury bonds provide extra support on portfolio liquidity that is often lacking in the long duration segment.

2016.12.31 Outstanding Bond Maturity Distribution by Main Bond Typs (100 Million CNY) China Bond, 中债登

7.6.4 Mutual Fund Investment, a Mixed Asset Pool to Start With

Mutual fund applies active bond trading strategy with less regard to index bench-marking that is often the standard practice in the US bond fund market. The other noticeable distinction its venture into equity-based assets in terms of hybrid bonds, and money market exposure. Repo is heavily used as a funding method.

7.6.5 Foreign Banks' Short Duration and Carry Trade

Foreign banks often have relatively short duration in their portfolio. These institutions buy liquid policy bank bonds, financed with interbank repo carry trade, and receive the difference between instrument yield and repo rate. This is a relatively safe strategy, with minimum liquidity risk. The policy bank bond has good liquidity support and can be easily sold when position needs to be unwound. On the financing side, PBOC manages money market via pricing target, which is the short end repo rate. Therefore a stable short repo rate is a high probability. This carry trade strategy is a low risk, low overhead strategy, preferred by foreign institutions at their developmental stage in Chinese market.

7.6.6 Off-balance Sheet Wealth Investment, a 3 Trillion USD and Still Growing Sector

Wealth management product appeared as part of the interest rate liberalization process. Similar to various financial instruments created in the US after 1973 to bypass Regulation Q and deposit ceiling, WMP was created in China to give savers market return higher than deposit rate so bank can attract resources to fund financial activities.

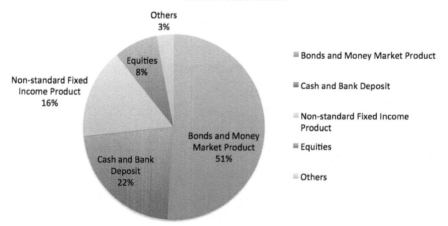

Wealth Management Product Asset Composition 2015.12.31 (%)
Market Observation

The largest destined usage of WMP fund includes bonds, money market products and bank deposit. The fact the largest portions of WMP go to bond, MM and
bank deposit determines the return of these liquid assets plus a management spread
will produce the prevailing WMP return. But the market has also observed on
occasions WMP rate rising sharply on its own when there is a shortage of funds, but
falling with difficulty since banks do not want to lose their existing funding base.
This has created uncertainty over the WMP profitability especially the return of
many other asset classes has generally come down substantially over the recent
years as growth moderated.

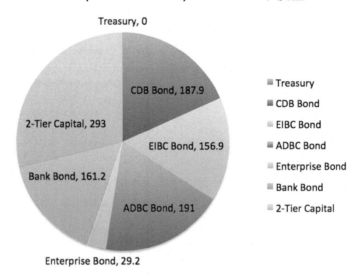

Net Bond Purchase by Wealth Management Product in 2015 (100 Million CNY) China Bond 中债登

At deeper level, even though WMP is assumed to possess credit risk from legal perspective, in practice banks were public institutions before market reform and many savers buying WMP from banks today still treat these products as risk-free financial investment. As a result, some of the analysts regard WMP rate as the risk-free non-sovereign market rate and the yield on trust vehicle as the real financing cost. Risk limit and liquidity requirement restrict WMP investment choices in strategy formulation. These combined with competition for funds in an increasingly more transparent market will continuously reduce WMP profitability.

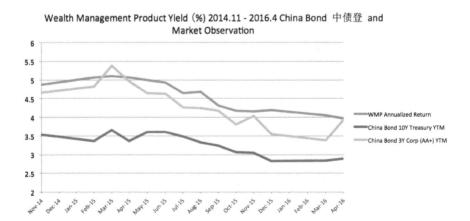

Wealth Management Product Yield（%）2014.11 - 2016.4 China Bond 中债登 and Market Observation

Next to standard bond and MM in WMP allocation strategy is the non-standard fixed income assets often associated with entrust loan and trust loan. Typically 1–3 year maturity, these non-standard assets have low liquidity but offer critical yield enhancement to make a WMP issuance competitive. At bank balance sheet level, this off-balance-sheet funding strategy of matching WMP with bonds and high yield is more important to share-holding commercial banks and urban commercial banks than large commercial banks. With substantial financing source coming from retail and institutional deposit, large commercial banks apply this method mainly to gain intermediary fee and maintain market share. Regarded as risk-free investment and most invested into less risky assets, large commercial banks WMP yield is lower than those offered by smaller peers. On the other hand, share-holding banks and urban commercial banks with smaller and more volatile funding base apply this strategy mainly to compete for and attract more expensive funding to support off-balance-sheet project financing with reduced risk capital expense.

There has been discussion and regulatory push to break the prevailing principal protection practice, to introduce more market-oriented pricing into WMP. One proposed approach is to introduce NAV routine to WMP. This has met difficulty in implementation for banks are concerned about losing WMP as an important funding source.

7.6.7 Trust-Based High Yield Regulatory Arbitrage Strategy, a Substantial Sector with Limited Potential

This was a popular strategy formed by borrowing from interbank and investing off balance sheet. Its borrowing cost is at interbank Shibor rate. The return from trust investment could be close to 10%, much higher than banking loan or high yield bonds.

The trust investment is off balance sheet. The capital weight for interbank borrowing within 3 months is 25%, while a normal lending would be 100%. Compared to a normal lending assuming 20% capital reserve ratio and 10% capital return that costs capital expense around 200 bps, funding trusts with interbank borrowing saves 150 bps, on top of high yield offered by trust vehicle. The trust investment strategy basically formed around capital requirement arbitrage by banks, therefore was always under close scrutiny by the regulators. The strategy does provide critically needed capital to certain projects.

7.6.8   Asset-Backed Securities Investment, Regulatory Capital Advantage, Risk Diversification, and Yield Enhancement

ABS packaging is designed to meet investors' demand while maximizing issuer's capital expense saving by offloading risky assets from balance sheet. An investor often makes portfolio investment decision based upon ABS yield spread and liquidity that is mapped to seniority, rating and maturity of the most recently issued ABS of comparable quality.

The very senior tranche with short maturity that is between a couple of months to a half year often has planned amortization schedule. A mutual fund may be interested in this tranche with yield often at a dozen bps above commercial paper of comparable quality and maturity since its short maturity reduces liquidity concern of bond fund during redemption. Often rated AA− and above, the risk capital requirement can be 20%, which cuts holding capital expense by 80% at 160 bps. Lower rated senior tranche between A− and A+ requires risk-holding capital at 50%, which cuts capital expense by 50%. Assuming 50% * 20% capital reserve ratio * 10% capital return will produces capital saving close to 100 bps. These tranches offer higher yields than comparably rated quality bond hence are suitable for institutional investors interested in portfolio yield and liquidity trade-off.

Less senior pass-through tranches with between 1 and 3Y maturity rated at BBB − to BBB+ require capital allocation at 100% and those rated at BB− to BB+ at 350%. These tranches will produce less capital saving. Since an issuer is required to hold at least 5% of each issued tranche hence the issuer has the incentive to minimize the sizes of these less rated supporting tranche to reduce capital requirement as long as protection for the more senior tranches is not compromised. Lacking instrument liquidity and amortization speed certainty, they offer yields above high yield bonds. Banks with ample cash flows are often less concerned with amortization schedule risk and portfolio liquidity risk and are generally more comfortable with these lower rated tranche assets issued by other banks, hence these assets are often purchased by WMP to enhance portfolio yield.

The equity tranche requires capital allocation at 1250%. Not rated, with high liquidity risk and amortization schedule risk, its investor base is rather limited. Interested by PE, they could produce return yield around 10% with further yield risk sharing on top of that.

7.6.9   Convertible Strategy and Callable Implications

Accurate convertible bonds risk hedging in their current state is difficult and the return on convertible is driven largely by investor's expectation over unhedged return. The largest investor group is type 1 bond fund from mutual funds that can allocate up to 20% in stocks and convertible bonds. The return upper limit could either be the bond call price, which acts as a protection for issuers from rising equity price, or the equity conversion value, very much dependent upon issuer's willingness and capability to convert bonds to stocks. A large bank may prefer a bond call in an equity bull market to avoid diluting shares that could lead to complicated change on corporate management structure. Some corporations may prefer giving stocks to avoid dispensing large sums of cash. The difficulty in quantifying issuer's willingness or capability in stock conversion exercise reinforces the flow-driven valuation for convertible bond. Since the valuation can be subjective in nature and may lack quantitative precision, an investor may approximate the value floor of a convertible bond, when holding stocks is not likely, with the value of discounted cashflow of the convertible bond. When holding stocks is likely in possibly a bull market, the value floor is converted equity value.

When compared against corporate bond, the convertible bond has low coupon rate and display strong equity-related characteristics; on the other hand, when comparing against other equities, within certain range, it can be undervalued for its various clauses. When a convertible bond can be repoed, in a bull market, holding convertible bond may generate substantial return due to leverage.

A low volatility of convertible bond price is typically associated with low probability of converting to stocks. For example, when the issuer is unwilling to convert bond to stocks, and bond will mostly function as a bond asset, hence very low volatility compared against a bond with higher probability converting to stocks.

Convertible bond is essentially an equity strategy play after taking into account issuer's bond call price protection, willingness for conversion and possible leverage usage in fixed income market. A trader could choose to sell before the bond call price is reached. A trader could choose to buy when the convertible bond is oversold, or the stock market is oversold.

7.7 Trading and Investment in Gold

7.7.1 Physical Gold Segment

Gold is an important investment asset class within the larger world of commodities and precious metals. Physical gold price on Shanghai Gold Exchange hit its peak between 2010 and 2012, during which the global gold price was also at its high peak. The Shanghai price closely tracks global gold price, mirroring the fall of US dollar index during the Great Recession and its subsequent rise following US economic recovery.

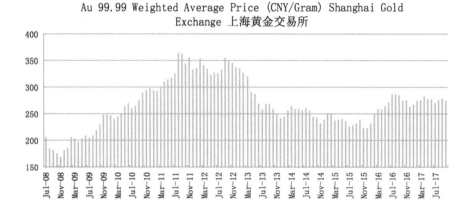

Au 99.99 Weighted Average Price (CNY/Gram) Shanghai Gold Exchange 上海黄金交易所

Regarding gold trading volume, the general pattern has been the lower the price of CNY in terms of USD, the higher the transaction volume. This suggested that physical gold activities were heavily driven by domestic anti-inflationary purpose.

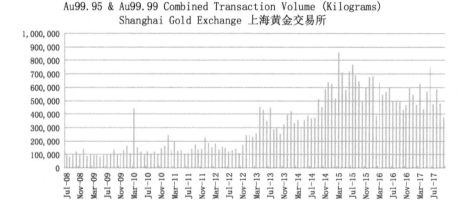

Au99.95 & Au99.99 Combined Transaction Volume (Kilograms) Shanghai Gold Exchange 上海黄金交易所

The gold price quoted in domestic CNY on exchange may diverge from global gold price in USD translated with USD-CNY exchange rate. One of the two large divergence peaks happened during 2013. During that time US economy was moving out of recession and USD could move higher versus CNY. The second peak was the end of 2016 during fed fund rate increase. This suggested the CNY hedge applications on top of USD in domestic physical gold strategy versus USD hedge application in international gold market.

Au99.99 Price - Global Gold Price (CNY/Gram) Bank of England 英国央行
Shanghai Gold Exchange 上海黄金交易所

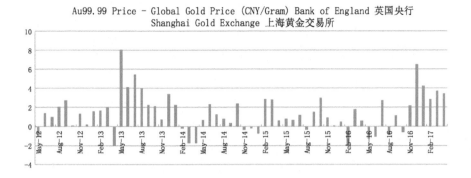

7.7.2 Deferred Delivery Gold

Gold can also be traded with deferred delivery contract, which is a leveraged trade in nature. The acute volume peak during the mid of 2015 coincided with the large stock market crash. The other volume peak at the end of 2015 coincided with the capital flow volatility amid fed fund increase. This suggested the fast and speculative nature of the deferred delivery gold segment. Fast moving leveraged buy sell trading during broader market uncertainty should be its main strategy application.

Au(T+D) Transaction Volume (10K CNY) Shanghai Gold Exchange 上海黄金交易所

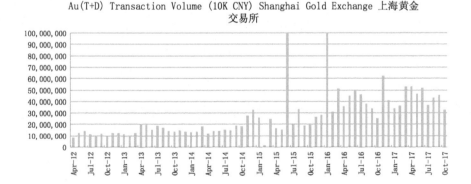

Chapter 8
Risk Management Practice

Progressive financial statements demonstrated banking industry's continuous improvement on risk management practice. It has become such an import part of investment and trading business, leaving it out might render this book incomplete.

Some of the well accepted practices include that all accounts be classified into either trading accounts or banking accounts, and market risk, credit risk and operational risk management are applied in managing relevant business lines. For capital adequacy control, tier 1 capital adequacy ratio and capital adequacy ratio are important measures based upon risk-weighted assets. In addition, financial statements also often report RWA to total assets ratio and total equity to total assets ratio. For liquidity management, liquidity ratio is widely used. Leverage ratio is required in the annual filing of bank statement. As banking industry in China modernizes, the leverage ratio also came down, especially for the larger banks. This enables them to withstand more volatile economic condition, and therefore offer critical support before economy and loan quality improve.

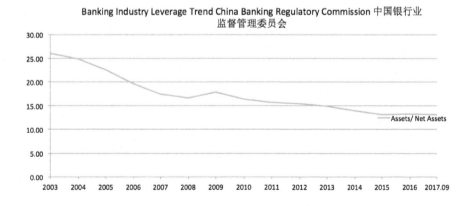

© Springer Nature Singapore Pte Ltd. 2018
X. Zhang, *Capital Markets Trading and Investment Strategies in China*,
https://doi.org/10.1007/978-981-10-8497-3_8

Using comparable logic to calculate insurance industry leverage and the result demonstrates that the industry has overall kept the same level of leverage, while loosening slightly over the more recent years. This has more to do with the initiative to update industry's risk management practice from controlling the input asset quality to overall outstanding risk exposure, a significant step in modernizing the insurance industry to measure up with the international standard.

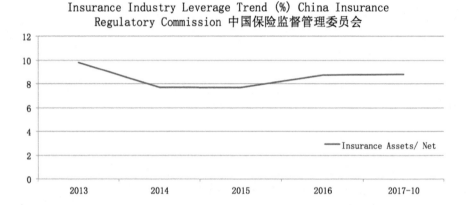

A segment worth watching for risk managers for its general less standardized operational practice, the trust industry had provided very significant funding to various projects, many facilitated by banks. While the return had come down over the recent years, the leverage ratio remained high.

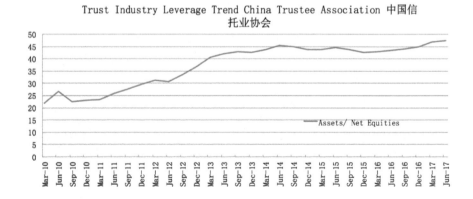

International spotlight has been put on capital markets division of all banks around the world, and Chinese bank system is no exception to that. BASIL implementation is a continuous progress for many banks. According to BASIL III, identified areas of capital market risks include credit risk, market risk and operation risk. Credit risk can be further divided into investment credit risk, which covers fixed income market, money market, and non-interest bearing assets; counterparty credit risk, which covers OTC derivatives, and security lending when outright Repo was used. Market risk covers general market risk and specific market risk, which covers OTC derivatives.

8.1 Trading Accounts Limits Allocation

For market risk management in FX position, PV01 is allocated to traders and desks. For market risk management in interest rate and credit positions, IR DV01 is allocated. Various 01s are aggregated to contribute to unit volatility of VAR, which is the foundation of market risk and specific risk management. Other possible risk management parameters include Maximum position limit is to control the exposure part of the VAR; single transaction notional limit and maximum loss limit are utilized to control trader and desks from taking too much risk.

A large fixed income desk may use duration other than 01s to benchmark risk against bond universe. Portfolio duration and key rate duration are applied to manage risk for the whole portfolio or risk by instrument within portfolio.

8.2 Investment Accounts Risk Allocation Practice

Investment Accounts have to manage issuer risk and counterparty credit risk when cash is deposited at counterparty or loan has been made to counterparty. Investment accounts also have to manage counterparty credit risk when outright repo is executed. Specifically for fixed income desk, Credit Limit by Issuer is used. For money market desk, besides Credit Limit by Issuer, Credit Limit by Counterparty can be applied for two risk management purposes. One is the counterparty risk when outright repo is executed for money market desk financing. The broader usage of Credit limit by Counterparty within a bank including money market desk is the credit risk when a loan has been made to a counterparty or cash is deposited to counterparty. The aggregation of various credit risk at the desk level is managed via the so-called Credit Limit by Lines of Desk Management